★ *THE*
# *HIT CHARADE*

# ★ THE
# HIT CHARADE

LOU PEARLMAN,

BOY BANDS, AND

*THE BIGGEST PONZI SCHEME*

IN U.S. HISTORY

# TYLER GRAY

**COLLINS**
*An Imprint of* HarperCollins *Publishers*
www.harpercollins.com

HarperCollins books may be purchased for educational, business, or sales promotional use. For information, please write: Special Markets Department, HarperCollins Publishers, 10 East 53rd Street, New York, NY 10022.

FIRST EDITION

Designed by Jaime Putorti

Library of Congress Cataloging-in-Publication Data
Gray, Tyler.
    The hit charade : Lou Pearlman, boy bands, and the biggest Ponzi scheme in U.S. history / Tyler Gray.—1st ed.
        p.  cm.
    Includes bibliographical references and index.
    ISBN-13: 978-0-06-157966-0
    ISBN-10: 0-06-157966-1
    1. Pearlman, Lou.  2. Sound recording executives and producers—United States—Biography.  3. Swindlers and swindling—United States—Biography.  4. Ponzi schemes—United States—History.
I. Title.
    ML429.P35G74 2008
    364.16'3092—dc22
    [B]                                                        2008029671

08  09  10  11  12  DIX / RRD  10  9  8  7  6  5  4  3  2  1

**May 2009**

*This book is dedicated to those whose patience*

*and encouragement allowed me to write it:*

*my son, Cash, and daughter, Ida; my mom, Mary*

*Lynne; my sister, Jessica; and especially Sia.*

*It's also for my dad, Michael Earl Gray,*

*whose inspiration outlasted his life.*

# ★ CONTENTS

I became Backstreet-aware in 1994. I was working my way through school as a waiter at an Italian restaurant in Orlando called Trastevere. Kim, my coworker, was dating one of our regular clients, Alan Siegel, a dark-haired, glimmering-eyed, charming, wheeling-dealing New Yorker (and quite the catch for Kim). He was well regarded by the family-like staff of the restaurant. He came off kind of like a big bro, but he wore a man's suit. When he showed up with a group of other executives, we tried to help him look like a player. We knew his standing order and it probably made him feel cool in the company of other business types when we'd say, "The usual, Mr. Siegel?" Kim wouldn't shut up about the pop music act Alan was working with, a bubblegum singing group. Having graduated from the suburbs straight into the local hard-core punk rock scene, I often wished she would. I had a college radio show then that played bands I'd describe as the antitheses of candy-coated, mass-appeal pop bands, and I frequently chided Kim for liking something called a Backstreet Boy. Nevertheless, shift after shift, she preached the gospel of Trans Continental Records, the company Alan helped run: "Just wait," she'd say, "they're huge in Europe already. Wherever they go, their bus is literally mobbed with fans. Watch. They're going to be huge here." Then someone's osso buco would come up in the kitchen window and Kim would be summoned back to Earth to deliver it promptly or risk getting stiffed on her 15 percent tip. Eventually, she traded in her wine key and pomodoro-stained apron for a position as the wife of Trans Continental Records vice president Alan Siegel.

Alan's boss, Lou Pearlman, with his blue Rolls and limos, started making a name for himself around town about this time, too. His bands were already farther along than I—or most people in Orlando or even the nation at large—imagined then. He'd organized a team that put together the band by 1993, and by 1994, they had perfected dance moves and vocals in a section of Lou's blimp parts warehouse on Michigan Avenue in Kissimmee, a couple blocks from where I later lived as a cub reporter on the county government beat. No girls mobbed the inconspicuous spot, and the boys came and went without anyone batting an eye—no one really cared yet.

Nothing pissed me off back in my grizzled restaurant days like the idea that a prefab pop band could strike it rich. But Kim was right. The Backstreet Boys were blowing up. Alan (and Kim) got rich. Lou Pearlman put my hometown on the map as boy band central. I went to work for the *Orlando Sentinel* and finished college (in that order). One of my first bylined stories for the paper ran on the dress page of the

Business section on May 27, 1997. It mostly doted on ShapeCD, a Pearlman-backed company run by Alan that pressed compact discs into novel shapes, like Christmas trees and Backstreet Boy heads. A few years later, still at the *Sentinel* but covering nightlife, I listened to Bob Fischetti, the executive vice president of Trans Continental, blow smoke about his yet-to-be-constructed all-class dinner-and-dancing club, the Vanguard Room (it never opened). I even got a tour of Trans Continental studios' grand space where it recorded artists I really couldn't care about. I did whatever I could as the nightlife writer to avoid anything having to do with Trans Continental. It felt so fake. Fischetti, though, seemed genuine, nice enough. He started a singer-songwriter night, which mostly featured the hitmakers behind boy band tunes and other pop songs. "He's N' Sync with the Boys," I wrote of Fischetti and his self-touted music industry contacts. Far more than a groundbreaking pun, it was a wink to a segment of my readers who shared with me the feeling that Fischetti and his ilk were riding a wave of hype that would soon peter out—wishful thinking. I always peppered any and all nightlife references to Pearlman or his people and their projects with skeptical undertones. I was half-wrong. The boy band thing was there to stay. But I should have paid a lot closer attention to what Lou was up to.

I was around to see Backstreet Boys, then *NSYNC, sue Pearlman. It looked rough for him for a moment, but he never stopped showing up in the VIP sections of the swankiest clubs downtown. He launched more bands that had some hits, and he only seemed to get richer and more famous. I departed Orlando just as Pearlman bought and moved into Church Street Station, a darkened tourist-destination-turned-eyesore in the heart of downtown Orlando. He'd opened a steakhouse, a deli, a pizza place, and was converting the former tourist trap— where I spent many a teenage night—into his lavish executive headquarters. He'd convinced city leaders that he'd save the vacant core of downtown O-Town by turning it into boy band central. It was the kick in the pants that helped send me packing. In 2003, with a thousand miles of distance on Central Florida, I started to realize what a strange and fascinating story Lou and his Orlando pop empire were, but I wasn't quite ready to revisit my roots. Then, later that same year, Lou's long arm found me in Times Square. I was walking there when an attractive female stranger approached and said, "Excuse me, have you ever considered modeling?" I hadn't, as a matter of fact. I also hadn't developed that preternatural New York standoffishness and probably still looked like Axl at the beginning of the "Welcome to the Jungle" video, straight off the bus.

"Um, well, no, but that's nice of you to say."

"You could really do it," she insisted. "That height! Let me give you an invitation to an open casting call tomorrow at seven. . . ." I walked away feeling puffed up, but there wasn't a chance in hell I was going to waste any more of my time following up. For a brief moment, however, I pondered a career in high fashion, griping because I'd clearly demanded that the caterer provide *Greek* yogurt and *Fijian* water. Then I caught my crooked smile in a T.G.I. Friday's window and remembered I had opted out of braces in high school and now sport a dental scheme that polite people say gives me "character."

Unbeknownst to me at the time, thousands of people in cities all over the United States—even New York—were falling for the same modeling pitch. When they showed up to the casting calls, salespeople gave them the hard sell on a picture and promotional package that would kick off their glamorous lives in front of cameras. The investment in their career as a model was a mere $1,000 to $2,000. The company, Trans Continental Talent (which sounded familiar to me even back then), worked with top talent agents to get its clients high-dollar work and placement in top fashion magazines, they said. The only real value customers got out of the package—which was essentially a spot on a website—was the set of pro photos. I knew this because just a few weeks after a model scout approached me, I got a call from a friend, Wheat Wurtzburger, who had worked with me as a freelance photographer during my days at the *Orlando Sentinel* and had sidelined in model photography. He was on his way to New York on what he called a "photo tour" and wanted to know if I wanted to get a drink and catch up. He had picked up an assignment working for a model-scouting agency, he told me, with a tone that sounded a little embarrassed. It didn't take long for us to figure out he was shooting for the same scouts I'd run into. He felt a little slimy, he told me, not because he wasn't taking quality shots, but because the owner of the company was the same guy who'd started Backstreet Boys. He was working for Lou Pearlman. What's more, Wheat was having trouble getting paid. Checks that were supposed to have covered his and his team's expenses for their Manhattan jaunt had bounced just before he'd left to come to the city, he told me over drinks. I bought the beers.

He'd also discovered exactly how Pearlman's model-scouting business worked. In his hotel room, he pulled out his digital camera and scrolled through recent shots he'd taken. The subjects, most of whom had paid close to $1,000 apiece, were not what the average person would consider model material. Yes, their makeup was impeccable—among my friend's photo crew were professional makeup artists who carried their own arsenal of tints and shades. And my friend had an eye for choosing angles and locations. He packed lighting for every condition, too. In most of the shots he took, he'd used Times Square as a backdrop—the public nature of the shoots did wonders for the egos of the subjects. Even the guy with the lazy eye.

Wheat didn't exactly know what to tell him when he'd showed up for his turn. He treated him as if he were the next

Brad Pitt, and the guy walked away hopeful that he'd land work. There were others with features or flaws that, sadly, precluded them from ever making it in the mainstream modeling world. "They got good photographs," Wheat said, "but the whole thing was a scam." Orlando news outlets eventually exposed Lou's modeling business as a fraud. It never lived up to the hopes it sold to its clients. Lou had taken over the business a month after the Florida state attorney's office started investigating it. The government suddenly dropped its case, though, just before charges were filed, leading to all kinds of speculation about a backroom deal between Lou and then-state-attorney Charlie Crist—who later became governor. The business never recovered from the bad press, and it went bankrupt. The whole thing left a stain on Lou as a huckster guilty of greater crimes than his bad taste in pop music.

Pearlman, with his downtown megaplex and dozens of businesses and bands in the works, was deeply entrenched in the heart and soul of Orlando when, in 2006 and early 2007, it all came tumbling down. I was working for *Radar* magazine as a senior editor when I learned that state and federal authorities were investigating his massive investment scheme. Then he vanished. As the FBI raided his offices and home, the three-hundred-plus-pound man with a penchant for bright blue clothing was said to be in hiding, possibly somewhere in Europe. That's when I got interested again in Pearlman and the O-Town story. I pitched it to *Radar,* but neither I nor anyone else—including the FBI—had a lead on where he might be hiding. He was spotted in Bali in June 2007 by a German tourist who e-mailed *St. Petersburg Times* reporter Helen Huntley. With the tipster's permission she forwarded his info on to the FBI, who swooped in and eventually got Pearlman to Guam, where he was indicted on wire and mail fraud charges. He was flown via Con Air back to Orlando, where he awaited trial in a cell at the Orange County Jail at Thirty-third Street.

Having learned from watching and reading seasoned, hardcore cops and investigative reporters such as Lenny Savino, Henry Pierson Curtis, and Jim Leusner at the *Orlando Sentinel* (Leusner was still breaking news on Pearlman for the *Sentinel* in 2008) and having covered my own share of criminals there, I knew the Orange County jail and Florida's public records laws pretty well. The way it works is that almost anyone can visit almost any prisoner, as long as he's not seeking special media access or hasn't been otherwise prohibited. I had mailed several written requests for an interview to Lou himself the moment his prisoner number popped up on the jail's website. He never wrote back or called, as I'd requested him to. And he didn't expect me to show up. From JFK airport in New York I called the jail and signed up to drop in just twenty-eight or so hours in advance (the rules require twenty-four hours' notice). Neither Lou nor the local media, which watched the public visitor roster with hawklike intensity, had time to spot or recognize my name. I knew that the guards wouldn't question who I was or why I'd come calling and that they'd at least bring Lou out of his cell and up to the conference center without even giving him a choice in the matter. He could get up and walk away after he saw me through his monitor, but I'd have at least a few seconds to sell myself, and I knew Lou as a guy with a reputation for face-to-face courtesy, someone who'd bend over backward to appear helpful and cooperative. I knew he hated to say no.

On July 16, just before two P.M., I signed in, turned over my driver's license, and took a seat on a hard bench next to a fan in the outdoor waiting area. Judging by the T-shirted and flip-flopped throng more appropriately clothed for the summer heat, I was way overdressed in a black suit. When our two P.M. appointment time rolled around, we were herded into a stark cinder-block room, informed for the umpteenth time that no cell phones or cameras or recording devices of any kind were allowed, and ushered to seats by lingering guards in front of videoconference monitors. The large woman seated a couple of feet to my right saw her man appear and nervously began a conversation that was obviously the culmination of a series of love letters to her incarcerated Casanova. Within seconds she was speaking with the man on the other side of the monitor about her own abusive past and then seconds later talking about putting money in the man's commissary account. To my left, another visitor had initiated her conversation. In fact, people all around me were well into their visits, but on the other side of my monitor there was only a blank wall. A guard behind me noticed this and got on his radio, muttering something about "Pearlman." Lou had categorically declined all media interviews—special arrangements made by the jail and hosted by its dutiful public information officer, in which reporters were allowed to bring in cameras and gear and meet face-to-face with inmates. But I hadn't asked for anything special. I had signed up in accordance with the rights of any other citizen, and I had presumed I'd get at least a few moments with Lou, a feat no other media outlet had accomplished by the time this book went to press. But he wasn't showing up. *Could he have somehow refused my visit already?* I wondered. *Did he refuse to go to the conference center? Are they on to me?* Someone radioed back to the guard hovering behind me. There was a brief back-and-forth chatter. Lou never showed up on time to meetings. Not as a kid. Not now. "He's on his way," the guard leaned in and said. And moments later, I saw Lou hobble into frame. He was wearing his standard-issue prison jumpsuit, which was almost the same shade of blue as his old Rolls-Royce—his favorite color, cornflower blue. Once a husky, ginger-haired boy, his thin thatch was grayish blond and stringier than it usually appeared in pictures (he ordered dandruff shampoo and pomade from the commissary, I later learned). He wore a forced half

smile that didn't quite conceal a suspicious squint. He hobbled to his chair (he'd been suffering from back problems)
and said "hello" in the form of a question. This was my audition for Lou. I was on.

First I apologized for the cold call but mentioned the
letters I'd sent him seeking an interview. Surprisingly, he
apologized, too, for having no idea who I was and for not remembering the written requests. It was like a scene from
Pearlman's bio; he's the guy who bragged about convincing an
E. F. Hutton exec to bankroll his fledgling helicopter shuttle
business in the hallway of that institution after being turned
down by a loan officer, but this time he was on the receiving
end of a proposition. I told him I was a journalist, that I was
doing a story on his situation, that I wouldn't consider that
story to be complete without his comments, that I had visited
his old office and talked to many of his old associates, that
many of them had very nasty things to say about him that
begged for rebuttal. I told him I knew he'd declined all official
media requests since being incarcerated. He was nervous and
declined to speak on any specifics relating to his legal woes.
"I'd love to come out about a lot of things," he said. "I think
there are things missing from the story. Nobody's heard my
side, which is unfortunate, but my lawyer has advised against
talking about anything having to do with the case."

So I asked him to talk about his "legacy." And with that he
was off on a tear. He talked about his blimps and planes and

reality show, *Making the Band*. He said he was still working with US5, a group that seemed cloned from the best qualities of his biggest bands, Backstreet Boys and *NSYNC, who'd long since flown his coop. Backstreet was getting back together, though, he said: "We are still entitled to a share of the revenues." He went on to talk about his accolades, his World Award. "The other people who got that are Paul McCartney, Steven Spielberg, Michael Jackson, Morgan Freeman," he said.

After warming up and even laughing a few times—once when I joked that he, with US5, was like the band Spinal Tap at the end of the mockumentary *This Is Spinal Tap*, fizzled in the States but still all the rage overseas. "Exactly!" he said. "It's odd, because we usually start over there and break an act overseas." After about thirty or forty-five minutes of chatter, during which time he offered a window into his upbeat and disarming personality and exhibited none of the signs of a man facing 130 years in jail, he still declined to talk about his case. But he did indicate that he'd be cleared on the charges. "I'm planning on this chapter ending relatively soon," he said.

Forty-five minutes after I parted ways with Lou that day in July, I got a call from the jail's public information officer. He was abrupt. He wanted to know if I was a journalist, and when I said I was, he scoffed and sputtered a bit and said he had received a call from an angry local TV reporter who'd seen my name crop up on the brand-new visitors list—his *media* request had been denied. He had worked Orlando for a long time and recognized my name from my *Sentinel* days. He'd demanded to know how I was allowed to interview Pearlman when he wasn't. The PIO wanted to know why I thought I was allowed to talk to Lou when he hadn't authorized it, and he explained how he was caught looking like he was playing favorites. He said I'd "violated several jail policies" by going around the media request process. I insisted that I'd asked for no special treatment, nothing above and beyond what their website required of visitors. I asked if I'd broken any laws; I knew I hadn't, and he admitted as much. I apologized but told him I didn't care to differentiate myself from a member of the public who wanted answers. We made nice, and he was a consummate professional throughout my research, even if he did have to take a bunch of flak from his frequent sparring partners in the local media.

At the conclusion of our initial interview, I asked Lou if we might speak again in the near future, maybe ask the jail to let us have a longer sit-down. He agreed but never came through before deadline. He blamed his lawyer for blocking him from speaking, but he'd likely never planned to. In the end, I got a tiny taste of the heap of garbage Lou fed the investors who backed his bogus companies to the tune of hundreds of millions of dollars over the course of twenty years. He'd strung them along, kept them dependent on him, kept them in his game. Lou never planned to confess anything to anyone, let alone a journalist.

So I dug into his biography/business/self-help book, *Bands, Brands, and Billions: My Top Ten Rules for Making Any Business Go Platinum* (McGraw-Hill, 2002). It was a treasure trove, and without it as a reference, the job of telling Lou's early life story would have proved extremely difficult—not that his own recollections are anywhere near accurate. Quite the contrary, almost everything in the book is cherry-picked, exaggerated, or just plain made-up. I called the childhood friends he quoted in his tome—many of them had never read the passages in which they were named, and when I shared the way Lou described things like his childhood lemonade stand or his newspaper route, they laughed or scoffed and almost always said "Louie's" recollection was just plain wrong. Alan Gross was particularly helpful. Gross knew Pearlman since the two of them could talk. They were neighbors in Mitchell Gardens, a Queens, New York, high-rise complex. Alan still lives there. And his apartment is the repository of his own and Pearlman's histories. He had a bone to pick with Pearlman, his childhood chum who'd cheated him out of a stake in a blimp company, and he's kept every scrap of paper and photo to back up his claims.

Everyone in this story had an angle. For many, that angle was keeping their own tail out of jail. Pearlman surrounded himself with hucksters, ex-cons, and loyal friends to whom he awarded bogus titles and paid inflated salaries. In exchange, they did exactly what he told them to do and kept their mouths shut. A few did speak to me, usually off the record. I tried to avoid relying on those off-the-record conversations while researching this book, but when it was necessary to get a more complete picture of Lou's world, I tried to corroborate those conversations with public records or leaked documents that lots of former Trans Con associates have kept. There were thousands and thousands of pages of records that helped tell this story and, as one might expect, hours and hours of interviews with the many people Pearlman touched (literally, in some cases). Many of those who were the most exposed legally, the ones who had already been interviewed by the FBI and were possibly facing indictments of their own, offered the same basic excuse: They had no idea that Pearlman had created a fake company with few assets and then used it as bait to lure more than a thousand investors. Even as they marketed and promoted Lou's investment schemes and signed deposits into his accounts, they had no idea it was a scam, they said. They often said they had invested their own money in Lou's fake savings accounts and lost it as a result of his downfall. A few were truly ignorant, but some of the associates closest to Lou enjoyed the fruits of Pearlman's shady schemes and made out like bandits. They lived luxuriously for years on swollen salaries and executive titles their credentials didn't merit in the real corporate world. They might have turned a blind eye to the specifics, but they knew something fishy was going on.

Julian Benscher was a different case. The son of Gabi Benscher—the eccentric Campari Group Chairman and CEO—and a swashbuckling businessman himself, he was an important figure in the telling of Lou's story. He spent a lot of time as Lou's business partner in the blimp, boy band, and airline (or so he thought) businesses and told an amazing tale of how he came to work with and even befriend Pearlman. Though he has a knack for embellishing his memories to give them a better narrative sizzle, documents he shared (and I vetted) and independent sources corroborated his stories. Some bilked investors have criticized Benscher as a party to Lou's fraud, but the truth is that he started to untangle himself from Pearlman as soon as he suspected Lou was up to no good—it was in his best interest as an intensely creative but legitimate businessman. Like those who lost millions with Trans Con, he couldn't fathom the depth of Lou's fraud, even when it was staring him in the face. That was a theme among most of Pearlman's victims, investigators, associates, friends, and family I interviewed for this book: No one could believe one man was capable of masterminding such a long-running, convoluted scam.

Another important figure was Tammie Hilton, the woman Lou called his girlfriend. I cold-called her after visiting Lou in jail, having scored her cell phone number from the jail's visitor roster. We talked for months—on background in the beginning, but Tammie always understood I wanted to use the information she was giving me and quote her. All she asked in return was that I wait to do so until the whole drama played out and I was able to get a full picture of Lou. At first, she was his biggest defender. She met with him three times a week at the jail. She talked to him on the phone even more often. She passed on things Lou wanted me to know. But as his case stretched out, the stories he told her stretched thinner, too. During one dinner at a Disney restaurant, Tammie incredulously claimed that several of Lou's longtime employees had stolen money from him. He let it happen, she said, because he trusted them too much. Now he was in jail for things *they* had done. Lou had ceded much of his operation to his triumvirate of insiders, she explained—Alan Siegel, Greg McDonald, and Bob Fischetti. None of them, not even Alan, to whom I'd served dozens of delectable pasta entrées, would talk to me for this book. Once, as Tammie and I ate dessert, her cell phone rang and she took the call. It was Lou. Tammie didn't say much. She seemed to be taking orders, asking cursory questions about how things were going here and there but getting nothing incredibly revealing in Lou's replies. The last thing she said before hanging up was, "Love you, too."

Another important thread in the unraveling of Lou Pearlman's monumental scam was Helen Huntley's Money Talk blog and stories for the *St. Petersburg Times*. She was the reporter who first passed on information on Lou's whereabouts to the FBI, a sighting that led to his arrest in Bali, Indonesia. From that point on, she covered the daily and weekly developments in the case, often posting vital advice or information for investors who'd been cheated out of thousands—or combined millions—by Pearlman. Beneath every post, a digital horde of commentators added their own bits of information, some true, some planted by those with agendas of their own. Almost none of it could be verified—commentators on her blog were anonymous or could have been posting under fake names. They frequently turned on each other and remarks often spiraled into nonsense. But they did provide a glimpse into the vitriol and heartbreak wrought by Pearlman. Helen tried to moderate them when she could, and no one blanketed the day-to-day drama like her. Fortunately, she never had any interest in writing a book.

Other books were vital in researching this one. Les Henderson's *Under Investigation* (Coyote Ridge Publishing), about the model-scouting business Pearlman purchased in 2002, is nothing if not an obsessive anatomical study of a scam. Broadly sourced, it tells the insider's story of one of Lou's relatively smaller schemes—the one that eventually turned the tide of press and public opinion against him and threw his juggling act out of balance. Lance Bass's 2007 memoir *Out of Sync* (Simon Spotlight Entertainment) revealed several intimate moments in boy band history and offered an unprecedented peek behind the scenes. Bass's book was especially helpful since none of the former members of *NSYNC or current members of Backstreet Boys would speak about Pearlman—or even anything remotely related to his story. Even Bass turned down numerous requests to elaborate on his recollections. And when confronted at red carpet events, other former and current boy band members shut off and just walked away.

Part of the problem was that they had been dogged by the same rumors I first heard regarding them and Lou when I was working for the *Orlando Sentinel.* The fact that he was a man in his late forties who constantly surrounded himself with attractive, often underage males led many to believe that he wasn't just in it for the music. But it's a dastardly thing to accuse someone of pedophilia in print, especially considering the impact the implication has on innocent victims. I chased down a few rumors as a reporter for the *Sentinel.* They all led nowhere. Someone always knew someone who knew someone who had "allegedly" done something with Lou. It was tantamount to high school locker room talk, though, and the paper's ethical standards would have never allowed us to even raise the specter of Lou having inappropriate relationships with his artists. But magazines are different animals. As I was researching this book, *Vanity Fair* published a story by writer Bryan Burrough that vividly exposed Lou's business shenanigans but seemed to focus primarily on his fondness for young boys. No one in the *Vanity Fair* story said he had sex with Lou, but it carefully navigated claims to leave the impression that Lou lusted for the young males he promoted. I talked to some of the same people who made those claims in *Vanity Fair* and found their tales much less damning than they sounded in the magazine. But most of the former band members and Pearlman assistants quoted in the piece, and new sources, told me they saw plenty of things they considered inappropriate between Lou and young men. No one ever saw him have sex with a boy. No boy has ever come forward to say he had sex—consensual or otherwise—with Lou, even after *Vanity Fair* paved the way for someone to do so. It was obvious Lou would deny any wrongdoing, but I asked the man himself about the rumors of inappropriate sex between him and his artists. His comments were conspicuously absent from the *Vanity Fair* story.

"We are all good friends and had a normal friendship with no inappropriate activity," Lou said in a letter. For the record, he vehemently denied any allegations of inappropriateness. Asked about specific claims that he gave massages to several of his boys, Lou denied it and alluded to another famous entertainment figure who was frequently accused of inappropriate relationships with boys, Michael Jackson. "I paid for professional masseuses to give massages to our artists," he said. "It is also true that I do not own a 'Neverland Ranch.'"

He wasn't the only one who came to his defense on the

sexual allegations. Even the lawyer he stiffed on a $15.5 million bill, J. Cheney Mason, said he never knew of Lou engaging in any inappropriate behavior with his boys. Ditto Julian Benscher. Brad Fischetti of Pearlman band LFO said he never saw anything inappropriate happen between Lou and his artists. And Ben Bledsoe of Lou's band Natural, a guy who spent years in the company of Pearlman, said, "It could be totally true, but I, personally, have no clue." I had the same answer when *Radar*'s editor in chief, Maer Roshan, asked me about the allegations as I was researching my Pearlman story for the magazine. He asked if Lou was gay. But it wasn't as simple as that with Lou. He denied being interested sexually in men, but his actions over the years seemed to confirm his cravings for affection from boys. He had a girlfriend, even though their relationship turned out to be anything but typical. He just didn't seem to have the capacity for an adult romantic relationship—gay, straight, or whatever.

In February 2008, Pearlman struck a plea deal. He copped to money laundering and bank, bankruptcy, and investment fraud charges. On March 3, his deal went public, as did a forty-seven-page document outlining two decades' worth of fraud. It legitimized and often corroborated much of what I'd learned from sources and documents, and the deal and Lou's subsequent court appearances made for scintillating daily paper fodder and a convenient ending to his story. After he was sentenced on May 21, however, a palpable sense of dissatisfaction hung over the heads of investors who lingered in the courthouse hallways. Sentence aside, Lou made their money disappear—about $424 million according to prosecutors, as much as $500 million according to several investors' math, which included exorbitant interest returns Pearlman promised. [Note: This figure comes from claims made by prosecutors at a restitution hearing held after the deadline for this draft.] It didn't feel like an end or even much like justice for those who would never see their hard-earned savings again. They were left burdened by the questions investigators and lawyers couldn't answer: How could Lou keep this massive fraud organized in his mind for so long? How could he lie so effectively and stave off angry investors, banks, and government investigators? What kind of person is capable of such a massive lie? And most importantly, how did he spend *all that money*? As the daily drama of Lou's legal case unfolded in the press and as the aftermath of his fraud continues to unravel, those are the big questions this book answers.

## CHAPTER 1

# *TRANS CON*

*O*n a typically sunny Orlando afternoon in January 2006, an ac-
countant named Paul Glover arrived at the ragtime-themed
offices of Trans Continental Enterprises, a collection of travel,
entertainment, restaurant, and retail operations presided over
by fifty-one-year-old boy band impresario Lou Pearlman. He
walked past a flowing indoor fountain beneath authentic
World War I planes hanging from the ceiling and rode a glass
elevator to the third floor, filed past gold records and framed
accolades touting the successes of Pearlman's various pop
groups, and nestled into Lou's corner office, the one with the
faux-tiger rug and electric draperies that opened to a pan-
orama of downtown Orlando—"O-Town," as Lou had rechris-

tened it when he put it on the international entertainment map. The middle-aged mogul had burst into prominence in the '90s, back-dooring his way to the top of the pop charts with bubblegum acts Backstreet Boys and *NSYNC, followed by O-Town, LFO, Natural, Take 5, US5, Aaron Carter, and more. To frame it in the simplest present pop cultural terms: Without Lou Pearlman, there would be no *Making the Band*, no Lance Bass or bestselling Lance Bass book *Out of Sync*, no *FutureSex/LoveSounds* or other albums from Justin Timberlake, no Aaron or Nick Carter public train wrecks to gawk at—a horrific alternate dimension for millions of pop culture consumers. More than anything, though, he scored the soundtrack for the coming of age of an entire generation. He beat impossible odds in the entertainment business not once but twice, doing as a lone entrepreneur what entire music conglomerates couldn't. He shattered sales and revenue records with his seminal quintet, Backstreet Boys, then he trolled Central Florida's pool of Disney darlings (and scoured the back burghs and hollows of Mississippi) to do it all over again with *NSYNC. As one record executive put it, "It was like finding a needle in the haystack . . . *twice."* But Glover didn't come for an autograph. He was sent to save Lou from financial ruin—and maybe jail. As it turned out, the only thing more astonishing than the unlikely fame and decades-long success of the boy band Svengali was the monumental fraud that underscored it.

Born on June 19, 1954, in Flushing, Queens, Lou Pearlman grew up on the third floor of a different kind of complex,
a modest elevator building in Mitchell Gardens, a brown
brick, middle-class cluster of high-rises set apart from the big
city by open spaces and green lawns. He was his mother's son.
Reenie Pearlman had him well into her thirties, and once she
brought Lou into the world, she was sure to keep him happy
and well fed. His father was the late-'50s model of a working-
class family provider, Ward Cleaver with a Queens accent (and
a dark streak). He ran a humble custom dry-cleaning business
and even taught Lou the merits of customer satisfaction—and
the best places to feast on roadside meals—on dry-cleaning
delivery ride-alongs, his version of quality time.

By age nine, Lou had styled himself as an entrepreneur,
too, the proprietor of a lemonade stand by a neighborhood
bus stop. In the years that followed he assumed the roles of
hustling paper delivery boy, math nerd, "helium head" (slang
for a blimp groupie), and onetime guitarist turned manager of
a successful local rock band called Flyer. Music, he would frequently say, ran in his family—he's folksinger Art Garfunkel's
first cousin. While other kids played stickball and chased girls,
Lou retreated indoors, where he created fantasy worlds and
fake businesses, usually involving rock 'n' roll or airships, and
he made himself a fabulous player in them all. He studied accounting at Queens College, where he breezed through classes
and formed the ideas for his first real business—a helicopter

commuter service—as a final project. After graduating he started the helicopter service, then a fledgling charter airplane business, both run from his Mitchell Gardens home base. Then, as the helicopter service merged with a larger company and the airline business took off, Lou finally moved out of his parents' place and built his first blimp. In reality, he was never the sky captain he made himself out to be. In 1981, Lou's first airship crashed. In the years that followed he wrecked three more. After each, he pocketed insurance money for his next move, and his blimp company even went public, but it was his private airline company, Trans Continental Airlines, and its travel service that funded dozens of other air transport, food, and entertainment ventures in Lou's Trans Con empire.

By 1991, the boy from Flushing had outgrown Queens. He moved a ragtag but loyal cadre of workers to Orlando, Florida, where the climate was friendlier for both flying and reinventing oneself in a swashbuckling style. A malleable media came to know Lou as a jovial merchant prince who'd banked his first million by age twenty-one and his first $400 million by age twenty-four. At home in Mickey Mouse's backyard and approaching forty, Pearlman plunked down millions of dollars—or wrangled investors who helped him cover the tab—to make Backstreet Boys pop stars. When Lou did finally crack the code in the entertainment business, pop music would never be the same.

Along the way, he cultivated his own outsize impresario character, a Caucasian Berry Gordy, a deep-pocketed puppet master of pop who dreamed large, lived large, *was* large. By 2002, Pearlman had almost single-handedly lured pop music fans out of their dark and gloomy grunge phase with a squeaky-clean bevy of bleached, buffed, and meticulously groomed idols. He lived the high life, reaping the spoils not only of his success but of successes he only imagined he'd land in the near future. In Orlando, he was as much an icon as Mickey or Goofy. He sported a $250,000 Rolex. He rented out entire nightclubs for parties. He whisked his band members to gigs on his own Gulfstream jet. He took his entire office staff on vacations to the Bahamas on his charter planes. He feasted on three-pound lobsters at his own signature steakhouse and rarely dined with less than a dozen people. He always picked up the check. He zipped around in his stretch limo or his cornflower-blue Rolls-Royce Phantom, usually driven by wannabe singers and dancers and chiseled young dudes in tank tops. He frequently appeared alongside his pop stars, reminding the world that his boys would be invisible without him, the sixth Backstreet Boy. He guided tours for media and a never-ending stream of investors through his multimillion-dollar O-Town recording compound. He cultivated a far-reaching reputation as a lucrative mogul who could spin gold records out of nothing at all. Everyone wanted in. Even banks tripped over themselves to front him tens of millions for his new projects in the entertainment industry— an MTV show, an *American Idol*–style talent series, and more. As collateral he offered stock in his Trans Continental empire, which had swollen to include planes and travel, fashion, modeling, food, jewelry, CD manufacturing, and even a male stripper business. There were eighty-four corporations and limited partnerships at Glover's last count, and no one but Lou knew exactly how they were all strung together. City leaders were eager to help him turn the once thriving but darkened city-block-size tourist trap called Church Street Station into his bustling base of operations. He promised to give it a vibrant boy-band-style makeover, and in return the city council pledged $1.25 million in taxpayer-funded incentives to help him along. Then they literally handed him the key to the city.

Unbeknownst to them and many of Lou's closest executives, friends, and relatives who'd helped float Lou and his operation—Art Garfunkel and the folk music star's brother and mom among them—they had joined in one of the farthest-reaching, longest-running cons in U.S. history.

Behind the scenes, the companies that buoyed Pearlman's mid-'90s hit parade and lavish lifestyle had fallen into financial shambles by the time he moved into his Church Street complex. Time after time, rather than blowing the whistle, investors and investigators took Lou at his word when he explained away a gaping sinkhole of bad debt and broken promises. Even those who had started asking for their principles back let Lou keep stalling them, hoping all the while that he'd make them whole or even wealthier than they could imagine. He was, after all, the man behind Backstreet Boys and *NSYNC. And Trans Con was just about to go public, Lou perpetually promised.

Instead, a series of Lou's dirty deals went public. In 2002, news that his new model-scouting business Options Talent was at its core a bait-and-switch-style scam broke just as he was scheduled to close on his fancy new offices. His customers, wannabe models who'd paid a thousand bucks apiece for a promotional package, never got work in the industry and were telling their stories in local news "gotcha" reports. The bad press from Options rocked his investors' confidence. Soon, security guards once tasked with fending off starstruck teens or wannabe pop stars with demos in hand were forced to repel angry, elderly people showing up at the Trans Con gates. Some had traveled hundreds of miles to demand in person the return of their investments in what would turn out to be a dastardly scheme, a so-called savings plan hatched in thin air and anchored only in Pearlman's pockets.

In 2006, Trans Con suffered a fatal blow. Frankie Vazquez Jr. was Pearlman's lifelong chum from Queens, the son of the super at the Mitchell Gardens apartments and one of Lou's few close friends. He'd dedicated his whole life to Pearlman's businesses, rising to vice president of operations at the company and handling a huge chunk of responsibilities. But when investors and banks came clamoring for repayment, Vazquez started to realize the ugly truth behind the business he'd helped build. He got his first real glimpse of the whole picture as investigators closed in and Lou kept right on pocketing hundreds of thousands of dollars in investor money. In November, Vazquez climbed into his white 1987 Porsche, cranked it up, and lowered his garage door, asphyxiating himself to death.

With raids of Pearlman's home and offices by the Justice Department and IRS just around the corner, the corpulent mogul, who often demanded his underlings call him Big Papa, scrambled to keep his juggling act going. Behind the scenes, he was desperate to liquidate any assets he could find to buy himself some time. He'd been leveraged to the gills before. He could dig out again, he believed. The next great idea was just around the corner, the one that would save his bacon. It had to be.

That's when Glover got involved. The forty-nine-year-old mild-mannered CPA was assigned to Pearlman's operation in an effort to save it. But even that anguished maneuver was spearheaded by another shady character in Lou's world: Frank Amodeo—a disbarred attorney, convicted felon, and self-styled "distressed business manager" with connections that stretched all the way to the White House. He gave Glover a rough sketch of the mission and sent him headlong into Pearlman's operation. Trans Con's crackerjack executives were dying to cooperate, and they opened the books to Glover. Transparency was the only thing that would save them from being dragged down with their boss—or suffering the same fate as Vazquez, whose suicide had served them with a wake-up call. Besides, Glover was presumably on their side, having been brought in directly by Lou. But unlike those before him who had stumbled upon the telltale signs of fraud in Lou's books and tiptoed quietly away, Glover didn't have a stake in Trans Con, and he wasn't beholden to anyone who did. A straight-shooting Eliot Ness of the accounting world, he zeroed in on Pearlman's in-house retirement plan, which he called Employee Investment Savings Accounts, EISA for short. Offered first to his employees and then to the public at large, the scheme traded on Lou's notoriety and success as a music mogul and promised slightly better returns than traditional savings accounts. He and his sales agents first targeted friends, family, associates, and long-standing owners of shares in Trans Con. Then they expanded the program to anyone who'd bite. Particularly susceptible were elderly retirees eager to grow their nest eggs, inheritances, and fixed incomes. Local salespeople or Lou himself solicited checks and transfers. They sometimes bundled Trans Con's EISA with other investments in funds to make it seem even more legit. Even respectable money-managing corporations were duped into transferring their investors' IRA earnings into EISA upon request. Everyone was assured in brochures and in face-to-face meetings that the savings plan was backed by the FDIC and insurance companies AIG and Lloyd's of London. Plus it sounded a hell of a lot like "Employee Retirement Income Security Act" (ERISA), a legitimate U.S. Department of Labor regulation that covered all kinds of savings plans. The accounts were not, however, insured or guaranteed in any way. In fact, there were no accounts. In January 2006, Glover found document after document indicating that a half billion dollars in EISA money was going straight into Lou's hands. *This is a Ponzi scheme,* he thought.

That's "Ponzi scheme," the illegal system of raising new money to pay old debts. Named after 1920s Boston huckster Charles Ponzi, it's a decades-old system of fraud that's not too different from a pyramid scheme, a shell game, or "robbing Peter to pay Paul." In Lou's case, he and his agents fanned out among the gullible golden age set and gathered up checks— about $340 million worth, all told. The investment plan was incredibly simple and alluring in its modesty. Pearlman wasn't offering a get-rich-quick scheme. EISA's interest rates were only a few percentage points better than the rates investors would get if they put their money in CDs. A long-term investor who sank his nest egg in an EISA wouldn't become an overnight millionaire, but he might find himself with a few hundred thousand extra dollars come retirement age, or he might live comfortably off of the interest checks he'd draw over time. Pearlman was allegedly able to negotiate these prime rates for his investors because of his decades of success and his deep ties to banks and businesses, particularly those in Europe. Some early investors were even able to take out their savings—with interest. Ponzi schemes often work because the benefits are believable. Like any successful scam, it's built on a tiny kernel of truth. Eventually, though, too many people started asking for their investment back, and that's inevitably when any Ponzi scheme falls apart. It's exactly where Lou was by the time Glover dove into his books.

As storm clouds gathered over Trans Con that winter day in '06 and the sun set on Church Street, scrambling execs and secretaries just kept forking over to Glover more and more evidence of fraud. There were hundreds of pages of documents, ledgers, and angry certified letters from investors. But it was one of the most boring details in the EISA accounting statements that bothered him the most: fine print that most would have overlooked—and most did. The red flag was the documents' standard disclaimer, the seemingly innocuous industry-wide statement that CPAs agonize over and constantly reform at annual conventions. On the EISA statement, it was years out of date. The program's auditing firm, Cohen & Siegel, should have caught that. "I've seen poor accounting work before, but I thought, *Wow, this is a shoddy firm,*" Glover said. It was this little detail that nearly convinced him he was neck-deep in a massive fraud. As a matter of ethics and to satisfy his own professional curiosity, Glover switched his mission that day. And at the end of a grueling ten-hour stretch—the beginning of the end for Pearlman—he would scurry out the front door of the ornate band headquarters carrying enough evidence to topple the impresario's pop empire and implicate most of the people who helped run it—the same ones who had brought him entire trees' worth of damning documents.

Unlike those who had previously inspected Lou's books, Glover handed over to authorities evidence that would brace the case against him. It would be a spectacular fall for Pearlman. The balls he'd juggled for two decades would come crashing down. His myth would unravel. Investors would lose their life savings. Banks would never recover their loans. His cars and planes and home would be seized. The hearts of friends and relatives who once entrusted their dreams to Pearlman would break. And the masses who once lined up to buy his products or get in on the ground floor of whatever new scheme he'd hatched would start to wonder what kind of monster Lou really was. What kind of person could perpetrate such a massive scam? How could someone live a lie for so long, and just how deep did it go?

But first, Glover gathered one last bit of evidence that he was, in fact, staring down an egregious Ponzi scheme. All of the EISA statements and almost all of the Trans Con financial forms had been audited by the slipshod Cohen & Siegel firm. So Glover decided to ring them at their Coral Gables, Florida, office. He dialed and hit "send" on his mobile phone, half expecting at that late hour to get an answering service. But then the phone on Pearlman's desk started buzzing. "When I hung up my phone, the phone on his desk quit ringing, too," Glover said. He was nothing if not a thorough accountant. So he dialed Cohen & Siegel once more. And Lou's line lit up again.

## CHAPTER 2

# LI'L PAPA

*T*he most honest business Lou Pearlman ever ran was a lemonade stand.
His parents might have purchased the raw materials for him,
but he manufactured the product, handled distribution, and,
of course, masterminded the marketing and sales schemes.
He was eight.

In July 1962, little Lou set up his beverage outfit on Union
Street, near the apartment where he lived with his parents in
Mitchell Gardens, a cluster of six-story brown brick buildings
at Union and Twenty-sixth Avenue in Flushing, Queens. He
plopped down near the Q14 bus stop to capture the attention
of parched Con Edison workers and commuters on their way
home. Even then, he understood one of the most important

principles in business: location. Generations of dirty-water-dog vendors and subway-side bodega owners had taken up the same sort of perch. Lou's lemonade recipe was simple, tried and true—sweet with a little sour, thirst quenching with just enough bite to leave them wanting more. Not that anyone walked away saying it was the *best* lemonade ever to pickle their puckered lips. Lou's real gift was his understanding of profit, a preternatural instinct that bordered on greed, even back then. He started off charging a nickel a cup, pocketing two cents per sale, but even a 60-plus percent profit wasn't cutting it for the husky hustler. After a few meager $20 weeks, Lou set his junior achiever mind to raking in real coin—he raised his price to seven cents a cup and doubled his profit to more than 100 percent. But that still wasn't the grift. He'd noticed that most customers carried only dimes and nickels, and when he changed his price to seven cents, they'd toss him a dime and tell him to keep the change. "It helped that I didn't keep any pennies around," Pearlman wrote in his 2003 biography-cum-self-help-book, *Bands, Brands, and Billions*.

Big from birth, Lou grew into a beefy tween. He looked like the Queens version of Spanky from *The Little Rascals,* minus the freckles and friends. Even in childhood pictures, "Fat Louie," as some called him, sported the spare tire of a man five times his age, which was accentuated unfortunately by high-waisted pants into which he'd tuck tight-fitting tees. Only one kid in the building took to him right away: Alan

Gross, the grinning tyke from apartment 4C just one floor up and on the other side of the building from the Pearlmans at 3F. Four years older, Gross helped babysit little Lou, and the two started palling around from the time they could communicate. Lou was especially shy as a child, particularly around adults, and he preferred the company of younger kids. Gross took him on as a sort of project to try to bring him out of his shell, but Lou still seemed awkward in his own skin. He made up stories that revolved around his adventures and claimed various expertises, mostly in piloting and in business. "He would tell tall tales and stuff . . . He was a weird guy," Gross said. One of Lou's go-to claims to fame was his relationship with folksinger Art Garfunkel. That one happened to be true.

He did occasionally try to join in the games other kids were playing. Gross said it never went well, though, and at least once it ended in a momentous disaster. It snowed heavily one year, Gross recalled, when he was eleven or twelve— Lou was probably seven or eight, and it must have been the winter just before he launched his lemonade stand. The sprawling, sloped lawn in front of Mitchell Gardens was transformed into virginal sledding grounds for the neighborhood kids. Played right, one could slide all the way from the tip-top of Union Street to the bottom of the front lawn, a beeline diagonal path that ended near the entrance to the garage around the side of the building. A few of the young pioneers packed down a groove, and before long they were whisking by in a blur, barely skirting metal pillars and chains that delineated a concrete walkway. When the other kids had groomed the run, Lou grabbed Alan's sled and demanded a turn. "Once he got to know you, he was very domineering in a way you wouldn't immediately realize," Gross recalled. He tried to warn Lou that day, but the thickset youngster was off. Gaining momentum, he followed the same path the others had taken safely, but, likely because he was heavier than most, Lou picked up speed too early in the run and started losing control by the bottom half. He was careening toward the metal pillars and chains, unable to steer or stop or make the pass around the side of the building. Gross watched and winced as Lou slammed into one of the pillars, dead-on. "I heard a snap," he said. The next thing he remembers is Lou wailing and holding his arm. It looked broken. "Everybody else was laughing at him," Gross said. "I took him to his mom."

Reenie Pearlman gave birth to Lou when she was in her midthirties after a couple of unsuccessful attempts at pregnancy. Even in pictures taken when Lou was very young, she looked perfectly matronly, tucked in, modestly groomed with dark, coiffed hair, and sporting the prescribed style of a 1950s housewife a la *The Honeymooners*. She lived for her boy, making sure he was spoiled on a day-to-day basis. Lou slept on a foldout Castro couch but it was in the only bedroom in apartment 3F. His parents, meanwhile, set up their bed in what would typically have been the living room. Almost everyone who knew Reenie back then described her in terms fit for saints and angels—sweet, adoring, heart of gold. She encouraged Lou to chase his dreams. She had ambitions of teaching but never made it to college herself. Instead, she volunteered as a milk lady and a teacher's aide at P.S. 21, Lou's gargoyle-adorned fortress of a grade school a few blocks away. She was, in Pearlman's words, "one of the most caring, big-hearted people in the universe." A synagogue in Southwest Orlando to which Lou later made a sizeable donation was named Ohalei Rivka Southwest Orlando Jewish Congregation in her honor, and a picture of her hangs on its wall with the inscription: "As Rivka of our Torah was known for her goodness and her kindness, so will Reenie be forever known for hers. May her life be a lesson and a blessing for us all."

Just as Reenie was cast in the classic role of a mid-'50s housewife, Herman (Hy, as everyone called him) Pearlman was the classic provider. Lou Pearlman's strongest memories of quality time with Dad involve him being carted all over Long Island in his father's Dodge—and, later, Plymouth— station wagons delivering laundered shirts and slacks. Hy owned Pleasant Laundry and Dry Cleaning, which he'd inherited from *his* father. He had a repertoire of well-rehearsed jokes he could pull out when the conversation lulled, and those who knew him recall him as being lively, funny. In pictures, his clothes are always well pressed and sharp. He had thinning hair and was a bit pudgy, especially in the cheeks—it was clear where Lou got his build. Among the details of rare time with dad that Lou remembers most fondly are the four-A.M. breakfasts they'd wolf down before heading out to deliver the day's cleaning. He'd learn from his father where to find the best roadside lunch fare in Long Island, too, at places such as Link's Log Cabin—little slices of home away from home for Hy, who spent marathon days working at the business or out on deliveries. When he did take Lou with him, his father would teach him about customer service, remembering each patron's preferences when it came to starch and hangers and folding; there were notes for each of them and Lou got the impression it was Hy's personal touch that made the business hum. Pleasant Laundry had two locations. Far from a cash cow, the store Hy solely owned provided the Pearlmans with a decent lifestyle, but he often dreamed out loud to Lou on long stretches of road about opening a whole chain of outlets. What happened instead was a fire—Hy's shop burned to the ground, and he was forced to go to work for the owner of the other Pleasant location. Lou called it a "soft trap" in his book. "I don't think my father was ever truly happy in his work. He wasn't unhappy. He liked the business. But he took no joy in what he did day in and day out. I came to see that as sad." Instead of a *career*, Hy labored at a *job*, Lou realized—not that he let his dad off the hook for sealing his own fate. He never took the proper time to think about what he really wanted to do and make it happen, Lou said. "That bothered me as a boy, and it stayed with me."

What he's never addressed is the rumor that Hy had a mistress. Several of the people who grew up with Lou knew, and it's hard to imagine that Reenie didn't catch wind. Lou found out eventually, too, and learned that his dad had fathered a child with this other woman. Though there's never been a DNA test to prove their kinship, at least one person very close to Lou says he has kept in cordial contact with his alleged half sister.

When spring came and others played stickball or touch football, Lou's parents' modest apartment became his lair. He typically sat indoors, often by himself, coloring or copying other people's drawings or art. He built model airplanes. He whiled away hours watching his favorite TV shows—*Sky King*, about the hotshot owner of a Cessna airplane who got into all sorts of predicaments, or *Whirlybirds*, a black-and-white show about the owners of a helicopter company who hired themselves out to people in various predicaments. All the while, Reenie frequently fried up bacon or hamburgers, the smell wafting out into the hallway of the building. Gross often visited Lou's inner sanctum in those days, but the food, he said, was always reserved for Lou and Lou alone. Just about everyone in the building came from the same working-class financial stratum, but Lou and his parents played it tight. Always one to share a snack or toys when he and Lou played in his own apartment, Gross remembered things going differently at the Pearlman abode. "His mom didn't like it when I played with his toys," Gross said. "But when he came up to my apartment, he had free rein." Lou could do no wrong in his mother's eyes, too. Neither Gross nor any of those who knew Lou as a kid could recall him ever being punished. When play turned to roughhousing—Lou loved to wrestle—and something in his apartment got broken, it was often Gross who'd get the blame.

By age seven, the spring and summer seasons did lure Lou outdoors more often, and after he outgrew the lemonade stand, he eventually took on a job filling in for the local news delivery boys, a pair of brothers named David and Danny Lebenstein. The gig involved dropping off papers to Mitchell Gardens' 120 customers, and Lou added a personal touch. He wrote down their delivery preferences on index cards (ring the doorbell, don't ring the doorbell, slide the paper under the door, etc.), a gimmick he picked up from his dad on laundry delivery runs.

But Lou's recollection of his delivery days and those of the others involved diverge. Lou told it this way:

His fifteen-year-old boss, David Lebenstein, outgrew the job and offered Lou the chance to take over his routes for $500. Lou didn't have that kind of cash any more than he'd had spare pennies for lemonade change, so he made promises to pay back the boys, who then essentially became his inves-tors. Recognizing that a whole generation of paper delivery boys was becoming more interested in girls than news, the entrepreneur, then four years younger than most of the elder newsies, made a sweeping offer to take over not just one but *several* of their routes. If he couldn't earn the money to buy the routes from their various owners within thirty days, he said, the original delivery boys could repossess them. Only a youth, Lou was already upside-down with his first massive debt, facing a seemingly impossible deadline—he had prom-ised to produce in a single month the presumed value of sev-eral entire routes, more than $1,000.

He wallowed in the financial predicament like a pig in filth. Suddenly the proprietor of a business he could neither afford to own nor service himself (running six stories' worth of stairs in six high-rises was not even a *young* Pearlman's style), he recruited a kid army, young boys mostly, to deliver his papers. After thirty days, however, Pearlman had only half of what he owed the older boys for their routes, so he bar-gained for more time, offering an extra $50 to $100 per route for another month's worth of time. Working at a breakneck clip, Lou continued pushing papers on the local gentry. He specialized in sales and offered discounts to customers if they'd subscribe to both papers he delivered, the *New York Post* and the *Long Island Star-Journal*. Short of that, he started delivering on Sundays, a chore his predecessors had dodged due to the heft of the Sunday paper. To make the load manageable, he got the newspaper distributors themselves to give him most Sunday sections for Saturday-morning delivery (all but news and sports sections are typically produced Friday night), evening out the weight of the weekend load and wowing his clients by delivering Sunday's news a day early. The masterstroke that finally allowed him to pay off his creditors involved buying in bulk—at cost—deep-fried morsels from the neighborhood Dunkin' Donuts and charging his customers extra for breakfast delivery with his newspaper service. Pretty soon, he said, people in Mitchell Gardens were blaming him for the fact that they never got out of their jammies on Sundays.

Interest. Refinancing. Delay tactics. Someone to do his dirty work (young boys, preferably). Entrepreneurial ingenuity. Fatty snacks. These became the hallmarks of Pearlman's enterprises. But there was one other trademark element to Lou's account of his paper delivery career, too: It wasn't true.

Former newsie and Pearlman chum David Lebenstein, from whom Lou said he bought his first paper route, laughed out loud when he heard the story as Pearlman told it. "He may have helped me out in a snowstorm or, you know, when I was sick or something, but I have no recollection of selling him the route." Lebenstein, four years Lou's senior, became a real estate broker in Manhattan, dealing mostly with nonprofits. "Five hundred dollars sounds like an incredible amount of money in 1964," way more than he ever had his hands on in those days, he said. Plus, when he gave up his paper route, he passed it to his brother, Danny, not Lou. "There was never any talk of Louie buying it," he said. Asked about Lou's version of the story, Danny Lebenstein erupted in a belly-laugh, too, and called it nothing short of a fantasy dreamed up by Lou. "He's really got an imagination," he said. He remembered Lou at that age not as a shy kid but more as a husky honcho. "He was outgoing and gregarious the whole time I knew him. He could talk you out of your shirt from day one, as I remember. Louie, he was fat. But he was the boss." It was, in fact, Lou's tall tales and flights of fancy that kept people hanging around, the Lebensteins both said, even though most were secretly laughing at the ridiculousness of them all. "The one thing about Louie that we thought was cool was that his cousin was [Art] Garfunkel," David said. "That was an actual fact."

At thirteen, Lou had his bar mitzvah at a Queens party hub called Leonard's. After a traditional Jewish service that summer day in June 1967, sixty or seventy people from the neighborhood, plus cousins and uncles and aunts, all came to the meeting hall bearing gifts—checks or cash, mostly. Gross's family gave him a check. There were early cocktails and snacks; the party, Gross remembered, was fairly unremarkable but for one special guest, Art Garfunkel. He was already a wildly popular folksinger by then, and he'd shown up just to pal around with his cousin. Lou stuck by his side for most of the evening, making sure everyone saw. "The fact that Garfunkel showed up to his bar mitzvah did a lot for his credibility," Gross said.

Lou had started coming out of his shell, too, venturing out of his apartment more. He went to the movies with Gross—the Beatles' *Help!* was their favorite. They took the Flushing line of the Long Island Railroad (the front car, so they could see out) to Rockefeller Center. Dressed in sports coats and clip-on ties, they'd sneak into NBC studios. It was a thrill for them both watching something live that would later show up on TV. They were both obsessed with the goings-on behind the scenes and spent several hours gawking. "A lot of my friends would have come with me, but I felt like I was Lou's older brother and I should take him," Gross said.

That same year, Lou saw his first-ever concert, his cousin's duo, Simon & Garfunkel, at the Forest Hills tennis stadium. It was a pivotal experience. Lou was always trying to hobnob with Art, hoping along the way that some of his cousin's fame might rub off, but as a VIP at his first concert, gazing out on an adoring audience from the same point of view as the artists onstage, Lou got a firsthand taste of Art's world—and it was opening act, The Doors, that made him want to become a rock star. He used his newspaper delivery money to take guitar lessons at Wabash & Babitsch Music Store in downtown Flushing. They were $3.50 a pop. His parents bought him a $250 Guild acoustic, a fancy guitar that would be worth much more today if he still had it. He paired up with a young organ player named Joey Kravitz, uniquely qualified because he bought the same kind of organ the Doors had, a Farfisa. Together with a few other young guys from Bleecker Junior High School 185, they played a few school functions as the Starlighters. Lou manned rhythm guitar. Over the years, the group would change members a bunch of times and add and subtract instruments, and in 1970, Lou changed the band's name to Flyer. They started playing paid gigs at nightclubs, opening for Kool & the Gang, Gloria Gaynor, Barry White, and Donna Summer. Feeling a stronger pull to the business side of the operation (and never quite fitting physically into the heartthrob mold), Lou would eventually give up playing in the band himself, go to work as its manager, and even flirt with getting his group a record deal. Ever since that summer day at the tennis stadium watching The Doors as a VIP on Art Garfunkel's guest list, he harbored hope of carving out his own place in the rock star world. But he set off chasing another dream before he found his way back to music and entertainment. As a young teenager, Lou was enamored with flight.

Around the time of his bar mitzvah, he made other friends, mostly outside of his building. One of the few women to have even noticed he was alive, Michelle Novak, describes him as a math whiz who tutored neighborhood kids at times. "Lou had a lot of hangers-on," she said. Lou and his friends were always tinkering with gadgets and dreaming up businesses and clubs. "These guys were the nerd squad," Novak said. Ray Seiden was one of them; a fellow member of the audiovisual team in grade school, he later partnered with Pearlman in business but would end up becoming a bit-part actor (he appeared most notably in the role of Dog Face in the 1989 cult classic *The Toxic Avenger Part III: The Last Temptation of Toxie*). Seiden, who's the same age as Lou, recalled him as a gregarious geek, too. "He had fascinating stories. He could talk circles around anyone," he said. No longer limiting his visitors to Gross, Lou hosted a revolving cast of kids in a couple of distinct cliques at his parents' place whenever they were both out. He ran the gatherings like business meetings and always seemed to be pitching people on reasons they should be his friends. "You'd come over to Louie's house. He would be hosting one group of kids who were there looking at pictures of his cousin, you know, Art Garfunkel, and you'd have another group who he was going to have over to try and take a blimp ride at Flushing Airport. It was very hectic," Seiden said. "He had dreams, that's for sure. He always dreamed of aviation and blimps." He even went as far as to have a local printer make up stock certificates for his fake blimp company. "I'm telling you that Mr. Louie Pearlman made up stock certificates for Airship International back then," former newsboy Danny Lebenstein said. "There was no company, there was just Louie just selling shares of a company. He went to a printer and made up a beautiful thing for Airship International—with a picture of the blimp."

In some of the rarefied times spent outside the confines of the cleaners or the delivery wagon, Lou's father took him to Flushing Airport, which was within eyesight of Mitchell Gardens, just across the Whitestone Expressway. Hy was a World War II vet, a former tail gunner. He'd buy Lou a Yoo-hoo, and they'd sit outside the airport fence for hours watching planes take off and land. Then in 1964, the Goodyear blimps rolled in for the World's Fair. They just hung there in the air, hovering quietly over Mitchell Gardens. And Lou's own story took another turn; he embarked on another flight of fancy that, once again, doesn't jibe with the stories of the other people involved—except in the case of Alan Gross, with whom Lou's own story jibed a bit too closely.

Lou first fell in love with blimps while watching them waft by his bedroom window. They were impossible to ignore, and he fantasized about what it must be like to peer down on his world from such heights. A kid from upstairs whose father worked in electronics scored Gross a radio that let him listen to the pilots talking to their ground crews, and he and Lou would wait for the airships to come soaring over, then sit and listen to the communications with the ground crews, picking up on the lingo in the process. Lou, who'd carved out a little world of his own in Mitchell Gardens, started to see airships as symbols of his lofty potential. They traveled the world, but they launched and landed just a stone's throw from his own abode. Gross eventually goaded Lou into venturing from his apartment complex to Flushing Airport, and the two crossed the Whitestone Expressway and started lurking near the Goodyear hangar all summer. Lou begged for a ride, but the crew told him the only civilians they took up for trips were members of the press. The next day Lou came back with a story he'd written for the school newspaper and the cooperative Goodyear PR man helped him get press credentials. Lou scored his first blimp trip. He even brought Reenie along. She was petrified at first, but Lou said his father's urging and the gentle hum and effortless flight of the airship put his mother at ease. Gone were the hydrogen blimps of the Hindenburg era, both Lou and his dad had assured Reenie, and before long they were floating above their own apartment building. "It went way beyond mere fun for me," Lou said. "It was like being aboard a giant cruise ship in the sky." Lou would go back to the blimp hangar all summer, eventually getting hired at $1.65 an hour to clean it up, wash the trucks, run errands, and even catch the ropes when the blimps came in for landings. Along the way, he scored plenty more rides, a boast he frequently shared with his Mitchell Gardens cliques. "I was infatuated," Lou said. "Riding high above Mitchell Gardens, I'd seen a whole new world."

Lou found his future at Flushing Airport. He called himself a "helium head," a blimp groupie. He has repeated the story of his summer romance with Goodyear and his foray into the blimp business in his book and countless interviews. It was one of the pillars of his persona. But he seems to have lifted many of the details from Alan Gross's life.

Gross grew into a mild-mannered former hippie with a head full of neatly coiffed, medium-short, swept-back salt-and-pepper hair and a mustache. He plugged away on part-time census survey work, living his whole adult life in the same Mitchell Gardens apartment he inherited from his parents. As Lou blossomed into a full-blown wheeling, dealing tycoon, Gross settled into being a kind of sidekick. But there was always a vital difference between him and his best friend. "I was never after money," Gross said. He got into airships solely for the love of the crafts, their simple bargain with gravity, and the timeless way they took flight. Compared to Lou, who saw blimps more as a means to an end, Gross's attraction to sky ships was more like an intense admiration or obsession.

On a winter day in November 2007, clad in shorts and a plain T-shirt, Gross parted the shades of his narrow, cluttered apartment, allowing the sun to cut a beam through the dark and dust. His living room was a maze of brown cardboard storage boxes and waist-high stacks of old VHS tapes of blimp events and Pearlman company occasions. Every once in a while one of three cats would dart between boxes of old documents he had cataloged only in his mind. The walls were adorned with hippie-ish art of galactic scenes, one called *Lavender Nebula* (Lou had the same one). Blimps were everywhere. He'd found plenty of time to nurture his passion: collecting blimp footage, blimp models, blimp mugs, stickers, T-shirts, toys, pens—anything airship related, really. His goal was once to become a public relations exec with the Goodyear blimp company, a job for which he's still singularly suited.

He believed for a time, too, that his future was with Lou, but he was dumped by his buddy. Then he was sidelined with leukemia. He never circled back to actualizing his airship dreams. Flushing Airport closed in January 1984. The view out of Gross's living room became the view of a *New York Times* production facility that was built just across the Whitestone Expressway, and he kept his shades shut, mostly. It was *his* perch, though, he pointed out—not the one in Pearlman's apartment—from which the pair watched blimps. Lou's window faced the wrong way, and unless he craned his neck and caught a glimpse of an airship as it passed directly overhead, Lou wouldn't have been able to see much from his own bedroom.

Gross told his own version of Lou's airship love story (and backed it up with documents and tchotchkes from his experience). Gross was into airships long before Lou started tagging along with *him* to the Goodyear hangar. It was Gross, not Pearlman, who first hung around the airport until *his* mom pushed *him* to ask one of the Goodyear guys for a press kit.

Gross still has it. It was that press kit that he, not Pearlman, used to write a story for the *North Shore News* in October 1964. He still has the clip, too (Lou's later story on blimps bears an almost plagiaristic resemblance). Gross's story got *him* and *his* parents a ride in the Goodyear blimp first. And it was *he* who first got odd jobs working at the hangar. At least initially, Gross said, Pearlman just kind of hung around in the background and generally "creeped everyone out."

"His story . . . is totally wrong," Gross said. "It was me, it wasn't Lou."

## CHAPTER 3

# HOT AIR

As a regular Goodyear gofer, Lou scored countless blimp rides throughout the late 1960s. Perched in the gondolas of the high-flying ships *Mayflower* and *Columbia,* he gazed upon Mitchell Gardens in its context. His building was an unimpressive little rectangle in the red-brown cluster of buildings. Manhattan stabbed upward just a putter away. The rest of the world teased him from just over the horizon. Airship trips inspired Lou to spread his own wings. His parents' Flushing abode would remain his base of operations for years to come, but as soon as Lou could drive, he hit the road with a giant hunger to make a name in business. To his eclectic assembly of friends—anyone who would listen to his tall tales about blimps, planes, and his close relationship to his famous cousin, Art—Pearlman was a husky, hyperactive kid who always put together an entertaining scheme. In his own mind, he was a player by age sixteen.

Ray Seiden, who later moved to the Aviation High magnet school in nearby Long Island City but spent most of his early high school days palling around with Lou, recalled him as an attentive student. He was a math whiz who tutored neighborhood kids for extra cash. Pearlman and Seiden often found themselves in the quieted halls wheeling projectors and record players to different classrooms. They were A/V geeks. It was one of the ways Lou became friendly with a cross-section of kids from different cliques—everyone from popular kids to math nerds, but mostly all guys.

When Christmas and New Year's break rolled around, Lou would spearhead vacations to Florida, sometimes assembling two carloads of people for road trips—again, all guys. He drove a boatlike two-door car with a white interior back then and packed it full of people for jaunts down the East Coast. The crew would stop over at the Days Inn in Orlando, meet up with the occasional Pearlman or Garfunkel family member, go to Disney for the day, and continue on to Miami or Ft. Lauderdale, where they would stay at the home of Lou's cousin Larry Zeitlin or some other family members, or even hotels. They swam somewhere every day in tepid pools or the relatively balmy ocean. They met up with girls. "Lou was a charmer," Seiden said, and he was quick to regale the ladies with tales of flying or hanging out backstage with Simon & Garfunkel. A few years into the tradition, alcohol seeped into the scene for some of the guys on the trips, but Seiden said he could never remember Lou taking a sip. He did remember him ordering virgin versions of whatever everyone else imbibed, then *acting* drunk. "I guess it was his way of playing along," said Seiden.

Like his father, Pearlman always mapped out the meal plan. "Lou always had his favorite restaurants," Seiden said. There was Chicken Unlimited, which was exactly what it sounded like, an all-you-can-eat chicken shack near Ft. Lauderdale. Over the course of an hour and a half or more, Lou could power down fifteen pieces—fried or barbecued—with sides of coleslaw and mashed potatoes and gravy. But it was at another local eatery, a slightly fancier place, where Lou truly flexed his remarkable intestinal fortitude. Seiden couldn't remember the name of the spot, but he remembered the name of its "challenge dish": the Plank. It was massive slab of meat on a wooden board. Anyone who could eat it all got it gratis (the digestive aftereffects, one might argue, were the price truly paid). Lou made quick work of it, finishing it inside an hour. "We used to joke that you'd see sparks when he cut it," Seiden said.

The Florida trips continued through the early college years; both Seiden and Pearlman commuted to Queens College, a few miles from Mitchell Gardens, and Lou lived at home. It wasn't a campus-life kind of school, and anyway Lou dedicated his spare time to scouring for business ideas. He cherry-picked shortcuts and tax loopholes from his business and accounting class lessons and worked them into his entrepreneurial exploits whenever possible. The trips to Florida, for Lou, always had a dual purpose. As young as sixteen or seventeen, Lou was already developing ideas for businesses based in Florida—a gym was one early plan that never came to fruition, for example. With Seiden in tow, he'd meet with owners of this or that who had ties to one of Lou's cousins or family somewhere, and he would toy with ideas for how to emulate their success in whatever business they'd started. Simply put, he was never merely vacationing, he was networking. "He always mixed business with pleasure," Seiden said.

By the mid-1970s, Lou had fallen back on his boyhood adventure as his best likely business, and along with Alan Gross and Ray Seiden he went to work for Goodyear at the Flushing and Teterboro, New Jersey, airports while he finished up at Queens College. He'd graduate with a degree in accounting in 1976, but not before garnering the attention of one of his instructors, David Deutsch, who summoned Lou to his office and encouraged him to try to turn a class project into a real business. Lou had imagined a commuter helicopter business that would shuttle busy downtown Manhattanites from their Wall Street offices to area airports. He'd worked out a lot of the details, too—much of the complicated permitting involved with flying a chopper in and out of Lower Manhattan.

Ideas and planning were never in short supply for Lou. What he lacked was cash and a helicopter. His first instinct was to hit up his rich cousin Art Garfunkel, who told him he'd have to ask his money man, his dad (Lou's uncle). Jack Garfunkel told Lou he trusted him, believed in the idea, and had full confidence his nephew would make it fly. Then he told him, "I'll gladly help you buy your *second* helicopter." A catch-22 for some, but glass-half-full Lou took it to mean he had one helicopter secured. He needed two (one for a backup) to be taken seriously as a bona fide commuter operation, so he started hitting up banks, getting no after no until, he says, an executive at E. F. Hutton overheard him mention the idea of a helicopter commuter service while being shown the door by a loan officer. Given a few moments, Lou blurted out his pitch one last time in the hall of the financial institution and impressed the man who would assemble his first group of angel investors. Commuter Helicopter Service Inc. was launched in 1975, backed by the Wall Street group that actually bought the choppers and leased them to Lou. He later bragged that his helicopter business earned him his first million dollars by age twenty-one. That was not at all likely. Commuter Helicopter might have appeared successful on paper, but Lou's upkeep on two helicopters was steeper than he ever bargained for. His whirlybird business bled cash.

Pearlman ran Commuter Helicopter for just a couple of years before merging it with Island Helicopters, which would become the largest tourist helicopter service in the city until it was evicted in 1997 from its Sixtieth Street heliport following noise complaints from new neighbors. He and Seiden were never official employees of Island, but they did enjoy a sort of cooperative agreement with the company that gave them access to aviation business insiders at several airports. It was a typical Pearlman arrangement that allowed him to string together a handshake network. Seiden, who first went to work for Lou's Commuter Helicopter Service in December 1975, said he was never really paid as an employee. "Basically as shareholders, we were putting money into this thing, not taking it out. The only one who seemed to have benefited at these times was Louie." All of the contacts Pearlman made through Commuter Helicopter and then Island Helicopter added up to a ragtag flight operation called Transcom Airways in 1976. He leased a Piper Aztec twin-prop plane and flew runs from Morristown Airport in New Jersey to Newark, John F. Kennedy, and LaGuardia airports. They were still shuttling business travelers, but it was cheaper to maintain leased planes instead of helicopters. Lou, who'd earned a pilot's license at age nineteen, took side trips with friends, too. He was always trying to lure new pals into going along with the promise of a cheap vacation, Seiden said, but for Lou, every trip had two or three purposes. While friends paid for fuel, for example, Lou got to log hours as a pilot. He and Seiden or others would fly to the Hamptons and mingle with the rich—they were all potential business contacts to Lou. "If he became friendly with them he thought that meant they'd invest," Seiden said. One of the richest men he met during his early days in the air transportation business was Theodor Wullenkemper, a German industrialist and airship manufacturer, head of the then twenty-four-year-old aviation company Westdeutsche Luftwerbung (WDL). Lou first learned about him while working for Goodyear. Wullenkemper, with his majestic fleet of airships, was a man with a reputation for precision blimp building, the sort of timeless titan who would literally bang on the table if the eyes of the person he was talking to veered from his own. He always traveled with an entourage, usually a couple of much younger, attractive women. His ground crews drove Mercedes docking trucks and wore matching jumpsuits, an aesthetic to which Lou was instantly attracted. Lou first greeted Wullenkemper the same way a thirteen-year-old girl might greet her favorite Backstreet Boy, with a sparkly present and a giddy grin. He found out Wullenkemper was trying to launch his own airline with international flights to New York and was coming to town around the time of his fiftieth birthday. Planes had started to earn Lou cash, and he labored daily to keep his hand in that side of the aviation business, but his boyhood blimp rides were what stuck with him. From his earliest days as a Goodyear gofer and "helium head," Lou had wanted to launch his own blimp. Wullenkemper, he believed, was the man who could back all of his high-flying aspirations. So he sent him a two-foot-tall glitter-and-construction-paper birthday card and offered the services of Island Helicopter while he was in town in exchange for a meeting. The German sent a telex message agreeing to an appointment. Lou, a doughy, grinning twenty-four-year-old, met the neatly tailored European tycoon at the airport gate. "I have an appointment with your father," Wullenkemper said.

Neither Seiden nor Lou's close friend and associate Alan Gross could keep up with all of the irons Lou had in the fire in the late 1970s. It was a crisscross of relatives, aviation contacts, and rich friends tied together by the remains of a helicopter service, the beginnings of an airplane transportation company, and the dreams of an airship business. "Things were always intertwined and it was never exactly apparent who he was working for or what he was doing," Seiden said. Neither he nor Gross, with whom Lou still shared his airship obsession, knew exactly what he was cooking up with Wullenkemper. No one but Lou knew. In a typical Pearlman move, he would put Seiden or Gross to work on one project while he met privately with bigwig partners on a new venture. "He always ended up having a lot of other people doing the things that he was supposed to be doing," Seiden said.

Instead of choosing a fancy restaurant in Manhattan in

which to talk business with Wullenkemper, Pearlman invited the former Nazi Luftwaffe pilot to Queens for a hearty Jewish meal with his mom and former World War II tail-gunner father. Tensions between Wullenkemper and Hy Pearlman were quickly assuaged, however, when Wullenkemper explained that he was forced to fly for the Nazis under threat of being shot for treason. He called Hitler a monster and said he had since traveled to Israel and met with Holocaust survivors. Reenie served rump roast. What Lou really got out of the meeting with Wullenkemper remains a mystery. He claimed that by the end of the visit Wullenkemper had agreed to build him a blimp for $1.2 million (astonishingly cheap) and help train his crew in Germany on how to handle the craft. But he was clearly inspired by his aviation scheme. Years later, Lou would tell a different deep-pocketed partner that Wullenkemper, who had his sights set on buying an airliner fleet of his own, originally partnered with Lou because of his connections at the various airports—Wullenkemper would need those to secure slots at the airport for his international flights at a time when Pan Am and TWA were trying to freeze out foreign competition. Together with Wullenkemper, Pearlman said, he formed Trans Continental Airlines. But in 1978, heading into 1979, the company didn't own any planes.

Under the loosely constructed umbrella agreement with Island Helicopters, Lou had been leasing planes for his side business, the one originally called Transcom Airways. These were the days before wire transfers, and banks were willing to pay to speed up the process of having loan payments—checks—transported to their clearinghouses. The less time they spent in transit, the more interest the banks, rather than the check writers, would earn. A few days' worth of interest on millions of dollars really added up. The banks would have more cash on hand to make more loans, too. So they booked Lou's air transport service—initially helicopters when Lou was running them, then leased planes—to haul checks across the country and back to New York. It was a quick-cash business that allowed Lou to lease even more commercial jets for a discount travel company. Seiden set up the logistics for what would become Trans Continental Airlines Travel Service.

By 1979, all of those connections to wealthy friends and family and regular passengers on his commuter choppers had started to pay off, Lou said. He tapped the upper echelon of investors who could plunk down a million or more apiece and started buying planes—big planes: 727s, 707s, 747s, and L-1011s. Lou would never disclose the names of these early backers. Calling upon lessons learned at Queens College, he had created a way for them to use the investments in the planes as a tax shelter. They were promised returns based on the company's growth. "I recruited friends and relatives, as well as a substantial number of people I'd met through my other aviation business, to form those partnerships," Pearlman wrote in 2003. "Today, those investors include corporate

executives, lawyers, doctors, professional athletes, entertain-
ers and celebrities of all kinds. I'd name some of them, but we
have confidentiality agreements built into the limited partnerships." But as was the case with his newspaper delivery tale
and his fond Goodyear blimp recollections, something didn't
add up. Neither Seiden nor Gross, the two who worked closest with him, could recall Lou ever really owning any jets.
"I've never flown on anything that said 'Trans Continental' on
it," Seiden said. And the only Trans Continental airliner Gross
ever saw still sits in his living room, a plastic model 747
adorned with the yellow-striped Trans Continental logo and
lettering. He and Lou took photos of the toy set against the
backdrop of John F. Kennedy airport in the late '70s. Just out
of frame in those pictures is the tail of the jet, where, Gross
says, Pearlman's fingers held it up. The shot was remarkably
similar to a shot Seiden had clipped from newspaper ads for
Trans Continental Airlines Travel Service, the booking arm of
Lou's airline subsequently set up to offer round trips from
New York to Paris on wide-bodied 747s. Lou did actually run
discount vacation flights on leased planes owned by other
people, but he didn't have any life-size Trans Continental–
branded jets of his own. He didn't disclose the names of investors in his fleet because there was no fleet. Neither he nor
Trans Con actually owned any jets.

In 1979, Lou set his sights on slower, more regal modes of
air transportation. He traveled to Tokyo, sent by his mentor

Wullenkemper to work on a WDL crew learning the ins and outs of the airship business. He joined German crews, donned a matching jumpsuit, and fell deeper in love with the majesty of German zeppelins. Seiden, meanwhile, kept the air transport business running. By the time Lou returned to the United States full time in 1980, he was ready to launch a blimp of his own. Airship Enterprises opened an office in Manhattan—right next to the offices of Trans Continental Airlines and Trans Continental Airlines Travel Service at 521 Fifth Ave. Trans Continental Airlines was incorporated in Delaware in 1981, but it was on autopilot by then, Lou said. Launching a blimp of his own became his full-time pursuit, but even with his close relationship with Wullenkemper, buying or leasing a WDL airship would have cost more than Lou had on hand, so he came up with a much cheaper—and flimsier—shortcut. He purchased an old industrial logging balloon used to lift trees out of dense forest, a V-shaped craft that could have been mistaken for a UFO. Then he ordered it hacked in two and had manufacturers reconnect it with scraps to form the traditional oblong shape. A metal fabricator designed fins and a gondola to replicate a much sturdier WDL airship. It was a patchwork plan if there ever was one. Even those who worked on the blimp never believed it would get off the ground. "It was a piece of crap," said Don Guth, who was a teenager in 1980 and worked on the skeleton—called the envelope—of Pearlman's first craft. "It was heavy when we put it together out in California. We'd take it outside and let the sun bake on it. As the helium on the inside got hotter it would produce more lift, but that was the only way it was getting off the deck. And its landing gear was pretty fragile, also. It was in the shape of an airship but it was never meant to fly."

Meanwhile, as the craft was being slapped together, Pearlman's one-man sales and marketing team, Paul Lofaro, went out hawking what he believed to be a fancier German-made blimp to corporate clients who would pay big bucks to advertise on its façade. Lofaro, now retired and living in Queens, recalled laying the groundwork in the '70s and '80s for most of Airship's future customers. He was lured to the company by the passion of Pearlman and his young associates and hungry for the 15 percent commission he was promised on substantial six- and seven-figure corporate contracts. Airship Enterprises, however, was no easy sell. At a pitch to liquor company Seagram, the executive who met with him uttered what would become a common refrain from clients passing on his proposition: "If you could tell me that I could open that window and see that blimp, I'd sign a contract right now with you." That was the rub, Lofaro said. He needed a client to sign a contract so he could get a German blimp shipped to the United States. He didn't know Lou was building a blimp in California on the cheap.

Lofaro found investors willing to take that leap of faith in the Nakash brothers, creators of fashion label Jordache. "I had a great presentation," Lofaro said. "I had a videotape that Alan [Gross] had given me, and it was all about the blimps in Germany and how they used them for marketing and how all the people in all the towns would gather around so they could get a close-up of the blimp and how they would run contests to give rides in the blimps." Plus, he had a secret weapon: an inflatable scale model of a blimp tucked inside a mysterious-looking "black box" that Lofaro carried on calls. On the model, there was even a mockup of the airship's night sign. "On would come our night sign with eighty-five hundred bulbs, I told them. And it's a moving sign . . . and I had one set up for Jordache. The brother Joe got so excited he said, 'I want to be your partner!'"

Israeli immigrants, Joe, Avi, and Ralph Nakash had opened four discount apparel stores in Brooklyn and Manhattan. A fire set during the 1977 blackout in New York destroyed their largest outlet in the city, but the brothers bounced back. They spent their insurance money on sexy ads touting the curve-hugging "Jordache look." In fact, the brothers had spent $120,000 hyping their jeans before they ever mass-produced them. The plan worked. Rabid demand fueled their quick production of thousands of pairs and made the Nakash brothers multimillionaires.

Pearlman was inspired.

With the Nakash brothers on the hook, Lou and Lofaro hatched a plan to have the airship fly in from New Jersey to

Manhattan and dock at the Sheep Meadow in Central Park for a fancy press-friendly party on October 8, 1980. But city officials considered the landing too risky and wouldn't approve it, so instead, Lofaro hunted down the developers of Battery Park City, which was under construction in downtown Manhattan. Eager to garner attention for their own massive office and residential project, the Battery Park people welcomed the stunt and all of its flash. The plan was for models adorned in Jordache looks to exit the craft on a catwalk when it docked just feet from a gaggle of press. There would be drinks, music, and, with any luck, headlines. Jordache would position itself as the label of choice for extravagant, jet-setting beautiful people who were so unique that they chose to travel by dirigible (and land in the new Battery Park City).

Back in Lakehurst at the launch site on that Wednesday in autumn, the mood was far from festive. Several earlier test flights had been scrapped. A day before the official launch, the craft was grounded by broken landing gear. The Jordache brothers had been out to inspect the blimp at the New Jersey hangar days earlier. They were beaming with anticipation over seeing the finished product. Lou had, after all, provided in his own handwriting to Jordache's PR people specs that described a 170-foot pristine airship capable of seating five people, in addition to the pilot. It could rev up to 70 mph, had a range of 500 miles, and could soar as high as 7,500 feet. The real craft, however, was nothing so sleek. It was slower, only

105 feet long, and would never reach 1,000 feet—or travel a single mile. The brothers left crestfallen at the sight of their actual airship, which was clearly the product of shoddy work and hot air. To make matters worse, the glorious gold paint they had chosen for the blimp's color turned in the sun a shade of brown Alan Gross described as "doodie." (Decades later he had a swatch of the painted fabric as proof.) The Jordache brothers skipped the launch.

On home video taken at Lakehurst on October 8, the blimp looked more like something out of a grade school science fair than one of the majestic German bullets shown in Lofaro's promotional video. It sputtered to about thirty feet up and floated limply before spiraling into a lopsided clockwise circle. It could *only* go right. Like an escaped party balloon, it corkscrewed toward the end of the airstrip and hung up on spiny pines. There, near a trash dump barely a mile from where the Hindenburg disaster unfolded, Lou's first blimp expired. The saggy mess splayed out like a flag for failure. The pilot escaped with just a scratch on his pinkie. Press outlets Lou could never quite coax into covering his PR stunt suddenly took interest. The Associated Press, United Press International, the *New York Times,* and various local news stations ran stories and pictures. One declared: "The blimp goes limp." Pearlman shrank from sight, emerging only briefly to order Alan Gross, then Airship's PR man, back to Queens, where he was instructed to tape-record all of the news reports on the crash. Lou, however, didn't seem especially distraught, Gross recalled. He was all business. "It wasn't the sort of publicity we'd hoped for," Pearlman later wrote of the crash, "but as I told the Jordache brothers, their name was all over the news that night. They were glad to get all that attention and relieved that no one was hurt." He had experience taking lemons and making lemonade.

Then came the insurance claim. Lou might have based a business on a monumental flop, but a policy worth several million dollars would fund his next venture—after a lengthy legal battle. In a January 16, 1981, memo, the aviation claims manager for insurance agent Marsh & McLennan Inc. wrote:

*Based upon our investigation, we have determined that the airship involved in this loss is not the same as the airship that was presented to us for coverage, and for which we issued the captioned policy [number HL 53-0078]. The airship presented to us for coverage was represented to have been manufactured in Germany by Westdeutsche Luftwerbung, and was said to have been of a type that had been operated for ten years in Europe loss/accident free. However, the airship which crashed on October 8th, 1980 in Lakehurst, New Jersey and for which a proof of loss had been filed, was an airship manufactured by Airship Enterprises, Ltd., which was not of a proven type and in fact, had never been flown. It is our position that the above constitutes material misrepresentations inherent in the underlying placement of the risk, and we therefore elect to rescind the policy.*

The company returned the premiums paid of $18,504.50.

It was a bait-and-switch, the insurance company claimed in court. A jury-rigged former logging balloon was being substituted for the precision German craft Lou had insured. But Pearlman's defense team presented its own documents, in which Pearlman provided the insurance company with specs of the new ship showing its actual length, its origin of manufacture, and its flying capacity. It was a nonchalant memo, but he had technically covered himself. Curiously, the insurance company never adjusted its coverage of the blimp based on Lou's new specs, which would likely have resulted in a lower premium. Just as curiously (and uncharacteristically), Pearlman never griped about paying the steeper rate for the larger, fancier blimp, even though he was really launching the Frankenstein's monster of dirigibles.

Outmaneuvered by an even greedier adversary, the insurance company agreed to a $2.5 million settlement for Pearlman—far more than it cost him to build his doomed airship and far more than the measly $18,504.50 Airship Enterprises had paid into the policy. Lou had the cash to fund his next move, which many close to Pearlman in those days assumed was the plan from the get-go: purchasing an actual blimp from Wullenkemper, transforming Airship Enterprises into Airship International Ltd., and taking the company public.

Pearlman circled back to the deal he'd struck with Wullenkemper and began to grow Airship International, but Alan Gross nearly smelled a rat. He had striven his whole life to secure a spot with an aviation company. He left Goodyear to go to work for Lou on the promise that he'd become a principal in the company. But he saw for the first time what time away in business school and a stint at the head of a real company was doing to his once awkward childhood chum. Gross had a 1979 roster of parts due to be shipped to Pearlman from Wullenkemper—it came just after the German's dinner with the Pearlmans, proving Lou had intentions of getting a WDL airship early on but didn't follow through. An expert in airships, Gross realized what a shoddy blimp Lou had built, although he'd tried to make it fly in his own way with crafty public relations and marketing. The crash was a wake-up call for Gross, and Lou's maneuvering afterward made him suspect that the Jordache deal might have been an elaborate insurance scam from the get-go. When he saw the insurance company documents disputing Lou's claim, he was convinced. He also realized that Pearlman and Wullenkemper were cutting him out of the next blimp venture. Feeling used in the Jordache disaster and fearful that he'd sunk a chunk of his life's work (and savings) into a business he would no longer be a part of, Gross wrote a letter to Wullenkemper on September 26, 1981, alerting him to what he considered to be Lou's backstabbing ways. He wanted the German to know that Lou was not the sole mastermind behind the blimp business. It was *he* who had done much of the legwork to get it going. When Pearlman caught wind of the letter, he called Gross (just before a scheduled one-on-one meeting with Wullenkemper in Germany), fuming. "We're not just talking about insurance money here, we're talking about the future," Pearlman warned, his raspy, nasally, Queens-tinged voice rising to a high, trumpetlike tenor. In the same breath, he agreed that Gross was owed money from Airship Enterprises and then threatened to cut him out altogether if his letter queered relations with Wullenkemper. "Alan, you're owed money," he barked. "You'll get money . . . I do have qualms about people trying to discredit me, deface me, and check me out, hurting me and maliciously trying to discredit me . . . People who bullshit and make phony accusations that they did work that they never did will get *zero.*" As Lou lectured round and round trying desperately to squeeze out of Gross info about his letter to Wullenkemper, he became strangely passive-aggressive. He hinted at snuffing out Gross's boyhood dream of launching a blimp of his own. Then in the next breath, he predicted that utter devastation would lead Gross to lash out at Lou. "I really think you're going to attack me . . . and try to do violence. If something happens to me it should be noted that you're the only enemy that I have." Then he made a threat of his own, too: "I'm a bitch when I have to be a bitch. If you want to be a bitch against me, we're going to fight each other and neither of us are going to win."

Alan Gross had already sent his letter to Wullenkemper. "I regret that your connections with Airship Enterprises are displeased," Wullenkemper wrote back in his quirky English. "Neither WDL nor I have had at no time direct connections with this company. Because of this I am not in the position to reply to all of your questions. As far as WDL will become active in the States we will contact you again." Whether it came across as tattletaling, whistle-blowing, or an attempt to ground an ego-inflated Pearlman, Gross's letter backfired.

With his insurance settlement, Pearlman did get his hands on a WDL airship, but he still needed a client. Having burned Jordache and almost everyone involved in the deal, he himself went to work on landing another big fish. By 1982, Gross was essentially on the outs with Lou and salesman Lofaro was gone, but their contacts and ideas for pitches remained. So that same year, Lou cold-called Dick Christian, then regional vice president of McDonald's in New York. After navigating around Christian's secretary, Pearlman crashed the McDonald's chief's office, stopping on the way into a conference room to set up a mysterious black box on Christian's office desk. He wowed Christian with a video presentation that showed a cartoon McDonald's blimp cruising over the Manhattan skyline, then on the way out, the two stopped by Christian's office, where a twenty-foot, self-inflating McDonald's blimp mock-up stretched almost wall to wall. "Dick loved it," Pearlman said. "He turned to me with wide eyes and said, 'Young man, I obviously need to talk to our franchisees about this first, but I think we might have something here!'"

It would take a couple more years for the construction and all of the paperwork to come through, but Christian, it seemed, was even more excited than Jordache's Joe Nakash.

Amid all of the finagling of his McDeal, Lou circled back to his other love, music. Throughout his exploits in the helicopter, airplane, and airship industries, he had remained a rock 'n' roller at heart. A child of the '60s, he'd come of age in a golden era of pop music, and thanks to his cousin Art, Lou had a backstage pass. True to form as an entrepreneur with more irons in the fire than anyone could count, he kept up his guitar study and occasionally played with musicians who would record under his band name, Flyer. In the decades that have passed, Pearlman has condensed his music history into a convenient narrative, describing Flyer as playing opening gigs for Gloria Gaynor, Kool & the Gang, and others and boasting how he came close to landing a record deal with Columbia—it was Simon & Garfunkel's split that nixed the deal. But Simon & Garfunkel parted ways in 1971, the same year

Lou said he got serious about relaunching Flyer. The group was an ever-changing assembly of players. Lou was the only permanent thing. But Flyer the *band*, a genuine ensemble, not the rotating roster of studio and one-off gig players, gelled in 1981. Lou had, for the most part, resigned from playing live gigs with the band himself but was working with a female vocalist, Jeri Blender. He needed a band to back her, so she found singer Willie Colon in Queens. She told him about her deep-pocketed producer, Lou, a fellow Queens boy done good. Colon and his group met with Pearlman and they, along with Blender, started playing under Lou's group name, Flyer. He immediately promised fame and fortune, but it was Colon and his crew who became the backbone of the band. They lugged their own gear, booked many of their own gigs, and drove their own van for years under Lou's management. The biggest show Flyer ever played was set up by Lou at My Father's Place, a Roslyn, Long Island, joint with a rep for featuring promising local and national talent (The Police famously launched a career there). The legend of Flyer's 1983 show there has bloated with age to epic proportions. The line to get in that Sunday night formed hours early and stretched around the building, band members said. The players were coaxed onstage by rousing chants of *"Fly-er! Fly-er! Fly-er!"* By the time they started their set, the crowd at the bar was eight people deep, and thirsty patrons were waving hundred-dollar bills, competing for the bartender's attention. Lou arrived in his limo and played the role of the fat-cat manager, but he didn't play guitar that night—or at any other subsequent Flyer gig, despite later claims to the contrary. He handled band business at best. "Get your passports ready," he told the performing members after the show, "'cause we are going to Germany." He set up a world tour, he said, that would swing through Europe, then Hawaii, then culminate at Giants Stadium. A record deal was always just around the corner, but Lou would back Flyer financially no matter what, he said. "I will tell you one thing right now. I will go ahead and I will stay with this group all the way until we get the record pushed and going, all the way to the point that I will back you with my company."

Pearlman had negotiated a $250,000 deal with Columbia records, he told members, but he went a step further in pledging his own assets, which he said were worth $72 million. "That's how desperate I am to want to see my songs promoted without Columbia—without people doing my songs. I want my *own* group that I want to be a part of, and if you're all part of this family here, I will promote it."

No deal, tour, or record ever materialized. Lou disappeared, but Flyer kept the name. It didn't take them long to figure out it was Pearlman who'd spooked a potential label—if there ever even was one—with his outsize persona and need to control every aspect of his band's business. Decades after their heyday, the current members were still keeping their dream alive, still playing and recording and reminiscing in the well-equipped studio in the basement of singer Willie Colon's Queens home, where they'd pledged to rock eternal. There was, however, a sense of "what if" that hung over every memory. They had watched as Backstreet Boys, then *NSYNC, took off and soared to unbelievable success, and they semi-jokingly started referring to themselves as "Lou Pearlman's first boy band." They were, after all, promised a German launch, a record deal, and unlimited fame and fortune—Pearlman's formula that worked so well for the bands that made him rich and famous. For years after his boy bands debuted, the members of Flyer would send Pearlman songs they wrote in hopes he'd record them with one of his bands and, of course, pay them royalties for their songwriting. He gave the three Flyer members a "special code" to include with CDs or music they mailed to Florida, and they always believed that the code would ensure that the songs were directly deposited on Lou's desk. As footage of *NSYNC at an arena show rolled during a 2005 interview with Flyer, D'Ambrosio said, "Naturally, there's a part of us that says, you know, why, why didn't it happen twenty years ago, when we had our shot . . . I know I think to myself, *Wow, that could have been us.*"

By 1982, Lou Pearlman was loaded. He's said he made more than $400 million from his helicopter, blimp, and airline transportation and travel businesses, though he'd told Flyer he had $72 million in assets—still impressive, if not consistent. He also had three offices on Fifth Avenue in Manhattan. But at age twenty-eight, he still lived in his parents' one-bedroom apartment. His father died that year, too. Lou never talked much about how that impacted him. His girlfriend of ten years, Tammie Hilton, said it bugged him that his father died before Lou could show him he'd done him better. "I think he's sad his father never got to see him succeed," Hilton said. "He saw him succeed in business, but he never saw Lou get, you know, famous, and I think that bothers Lou." It was also in 1982 that Pearlman finally moved into his first apartment—a penthouse in Queens at the Bay Club, a gated, guarded brand-new high rise complete with billiards and racquetball rooms, tennis courts, and an on-site deli, library, and movie theater; it's the borough's version of a Trump Tower, the kind of place that folks in the otherwise working-class neighborhood associated with new money (*"Oh,* the *Bay Club"*). Ray Seiden, still Lou's business partner, was aghast. For the eight and a half years he worked for Lou and his various companies, Seiden had to work a side job selling shoes at his father's shop just to make ends meet. Pearlman, who previously drove a cheap Dodge, suddenly started tooling around in a burgundy stretch Lincoln Continental limo ("for the business," he said) and a matching Rolls-Royce Phantom. He and friends would take one of the cars to Peter Luger Steakhouse in Great Neck, either paying cash for steak that started at $39.95 for a single à la carte serving or charging the whole bill to a restaurant account. Alternately, Pearlman and pals would cruise Northern Avenue on a Saturday night, stopping at Jack in the Box for burgers. Seiden couldn't figure out exactly where the money was coming from but he assumed cousin Art was pitching in. Plus, Pearlman confided in Seiden that he had as much as $50,000 in debt on his American Express card. "It was mind-boggling," Seiden said, but the whole point was to be seen living large. After his blimp crashed, Lou had a reputation to rebuild and new investors to gather, so he became his own best marketing tool. From this point on, the only thing Lou ever really sold was Lou.

It worked. Though Trans Con never went public and was not registered with the SEC, Pearlman gently lured friends, former neighbors, and family to buy shares of the company, usually at $5,000 a pop. There weren't any salesmen on staff and there never was much of a hard sell, just Lou in Mitchell Gardens letting friends and friends of friends in on the ground floor of his successful company. Ray Seiden became one of the first of many owners of a stake in Trans Continental Airlines Travel Service—he held a promissory note for 383 shares, worth about $7,000. Childhood acquaintance Michelle Novak, who'd watched Lou lead a studious "nerd squad" through grade school, said talk rippled through her family ranks that Pearlman was a "boy genius." They'd all seen him parading around town with his fancy wheels. Novak was unemployed at the time and was scouting around for a job with Eastern

Airlines and had heard Lou had connections. She even visited his penthouse with a group of others. "I went up there and I thought, *Gee, this guy really lives well.*" She and her family and many in Lou's expanding Queens circle were convinced that "everything he touched turned to gold." One of her family members (he asked that his name not be used), who had heard that the local kid had done good, contacted Pearlman and invested about $5,000 in Trans Continental Travel Service in the late '80s. "You were promised twenty percent interest on your investment," he said. "The interest grew on paper only, though." He never got his money back. Other members of Novak's family sank $10,000 or more into Trans Con, and a few put in their life savings—and even lived for a while off of the interest. "But I said, 'Here's the thing, can you get your money back?' and they said, 'Oh, yeah, any time'," Novak said. They never did, and a few of her relatives lost their life savings, she said.

With McDonald's on board for his first WDL blimp—and the first to actually fly more than a few hundred feet—Lou; his mom, Reenie; Wullenkemper; and others toasted the German airship at an intimate gathering in the Lakehurst, New Jersey, hangar in July '85. A beaming silver-haired Reenie reeled off lines to a camcorder: "I'm here at Lakehurst, where the Good-year blimp . . . ," she mistakenly said, then blushed and started over. "I cannot express my feelings toward my son. I am so proud of him. I want to tell the world how proud I am of my son, Louis, for creating this, and hopefully this blimp will fly very shortly." Lou, thirty-one but acting like a grade school cutup on a field trip, bounced into the frame and made goofy faces. Reenie giggled with pride. As Pearlman continued to hawk the private Trans Con to friends and family, he pushed Wall Street bankers and financiers to help him take his new blimp company public—Airship International, the one buoyed by a $2.5 million insurance claim on his crashed Jordache balloon. Lou had just one blimp and one client to lease it. But it was all he needed. In the fall of '85, he arranged a meeting in the conference room on the fiftieth floor of the City Midday Club near Wall Street. The top floor of the club looked out over Manhattan but Lou kept the draperies drawn tight while he played the same videos his earlier salesman Lofaro had used showing blimps soaring all over Europe—the PR presentation Alan Gross made. When the show on-screen ended, Lou dramatically pulled back the conference room shades and there, floating outside the window against the backdrop of the Manhattan skyline, was his yellow and red, golden-arches-adorned airship.

There would never be a better metaphor for Lou Pearlman than the McBlimp.

Wall Street was sold. Airship International (ticker symbol: BLMP) went public, underwritten by Norbay Securities, a now-defunct Bayside, New York, penny stock operation with a deep history of fraudulent sales. Lou was friends with

Jerome Rosen, a broker at Norbay who lived next to him at the Bay Club. Rosen had been banned from the securities industry in British Columbia for fraudulent trading, but from his Queens home base, he helped raise millions for Airship International, trading Airship's cheap stock in what some have alleged was a "pump and dump" scheme, in which shares are bought and sold several times over to make a stock look hot and inflate the price (meanwhile, the brokers' commissions skyrocket). Rosen later went on to sell Airship International stock at Prestige Investors and J. Alexander Securities, both of which were shut down in the mid-'90s after regulatory actions. By June 1985, Airship International Limited traded on the NASDAQ at $2 a share. McDonald's had signed a deal potentially worth $2.5 million to lease Airship International's blimp through 1987. Lou entered a new atmosphere, one perfectly suited to his skill set in many ways; his company's very existence would depend upon stockholder speculation and the perceived potential of its CEO. Whether or not Airship ever turned a profit, Lou would have to look like a success. The 193-foot WDL-built McBlimp performed flawlessly. Lou claims to have purchased it from Wullenkemper. Others said he merely leased it, just like the jumbo jets for his Trans Continental Airlines. Nevertheless, an IPO anchored in the McDonald's deal netted Airship International several million dollars. When the fast food company's lease was up in 1987, Metropolitan Life Insurance Company came on board and painted the former McBlimp blue and white and adorned it with its Snoopy logo. It was a multiyear deal potentially worth more than $8 million should the company continue to renew its yearly lease. But it was a toughly negotiated deal with Anheuser-Busch that established Airship International as a player in the skies. Though a deal with the beer maker wouldn't officially be done until 1993, the foundation was laid in 1986 by a friend Lou had met in the 1970s, Harry Milner. Before getting involved with Lou, he was a building contractor whose most notable work involved rehabilitating a few buildings at Edwards Air Force Base in California. Milner heard about Pearlman's budding public company and saw an opportunity. He knew Budweiser honcho Auggie Busch III and offered to talk to him about Lou's blimp business as a potential marketing tool for Bud. A novice salesman, Milner nevertheless piqued the interest of the beer honchos, who loved the idea of a Budweiser blimp hovering over gatherings of thirsty throngs. Budweiser would have come on board right then and there, but the company wasn't the advertising behemoth it is today. The marketing budget wouldn't bear the roughly $300,000-a-month cost of a yearlong blimp lease. "Next year," Bud execs promised Milner. Lou was impressed nonetheless by Milner's inroads. In 1988, Lou went back to Budweiser himself, never bothering to loop in Milner, and sold them on a long-term $3 million blimp leasing deal, plus deals for Shamu-the-killer-whale-themed blimps in Florida promoting the company's

SeaWorld theme park. Milner's son, Harold Milner III, insisted his father should have pocketed a $300,000 commission from the Anheuser-Busch sale. "Through the years it would have made him a millionaire," he said. His father frequently brought up the commission to Pearlman, but "Lou always blew it off with a promise of a great job or said 'we're going to take care of you,' " Milner said. Though Milner never drew a check from Pearlman or his companies, he's listed on documents dating back to the 1970s as financial officer for Trans Continental Airlines. It was a maneuver by Lou with a specific purpose that wouldn't surface for decades. For his part, Milner's son was uncomfortable around Lou, even as early as age thirteen, and came to see him as the man who cheated his father out of a fortune. "From the day I met him, I knew he was a strange guy. He was just weird. He just gave me that weird feeling." By 1989, Pearlman's underhanded dealings with Budweiser had driven a wedge between him and the elder Milner, and they never did business together again. Or so the Milners believed.

Airship International sold stock on the open market, but Trans Continental Airlines and Travel Service flourished in its shadows, luring even more investors in what they believed to be a growing fleet of airliners offering discount travel packages. Then, just as Lou hit his stride with Airship and Trans Con, he suffered a couple of deep blows. Reenie Pearlman suffered a blood clot and died in an operating room in May, on Mother's Day, 1988. "Lou was a mama's boy," Alan Gross said. By all accounts, Pearlman was devastated, but he carried on business without a hitch. Then in June 1989, his blimp for MetLife, his first WDL craft that was previously adorned with the McDonald's logo, was moored in Texas en route to California when a windstorm swirled up and ripped it to shreds. By November, however, he had filed an insurance claim and was touting the features of his new blimp, a $6 million Skyship built by English company Airship Industries, equipped with cameras and lights for nighttime signs. Some have since questioned whether Lou filed an insurance claim against a blimp he didn't actually own but leased from Wullenkemper—the German would later sue Pearlman overseas, but neither he nor Wullenkemper would discuss the details of the suit, and it was settled. Gross said Lou became more and more secretive and devious following his mother's death. "He no longer had her looking over his shoulder, so he intensified his scheming ways. He seemed to grow greedier and shadier, and the people he associated with had questionable moral values. As long as he had people to feed his ego, his negative propensities grew exponentially."

Unbeknownst to Gross or his longtime associate Ray Seiden, who'd cashed out his Trans Continental shares for $7,000 worth of Airship International stock, Lou had launched a new scheme, which he was already pitching to some of his earliest investors. Because they were share owners in Trans Continental Airlines or its travel service, they were eligible to participate in the company's Employee Investment Savings

Accounts (EISA). The program was insured by the FDIC for up to $100,000, Pearlman said in person and in brochures. The individual investor accounts, EISA literature stated, were further backed by insurance policies purchased through AIG and Lloyd's of London "as maintained on file in our office." There was a Lloyd's policy and letter confirming coverage, which Pearlman often showed to visitors and investors, but both were completely bogus. On some investor brochures was a picture of a Trans Continental jumbo jet, the toy plane he and Gross had photographed. His fingers (and the registration numbers) on the tail of the model plane were just out of frame. Attached to marketing materials for the EISA program was what Lou said was the "Lloyd's policy," which looked like the cover page of an insurance policy. Page two had policy number 823/AM9100780 and the "assured" was Trans Continental Airlines Inc. It was a forgery. There were no individual investor accounts and no insurance by FDIC, AIG, or Lloyd's of London, but no one would seriously question the authenticity of EISA or its insurance for years. And as Pearlman continued to helm his public company Airship International, he raked in hundreds of thousands in cash from shares sold in his private Trans Continental Airlines—which did not own forty to fifty aircraft or a fleet of jets in Germany as Lou told some investors. EISA was, from the beginning, a bogus scheme that would fund Pearlman's future businesses and help pay for his extravagant lifestyle.

For his part, Alan Gross was done with Lou's businesses

by 1989. Then on April Fool's Day, 1990, Gross sent a copy of his Airship International shareholder's agreement, his job description, a business card, receipts for expenses and services rendered, copies of canceled checks for his own personal investments totaling $6,300, and a handwritten letter to Lou. All told, he said, the only thing left of a friendship that blossomed when Lou tagged along with Alan to the Flushing airport was an outstanding balance of $19,704. "This amount does not include payments of damage or interest or the complete value of one of the shareholder's agreements," Gross wrote. "The amount also does not include money's [sic] promised to me for housing and feeding company personnel for several months prior to, during, and after the Jordache operation."

Pearlman's attorney wrote back on April 24, offering a $10,000 lump-sum settlement. They settled on $11,000. Later, Lou helped Gross buy a Hyundai.

Pearlman had latched on to a new friend in 1989, though, a debonair man who would become his longest, wealthiest business partner, a young lion from whom Lou would not only learn but whose lifestyle would deeply impact Lou's aspirations and whose genuine knack for deal making would help transform Airship International from a struggling startup into a temporarily profitable public company. Not since chasing blimps with Alan Gross as a boy had Lou found such a perfect partner as Julian Benscher.

## CHAPTER 4

# WINGMEN

Julian Benscher was everything Lou wished he could be.

As a boy, the proper Englishman was carted around in Rolls-Royces and jets, dined formally on meals prepared by teams of servants, and enjoyed—but joked that he was cursed with—an enormously wealthy upbringing with all the trimmings. He had a hard time ever settling for less. The money for his lavish childhood came from his father, Gabi, an eccentric world traveler and entrepreneur who'd earned his money building the publicly traded spirits company Campari Group. Just days shy of Julian's fourteenth birthday, Gabi came home for lunch to inspect a tiling job on the home's roof and fell from a scaffolding twenty or thirty feet, cracking his head on the concrete below. He died almost instantly, leaving his wife, Julian's mother, at the helm of his company. Devastated at the loss of a man he considered a superhero, he watched a scuffle ensue over his father's 22 percent interest in Campari Group. His mother ended up with the shares. Benscher didn't immediately get anything because "there was nothing to inherit," said David Kleeman, a lawyer who handled Julian's mother's financial interests after Gabi's death. Among the executors of Gabi's will was Julian's great-uncle. "He wasn't keen on the idea that the shares were left to the widow," Kleeman said. Nor was he keen on the fact that Benscher, who'd been milling about a bit aimlessly in his early teens and hadn't attended school, was now coming to him expecting an inheritance. The executors told Benscher he wouldn't receive his money until he finished school—his father had insisted. So he graduated. And he went back to the executors with open hands again. But they denied him again; his father had also insisted that Julian get a job before he could touch an amount he presumed to be in the millions. So he did.

Benscher scored a position as a merchant banker at one of the most exclusive institutions in England, BZW (a subsidiary of European financial giant Barclays PLC), then he returned to the trustees. Grinning, he said, they denied him the inheritance again, telling him this time that his father *further* mandated that Julian not be allowed to touch the money until he had made a million pounds on his own. Like Pearlman, Benscher had a boyhood fascination with blimps, so he quit the job at BZW and set out to launch his own business. He borrowed $20,000 from his mother and headed to Hong Kong, where he hatched a scheme to put an airship over the bustling harbor, a highly visible location where, in theory, he could charge top dollar to advertising clients for space. "[The executors] weren't pleased, nor was his mother that he had left this job at a prestigious corporate finance house," Kleeman said. But calling upon his family's connections in the business world, Julian had convinced representatives from Australian tycoon Alan Bond's blimp company Airship Industries to join him and the harbor's Civil Aviation Authority for a business meeting. When the time came, however, Bond's people suddenly had to back out of the meeting to attend to his collapsing operations—he had built an empire and even the iconic Bond Centre (known later as the Lippo Centre) in Hong Kong but would later go down as the perpetrator of one of the largest financial frauds in history. At the time, Benscher might have been preceded by his father's reputation, but on his own he was just a no-name twentysomething wheeler-dealer. The Hong Kong authorities were not impressed. Their response was, "Don't call us, we'll call you."

Left to fend mostly for himself once again, Benscher had almost burned through the $20,000 he borrowed from his mom on living expenses alone. But he saw an opportunity in Bond's troubles. Cash-poor, he devised a way to make a bid for Bond-backed Airship Industries' land holdings, a more modest, backdoor approach to owning a chunk of the blimp company. If successful, he'd become the landlord to Airship's manufacturing facilities. Besides, the properties, Benscher believed and real estate friends confirmed, were worth twice their book value, but only if he could open the parcels up to a slightly more intense industrial land-use designation.

Bolstered, once again, by his family name, as well as the merits of his plan and a background in finance, Benscher finagled a $12 million loan to buy 180 acres in the quiet English hamlet of Cardington, the Airship Industries land where historic military blimps were constructed. The deal was contingent upon him getting the property's zoning changed so future development would allow for homes and a shopping center—allotments that made the property more valuable. The local city council and residents were none too eager to see a chunk of their quiet town turned into a giant manufacturing facility or even a bustling shopping mall, but Benscher was able to convince the locals that he had no plans to transform their town into Manchester. They approved the land-use change and kicked his deal into high gear. The press caught wind and called him a "multi-millionaire" poised to inject $12 million into the ailing Airship Industries. Stories portrayed him either as the savior of Airship Industries or a young buck making a go at Alan Bond's empire, even though he was as cash poor as they come. The deal gave him his first million and then some in net assets. So Benscher strolled into a meeting with his father's trustees—this time, *he* was the one grinning, because he expected to strut out with his inheritance and promptly inform the suits that their services would no longer be needed. But they weren't wearing the long faces of men about to be fired. They were *giggling*, in fact, when they uncloaked the final piece of what they said was Gabi Benscher's design (or what could have been their own ruse all along). One last thing, they said. Your father stipulated that if you're able to come this far on your own, *you don't need an inheritance.* "With an equity base of nil, he had gotten himself an interest in an airship company. He went from having nothing but his charm, humor, and everything else he had to having an interest in the entity that manufactured the blimps flying over London," Kleeman said. "It was extraordinary at the age of nineteen or twenty that a man with no money was able to get himself into all of these things. I must say I was sort of mildly amused. I looked and I thought the apple doesn't fall far from the tree."

Benscher's helium-filled dreams of a blimp over Hong Kong harbor were not, however, deflated. As owner of Airship Industries' land and landlord over its manufacturing facility, he was poised to know just when to swoop in and take over the company, which was growing more and more desperate for cash each month. The money he paid for the land was immediately gobbled up by the banks to which Airship was indebted. The company's chiefs had to grovel to hang on to enough cash to make payroll. But Benscher's plan to buy out Airship Industries was detoured in the last week of January 1990 when the company invited some of its clients to meet some of its prospective buyers in London for a dog and pony show. Among the clients in attendance: a rotund young American entrepreneur named Lou Pearlman of Airship *International*—he'd purchased a blimp from Airship Industries and was poised to buy a few more. After a "fairly formal" meal at the Intercontinental hotel, Pearlman leaned over and whispered in Benscher's left ear, "Are you available for dinner after this?" A *second* dinner. "I'd had a pretty big dinner, and I thought that was a pretty funny question," Benscher said, "but I figured he wanted to talk." Full and flabbergasted—but interested in what Pearlman had up his sleeve—Benscher met the portly American across the street at a restaurant of Lou's choosing: the Hard Rock Cafe. Pearlman ordered and devoured a burger. Airship Industries execs had just finished filling his ears with boasts of making boatloads of cash from Benscher's land purchase, but he suspected Benscher had big plans in the airship business. A longtime student of artful business deals, Pearlman was curious to hear what Benscher got out of the arrangement with Airship Industries. So Julian told him how *he* was the one who made a healthy amount of money on the deal by securing the land-use change. Then he shared with Pearlman the basic story behind the bid—how he'd done it with the intent of unlocking his inheritance. Benscher left out the surprise ending, however, thinking he might need Pearlman to keep believing he actually got the family money.

Obviously, Lou did assume as much. He suggested that instead of investing in the ailing Airship Industries, Benscher should consider investing in Airship International, Lou's company. Benscher was intrigued. "To me it was funny that it was a public company, because it only had one ship." Lou's blimp for MetLife had been destroyed. With the insurance money, he had purchased an Airship Industries craft to replace it. But even with its lone blimp, Airship International had a fancy Fifth Avenue, Manhattan, address and its own hangar at a North Carolina airfield. He, too, was curious what his fellow airship entrepreneur had up his sleeve. So Benscher agreed to hold off on an Airship Industries bid and fly to the U.S. to check out Lou's operation. He landed in New York and was picked up in Pearlman's Learjet, whose tail number, Benscher noted, ended in "TC." "I couldn't figure how a company with one blimp could afford to be flying around in a Learjet, but he said, 'Oh, no, no, my private company pays for the jet,' " Benscher recalled. The "TC" stood for Trans Continental.

That's when Pearlman proceeded to unfurl his own saga, a slightly different version than the one he later told in his book and to reporters. It was the raw version of his myth, the one he would later smooth over and perfect with a combination of half truths or full-blown lies. Lou had already spooned out this story in bite-sized bits to associates, friends, family members, and potential investors until he had turned himself into a fictional character based only loosely on his real life. By 1990, Lou Pearlman the kid from Queens slipped into the shadows. Lou Pearlman, blimp baron and all-around entrepreneurial superhero, became his permanent public persona. For the first time, Lou had organized all of the pieces of his legend into a seamless narrative, and he laid it out for Benscher. Lou's idea for a commuter helicopter business in Manhattan, he told Benscher, was hatched in business school. He'd approached his cousin Art for the startup money. Art told him to go to his money manager—his father, Lou's uncle Jack—who told Lou he'd buy him his *second* helicopter. By Pearlman logic, he had one chopper taken care of. So Lou hit up a bunch of New York banks and was shot down but eventually caught the attention of an E. F. Hutton executive, who agreed to buy a helicopter and lease it to Lou. He let on that the chopper business was a money pit. "He basically said 'It was a cash flow nightmare—we were going from credit card to credit card,'" Benscher said. So far the story jibed with the truth, but then it diverged. Pearlman said he saw that big airlines, Pan Am and TWA back then, were rejecting proposals for landing slots in New York from international companies in an attempt to freeze them out. At the time, he'd also heard that a German industrialist and airship manufacturer named Theodor Wullenkemper was starting up an airline called LTU and had applied for an international route but was denied. So Lou applied for the route and won it. "No one bothered to object to the routing, because who cares about this kid with his two helicopters?" Benscher said. So Pearlman called up Wullenkemper and told him *he* now had the routes the German needed and he asked if Wullenkemper would be willing to meet during his next trip to New York. He did. Wullenkemper, Pearlman said, agreed to go into business with him and said he'd hand over some money for the international routes and buy the planes—mostly jets mothballed in the Mojave desert during the oil crisis of 1974, many of which now had liens on them. Because the whole deal was set up with various investors through limited partnerships, none of the planes would actually show up as being owned by Lou's airline company, should anyone check the tail numbers. Per the agreements, Lou said, the partners' names were kept secret. In exchange for the international routes and handling of the logistics for the flights, Lou could lease the planes from Wullenkemper and would own a small stake (12.5 percent, Benscher recalls, and later as much as 25 percent) in the company, called Trans Continental Airlines.

"That's where Trans Con came from. That's where the Learjet came from. That's how Lou explained it," Benscher said. Of course, the real reason none of the planes would show up as being owned by Trans Con was because they weren't. Wullenkemper was never a major shareholder in Trans Con anything. And the core of the story Lou told Benscher was totally bogus.

At the time it all seemed as plausible to Julian as it had to Lou's investors. Julian had himself swashbuckled his way into tycoon status by his early twenties, albeit legally, and Lou, he said, "struck me as someone who knew what he was doing. He had this aircraft leasing business that was obviously very successful because he's flying around in a Learjet. I loved his story." Benscher said he did pore over financials for Airship International, all of which were public. But he didn't look into Trans Continental. "You've got to remember my background: Yes, I had a successful family and a fabulous upbringing, but out of a standing start with twenty grand, I'd made millions on paper myself in this tiny short period of time. And, you know, I'm thinking that if you're determined and you know what you're doing . . . He had the same sort of blimp vision that I had!" Besides, he said, Pearlman wasn't trying to sell him on an investment in Trans Continental. Not yet. "I was curious, but I wasn't that curious," said Benscher.

The Trans Con story did bolster Benscher's interest in Airship International. He was not, however, interested in a one-blimp company. So he said to Lou, "If I can get a second blimp, can you get the client?" Pearlman had a client lined up, sure, but knew blimps were extremely expensive to buy and wondered how Benscher would come up with that kind of capital. "I told him, 'Watch,'" Benscher says. With a million dollars, he kicked off a scenario that would eventually win Pearlman a second blimp from Airship Industries and garner himself a significant stake in Airship International. By late 1990, the English blimp maker Airship Industries was truly hurting. Benscher knew this because he was the company's landlord. As such, he held strict covenants over Airship Industries that put him in the position to take possession of their manufacturing facilities if they missed the rent by as little as thirty days. So Benscher asked permission to call one of Airship International's debtors, the State Bank of South Australia, which he knew was after the company for cash. What followed was a deal structured like a delicate dance. It went like this: Benscher would buy a million dollars' worth of stock in Lou's company, Airship International. Due to a special clause in securities laws he—a foreign national—was entitled to buy it at half the value of the stock's lowest recent trading price. It worked out to about ninety cents a share. He'd get about 1.1 million shares in the deal. Pearlman's Airship would get a million-dollar cash infusion. With that cash, Lou's company would pay down a loan on one of Airship Industries' blimps, plus some of the $1 million would go to pay a few weeks' worth of Airship Industries' payroll. The English company was so short on funds it struggled to pay employees. Lou would get the blimp. Airship Industries would move $3 million in debt off of its books and onto Lou's. The Australian bank who'd loaned Airship Industries the $3 million liked the plan because the loan would get paid up to date—bad debt would be transformed into good debt. Lou liked the deal because it got him another blimp without up-front cash. Julian liked the deal because it gave him a heap of Airship International stock at a magnificent price, even though, under the foreign national special regulation, he had to hold on to it for forty days and couldn't sell it until it was registered, a complicated process. As it turned out, Lou decided he wanted to raise money by issuing Airship International stock just forty days after Benscher bought his, and as part of that process, the stock—including Benscher's million-odd shares—was registered. The trading price of Airship International stock at that point in 1990 was still about $2, a value that was strengthened in part by Lou's deal for a second blimp and the involvement of the man who had already been declared by the press to be making a move on Alan Bond's empire. Benscher sold off a third of his Airship International stock, instantly pocketing a 20 percent profit while retaining a big chunk of Airship International ownership. He had quick cash and a deep stake in the company.

Meanwhile, Pearlman and Benscher were becoming fast friends. Benscher even had Lou back to his family home, a palatial estate with all the trimmings. And just as Julian had latched on to Lou as a fellow boot-strapper, someone who had started with very little and built up an impressive business, Lou was impressed by Julian's family money. Suddenly Benscher's story about his Rolls-Royce-chauffeured childhood was in clear focus and right in front of his face. Pearlman sat down with Benscher's mother for a formal dinner, finger bowls and all. During dinner, Lou pressed so hard on a silver knife engraved with Gabi Benscher's initials that he snapped it in two. (He later sent Julian the money for a replacement.) Before long, Lou was even taking image advice from Julian, who suggested that, rather than flying around in comfy sweats, Lou should look more the part of a mogul, put on a blue blazer and some slacks. The next time Benscher saw him at the airport, Lou was wearing a navy blazer and slacks but proudly called Julian's attention to his shirt buttons. They were emblazoned with the Rolls-Royce logo.

In December 1990, Pearlman invited Benscher to the Bahamas, where he was meeting Wullenkemper, then believed to be the silent majority partner behind Pearlman's cash cow side business, Trans Continental Airlines. Wullenkemper had the two up to his home in Paradise Island. "He's referring to Lou the whole time as his *son,*" Benscher recalled. In the living room of his house, Wullenkemper walked over to a small stack of files on a wood shelf and, unsolicited, pointed to a small bunch of papers and said in his thick, domineering German accent, "Zis is my business." Then he pointed to a massive collection of documents and folders probably three times the size of the WDL documents and proclaimed, "Zis is Louie."

"First, it was none of my business, right?" Benscher said. "But it really lent credibility to the story. Now remember I'm not trying to verify anything. This is a casual visit. I'm interested, but I'm not invested in Trans Con or anything."

In yet another picture-perfect scene, Benscher said, "We were standing at one stage on a piece of property of Wullenkemper's, a big piece of property on a bluff overlooking the water, a *beautiful* piece of property. He said, 'I bought this to build a fabulous home here,' but then he said, 'I don't need it.' And he said, 'One day this will all be Louie's. He's my son. He's the son I never had.'"

It's a stark contrast to how Wullenkemper described in 2008 his affiliation with Lou. He wrote:

> *From 1986 to 1990 I had business ties with Louis Pearlman. They ended in anger and trials. When the differences were settled, we had a casual, personal friendship—mainly because I was a fan of his boy groups. I met Pearlman about once a year for a few hours within the scope of such events. We did not talk about business. It's correct though that I admired him for his success in the music industry. I never knew about his activities people talk about now.*

In retrospect, the Bahamas trip "could have been just a fantastic setup," said Benscher in 2008 in the airship-themed study of his luxurious but subtly adorned Italian-style home in exclusive Orlando gated community Isleworth. "It was done absolutely brilliantly if, indeed, it was done."

## CHAPTER 5

# BOYS ON THE SIDE

Friends suggested that since I'd held two or three jobs
during my teen years, maybe I was subconsciously trying
to recapture that time in my life hanging out with teenagers. Others said that since I missed my family, I was building a new one by surrounding myself with young people.
One friend said I was having a midlife crisis. Who knows? I
thought I was doing what I've always done, building businesses based on my interests and having a lot of fun
along the way.
      —Lou Pearlman, from *Bands, Brands, and Billions: My
      Top Ten Rules for Making Any Business Go Platinum*

*I*n 1989, Lou described Trans Continental Airlines as a low-maintenance
money mint, and no one questioned him. He was, after all,
renting out charter flights to the rich and famous, including
rock stars on tour such as Paul McCartney, Michael Jackson,
his cousin Art Garfunkel, and others. Then one day that year,
this band he'd never heard of called New Kids on the Block
booked one of his $250,000-a-month planes. They even paid
Lou with a brown paper sack full of cash. Lou had flirted (or
*teased,* the members of Flyer might say) with the idea of put-

ting together a group of his own and kept abreast of trends in the entertainment business. So how could this startup pop act he'd never heard of afford one of his planes? Asking around, Pearlman learned they were the creation of Maurice Starr, the man originally behind pop sensation New Edition. He heard New Kids had raked in $200 million in concert sales and another $800 million in merchandising revenue. A lightbulb went on, and Lou thought, *I can do that.*

It was his eureka moment, one he would repeat over and over for years to come, but no one other than Lou can recall New Kids booking a Trans Con flight. Jordan Knight, who years later struck a deal to put an album out with Lou's record company, wouldn't talk about anything having to do with Pearlman. Like other artists who once worked with Lou, Knight wanted to get as far away from Big Papa as possible, even though New Kids was staging a comeback. Starr, New Kids' creator, was very brief but said, "I don't remember seeing Lou Pearlman one day in my life with New Kids on the Block. I really don't."

In reality, by the time Lou got the idea for Backstreet Boys, he had started to abandon any real interest in planes and blimps. He needed to keep his airborne operations afloat, though. As the CEO of a publicly held company, he was certifiably legitimate, and he wore his ticker symbol on his sleeve as he lured a constant stream of new investors into his shadier schemes. In other words, Airship International was the bait; Trans Con was the switch. Airship International posted profits in 1989, but the public company nosed into a death spiral shortly thereafter. It reported a loss of $4.5 million in 1990 and $4.4 million in 1991. Pearlman tried to keep his chin up, offering demonstrations of faith such as a $2 million out-of-pocket investment and the deferment of his own $350,000 annual CEO's salary. For his part, Benscher was making deals as a major shareholder in Airship International that would keep the company alive but was also grabbing up pieces of Lou's neglected airship operation at bargain basement prices and setting himself up to make millions—legitimately—right under Lou's nose. In 1991, he had seen Airship Industries, the English company he once sought to take over, sinking further into bankruptcy. Several companies were circling like sharks, but as Airship Industries' landlord, Benscher had an insider's line on when to pounce. In the end, he was able to strike a deal with electric giant Westinghouse and airship gondola manufacturer Slingsby at precisely the right moment. The deal would give him and Lou access to the remaining assets of the Airship Industries' manufacturing operation, score a wealth of leftover airship components for Airship Interna-tional, and lock them into guaranteed low rates for the pur-chase of high-end Slingsby gondolas. It was the kind of deal Lou could have rested comfortably on for years if he'd been paying attention to what Julian was doing on the legitimate side of the operation. But he wasn't. By 1991, most of Lou's energy was spent perpetuating his Trans Con myth and his own reputation as the King Midas of Queens. The company was buoyed by investors all over Queens and New York who'd written checks for planes neither they nor Lou ever really owned, even though advertisements still touted cheap flights—$401 round-trips to Paris, for example—on wide-bodied 747s, one of which was pictured with a Trans Continental logo on its side. It was Alan Gross's toy plane again. Some of the Trans Con investors were already writing checks to their bogus Employee Investment Savings Accounts, too. Lou kept them believing those deposits were 100 percent safe and insured, even though they were not and did not go into individual accounts at all. They padded Lou's slush fund.

Then that same year, under the auspices of seeking sunnier climes and better blimp weather, Pearlman moved his airship operation and a loyal cadre of employees to Florida, that huckster's paradise teeming with gullible retirees and people chasing Disney-size dreams. It had been Lou's vacation destination of choice ever since high school, and he had already purchased a sprawling vacation home there by the time he decided to relocate permanently. He took with him his posse of Queens friends-turned-executives. Among the transplants were Frankie Vazquez, the son of the maintenance man at Mitchell Gardens who became a licensed aircraft mechanic at Lou's urging; Paul Russo, a neighborhood friend he knew from a bodega who'd become a driver for Lou for his

Queens-Manhattan commute; Frank Sicoli, the onetime guitarist for one of the early incarnations of Flyer; Alan Siegel,
another neighborhood guy who drove Lou's cars; and others.
Lou tried to get Ray Seiden to move, too. He had, after all, virtually run Trans Continental Airlines while Lou chased investors and other ideas—schemes, mostly—but Seiden chose to
stay in New York to pursue his acting career. "You'll never
make as much money as you will down here," Lou told him.

As Lou set up his new operation in the Sunshine State,
Airship Industries spied a glimmer of profitability in 1992,
thanks mostly to Benscher's maneuvering. The company
posted a profit of $104,000 in the second quarter and $513,000
in the third, not enough to cover Lou's personal investment or
the salary he'd deferred. Airship Industries needed quick cash.
So Lou momentarily retrained his focus on the blimp company and decided to issue a fresh batch of stock, with the
help of Colorado-based brokerage Chatfield Dean & Co. The
firm had underwritten legitimate stock offerings, including
Charter Golf and Isramco, and was a major dealer of John
Hancock Mutual Funds for years, but by the time Lou hooked
up with Chatfield Dean, it was already under intense regulatory scrutiny and had racked up $2.4 million in fines from the
National Association of Securities Dealers (the firm settled
with the association later) for questionable stock sales. Chatfield Dean subjected Lou and his Airship International to
the usual vetting—many of Lou's inflated figures and bogus

accounting slipped past the firm, just as they had slipped past investors and would go undetected by all sorts of legitimate institutions and regulators for years to come. Described nicely, Chatfield Dean was tireless in its selling of Airship Industries stock. In reality, it often operated like a boiler room. Making two to three hundred cold calls a day, Chatfield Dean & Co. reps would do their best to talk anyone who answered the phone into buying high-risk, low-value stocks with the lure of quick wealth. When the hard sell wasn't enough, several brokers for Chatfield Dean took it upon themselves to invest clients' money in stocks they'd never agreed to buy. In 1992, for example, a Boise, Idaho, professor bought fifteen hundred shares of a penny stock called Random Access from a Chatfield Dean rep over the phone. Later he found that his stocks had been sold without his authorization and that the money had been used to order—then cancel—the purchase of stock in a company called Plants for Tomorrow. In the end, the proceeds from the stock sale he never authorized went to purchase twenty-six hundred shares of Airship International. "The professor didn't even know what Airship International was," *Forbes* magazine reported in an alarming 1993 story called "Hello, Sucker."

None of that seemed to bother Lou, though. He had worked with shady brokers before, namely Jerome Rosen of Norbay Securities. The bottom line was what mattered to him. In his dealings with Chatfield Dean, Lou met one of its star brokers, Anthony DeCamillis, who had taken a hit with the rest of the firm's managers and been suspended from stock sales when the company got into regulatory trouble. But De-Camillis genuinely believed in Lou's money-making ability. He bought some of the same Airship International stock he sold, bought shares of Trans Con, and even sank tens of thousands of dollars into EISA—all told, his investment in EISA and Trans Con amounted to more than a half million dollars. In 1993, he was all aboard with Airship International and Trans Con and would partner with Lou on future deals, too.

Through its feverish stock sales, Chatfield Dean raised a staggering $17 million for Airship International, and by 1993, the blimp company was back in the black. Benscher visited Airship's senior execs, who were now flush with cash, and asked them, what's your plan for the next twelve months? They didn't understand the question. The CFO was measuring the size of a new desk he was going to put in the office he was getting in the new blimp hangar the company was building. "That said it for me," Benscher said. Even the guy tasked with keeping control of the company finances had planned to start blowing the new money. "I got a sense that Lou's heart was no longer in the airship story . . . He believed he could make a success in the music business." So Benscher gladly continued gobbling up most of Airship's assets. In fact, Julian's first trip to meet Theodor Wullenkemper in the Bahamas, the flights on the Learjet, and the ever-evolving fat-kid-done-good story of Trans Continental convinced him that the real money to be made was on the private side of Lou's empire, where he seemed to be focused. As fate would have it, the deal with Westinghouse presented Benscher with an opportunity to buy into Trans Con. For reasons he didn't yet understand, Lou had never let him purchase a significant stake, but as part of the Airship Industries buyout that Benscher helped orchestrate, Westinghouse had purchased as part of the blimp company's assets the original million-dollar promissory note from Pearlman—payment for his first Airship Industries Skyship, the one that flew for Budweiser, SeaWorld, and others. The note was still unpaid, and Westinghouse handed it over to Benscher as a commission for orchestrating the deal; all he had to do was collect. The bottom line was that Lou now owed *Benscher* a million dollars. He knew Lou didn't have the cash, so Julian offered up a proposition: He persuaded Lou, in exchange for him ripping up the note, to give him $1 million worth of shares in Trans Continental Airlines. Benscher wanted in. On top of the note, he put in $1 million cash and became a 7 percent owner in Trans Con. Lou had 12.5 percent of the company. A handful of other anonymous investors in the limited liability partnerships that had purchased the planes (mostly friends and family and a few famous people from Queens) had a sliver—about $6 million worth. Wullenkemper owned the majority, Lou told Benscher, then worked to keep him believing that lie for years. Benscher had every reason to believe it. He had met with Pearlman and Wullenkemper several times since the 1990 Bahamas trip, but Wullenkemper's stake in Trans Con was never discussed. "His business with Lou was his business, not mine," Benscher said. Plus, he was clearly a secretive man with a lot of money and a large fleet of blimps and planes. During one visit to Germany, Wullenkemper was showing Benscher a giant WDL hangar full of his vintage aircraft—a Messerschmitt and others—when the mogul flashed him a "conspiratorial" look and said in his thick accent, "I know you well enough to show you zis." He pulled a set of keys from his pocket and opened a door, which led to a spiral staircase. Benscher smelled chlorine. They slinked down the stairs and there, *under* the hangar, was a massive swimming pool and phone bank. "It was like something out of the movies," Benscher said. "Would it fit that this is a guy who owns numerous aircraft? Absolutely." Still, Benscher didn't dive blindly into Trans Con. On the contrary, Lou gave him an independent Dun & Bradstreet financial report, which detailed Trans Continental Airlines' revenues. It showed a yearly operating revenue in 1990 of $78,480,000—it had only grown since, according to other internal financial statements Lou gave Julian. All of the figures were audited by a firm called Cohen & Siegel. Benscher could hardly lose, he thought. But the auditing firm, the staggering profit reports, the figures upon which the Dun & Bradstreet reports had been based, and Lou's claims about Theodor Wullenkemper's deep interest in Trans Con were pure fiction.

Now a leader in the lighter-than-air industry and loving it,

Benscher spent his time hanging out in hollow hangars watching stress tests being performed on blimp fabric in order to determine which companies' airships would need new components and then figuring out how he could get possession of those components first and corner markets. Lou, on the other hand, was content to let his blimp interests deflate.

On June 1, 1992, in fact, another one of his blimps had done just that. MetLife was pressuring him to get his Skyship 600 adorned with its blue and white logo out of its Weeksville, NC, hangar and into the sky. Mechanics were rushed through their assembly of the blimp, and in their haste they wired the blimp's steering controls backward. When it was released from its mooring truck, it rose about 150 feet and then promptly took a dive right into the giant post on the truck, ripping the bag open and destroying the blimp. An investigation by the National Transportation Safety Board revealed the wiring foul-up and blasted the mechanics, ground crew, and pilot for failing to catch the mistake during mandatory preflight inspections. Once again, some suspected foul play. Burton J. Dodge, who painted the craft—and every other Pearlman ship—said the blimp was on its last leg. Mechanics did, in fact, learn about the potential wiring problem and told Lou about it in advance, but he insisted the blimp be rushed out and up, he claimed. "Lou Pearlman always had ulterior motives. He knew the thing would crash and he would collect the insurance money for it . . . People could have been killed." Fortunately none of the handful of passengers was hurt.

Although there was still plenty of legitimate money to be made on blimps, Lou wanted out. Instead of minding his airships or servicing clients, contracts, or worn-out craft, he got busy converting Trans Continental into an entertainment company. It wasn't too difficult given that it was mostly a false front for attracting investor cash. The only tough part was keeping all of the shareholders and investors—now including Benscher—confident in his schemes. Going from the air transportation industry to boy bands seemed like a weird leap to all involved, but Lou insisted business was business, no matter the industry. Lou instantly restyled his Queens chums, transforming them overnight from first-time airship executives to first-time music industry execs. Bob Fischetti, one of Lou's hometown friends, became Lou's right-hand man on all kinds of money-scouring operations. Alan Siegel, a Queens buddy and onetime limo driver turned Airship Industries chief, and Frank Sicoli, the former guitarist for Flyer turned Airship Industries exec, were tasked with starting Trans Continental Records, a division of Trans Continental Airlines. Scott Bennett, who'd worked PR for Airship International, did the same for the fledgling record label. Frank Vazquez, the son of the maintenance man in Pearlman's Mitchell Gardens building, took a spot atop the Trans Con empire, too, as an executive in charge of operations. They were all overpaid and underqualified and did exactly as Lou instructed without asking too many questions.

When Lou came to Julian Benscher in 1992 and told him

he wanted to start a pop band, something akin to New Kids on the Block, Benscher thought it was a smart move. He never pursued a career in the entertainment industry himself, but he agreed that since the departure of New Kids there was a gap in the market for teen pop performed by clean-cut boys, pop icons that were safe enough to fly under dads' radars and cute enough to entertain the moms who chaperoned their daughters to concerts. Plus, he and Lou had shared some ups and downs by this point. Lou had paid him to help sell stock in Airship International, and the two traveled together on Lou's Trans Con jet for cross-country road shows. Benscher now considered Lou, once the subject of detached amusement, a friend, and when it became clear that Lou's heart wasn't in the airship business, Benscher went in with Lou on his pop music dream, agreeing to put up half of the money to make a band—up to a million dollars (some was cash, the rest was traded for more shares in Trans Con). The move actually put him on par with, if not slightly above, Lou in ownership of Trans Con. It was never technically the Backstreet Boys in which Benscher invested; he owned a big chunk of the company that owned the band.

Somewhere, between juggling an ever-growing pool of investors in the mostly bogus Trans Con Airlines and Travel Service, its EISA investors, Benscher, Wullenkemper, and Airship Industries leftovers, Pearlman found the time and mental capacity to form Backstreet Boys. In June 1992, he brought on

Gloria Sicoli, an experienced singer working at Universal Studios Orlando and wife of Trans Con exec Frank Sicoli. She had ties to the local civic theater and some national music industry connections. She immediately made up fliers and hung them at high schools, the theater, and local teen hangouts. She and Lou took out a classified ad in the *Orlando Sentinel* that stated: "TEEN MALE VOCALISTS. PRODUCER SEEKS MALE SINGERS THAT MOVE WELL, BETWEEN 16–19 YEARS OF AGE. WANTED FOR NEW KIDS–TYPE SINGING/ DANCE GROUP. SEND PHOTO OR BIO OF ANY KIND." About four weeks later, they had a pool of about forty guys, and they ran them through auditions at Lou's house. Sicoli videotaped them while Lou watched, but after a couple of long days of nonstop drills, neither of them was blown away by the looks, talent, or attitudes of the guys in the herd. So Sicoli rifled through the Civic Theater archives and pulled two standouts from the stacks: Alexander James McLean, fourteen, and Tony Donetti, eighteen. McLean had performed in thirty theater productions around his home in Boynton Beach and had since worked for Disney and landed roles on the Nickelodeon shows *Guts, Welcome Freshman,* and *Hi Honey, I'm Home,* a sitcom about a 1950s sitcom family transplanted in real life 1990s suburbia—McLean played Sidney "Skunk" Duff. When he showed up at Pearlman's place with his mom, Denise, he was fresh off of a first-place win and a $1,000 prize at Miami's Latin Carnival for his one-man singing, dancing *puppet* show. He had just edged out a guy four years older whom he'd also befriended on the local talent circuit—Donetti. For his part, Tony had just missed a slot in the massive Latin boy band Menudo. The son of an Irish cop and a Puerto Rican mother, his weak grasp of Spanish cost him the job, but Pearlman and Sicoli were blown away by his audition and his polite, charming demeanor. They thanked him and agreed that Donetti and McClean were clearly the first two members of their group, but when they went to call back Tony, neither Pearlman nor Sicoli could find his number. They'd lost it. They searched fruitlessly via their talent contacts for Tony Donetti but were weirdly unable to find him. No one in the pool of performers they'd auditioned matched his skills. No one in the phone book matched his name. Pearlman and Sicoli were left frustrated and perplexed. McLean, who they discovered went by A. J. for short, was represented by a manager, Jeanne "Tanzy" Williams, a music industry veteran, former performer, and New York transplant with deep connections in the national music industry and the local young talent pool. Denise McLean asked Lou to loop Tanzy Williams into the scouting process. "[Denise] said this blimp company guy said he loved A. J., and in Christmas 'ninety-two, I get this call," Tanzy Williams said. "Lou says, 'I had you checked out'—I'll never forget that—'I had you checked out, and you're the real deal. I want you to put a group together like New Kids on the Block.' "

Not only could she deliver A. J., she told Lou, but she could line up a couple dozen other talented singers and dancers to audition for the remaining slots in the group. Early on, Sicoli left to pursue other projects, so Pearlman tasked Tanzy Williams to help with the search and offered to pay her with a hundred shares of the band, which he'd incorporate as a business. He also later agreed to pay her and her fellow talent scout/manager Sybil Galler $750 a week to go to work making the band. First, they had three more members to find. Just before the Christmas holidays in 1992, Tanzy Williams hit up her roster of boys and called agents for headshots. Galler got a hold of a sound setup and moved the auditions from Lou's house to his hot, cavernous blimp parts warehouse on Michigan Avenue in Kissimmee, a neon-stripped town on the outskirts of the attractions area that's best described as Orlando's gaudy discount outlet. The glossies and bios came pouring in via FedEx and overnight mail, and for days before the auditions, Tanzy Williams and her husband shuffled through the stacks, weeding out boys who just looked wrong or were too old or too young. One young blond just beamed—Nick Carter—but he was only a babe. Pearlman wanted young-looking guys, but Nick was thirteen. So Tanzy Williams kept pushing his headshot aside. And her husband kept subtly sliding it back in at the top of the stack. "I pondered over his picture because he was so adorable," Tanzy Williams said. What they didn't know at the time was that Nick was a seasoned veteran. At ten, he had started performing with the Tampa Bay Buccaneers cheerleaders. He'd been offered a role on the Disney Channel's *Mickey Mouse Club,* too, but was more interested in becoming a pop star. Tanzy Williams invited him to the audition along with fifty-nine other boys, who over two days would sing and dance their way through routines lasting up to twenty minutes apiece. They filed into the back of Lou's blimp parts warehouse, passing shelves of tools and drawers full of airship rivets, and performed on an unforgiving concrete floor. Lou situated himself and watched in the background. For his turn, Nick Carter sang Simon & Garfunkel's "Bridge over Troubled Water," a shrewd move obviously chosen to grab Lou's attention; it was a favorite among the songs his cousin sang. Nick did an up tune, too. "He had a whole little dance routine," Tanzy Williams said. But midway through, he pulled a cartwheel and flashed just a momentary grimace of pain. It disappeared and he kept right on singing, dancing, smiling. Tanzy Williams asked afterward if he was okay, and young Nick said yeah, he'd just hurt his wrist a bit but had wanted to finish. He went to the hospital after the audition. His wrist was broken. "What a little pro," Tanzy Williams said. "We knew immediately."

Auditions continued for a couple of days, and then, toward the end, a young man named Howie Dorough strolled in. His new agent had sent him to the familiar-sounding audition—he thought it might have been for a group that had already tried him out and passed, but the location was different, so Dorough took a chance. When he walked through the door, Pearlman recognized him instantly as Tony Donetti, the stage name given to him by his previous agent. Tanzy Williams met him for the first time and described him as a quiet, sweet kid with a stellar voice. For months after the audition, he addressed her as Ms. Williams, though she kept admonishing him to call her Jeanne. "He was the best kid professional that you'd ever want to work with," she said. "I think it was his Spanish Christian upbringing. Just good people." Reacquainted with Pearlman and crew and now going by his real name, Dorough, later rechristened Howie D, was given the job on the spot.

In the end, Tanzy Williams and Galler pulled two other boys from the pool of talent. Sam Licata was a community college buddy of Howie's and a talented singer and songwriter who came with his own roster of original music. They also picked Charles Edwards, an Orlando kid who was a bit weak vocally but had a look and showed potential. After the auditions, Tanzy Williams; Pearlman; his right-hand man from the loyal Queens crew, Bob Fischetti; and the parents took the boys to a local sub shop. Lou treated. And later the whole crew retired to Lou's place, where the boys took advantage of the pool and billiards table and dropped an endless supply of quarters in Lou's slot machine. Nick and A. J.'s moms accompanied their minor children. There was another kid along for the ride in the beginning, too, a rarely mentioned "little Spanish boy" whom no one could remember by anything but his first name, Jamie. Like an extremely short-lived, swivel-hipped phantom member of the group, he's since been erased from the Backstreet legend. "He was not a swell singer, but he was *wild*," Tanzy Williams said. "He did this dance with his pelvis that was so hot." During his audition, Pearlman's eyes were bugging out; he wanted Jamie as a sort of stand-in for the main five members of the group, but Tanzy Williams eventually convinced Lou that this wasn't Broadway, and they'd never get away with even occasionally replacing any of the boys once they became well-known pop stars—not even with the pelvic anomaly that was the mysterious Jamie. Lou relented.

With the five boys—A. J., Howie, Nick, Charles, and Sam—in place, Lou rented a four-bedroom house in suburban Kissimmee on Baltimore Street, near Tanzy Williams's place. Nick and his mother, Jane, who had traveled from Tampa, stayed in one room. Licata was in another. A keyboardist with the group took up another room, and the rest of the boys lived elsewhere in town but would come over each day. Pearlman completely furnished the pad and converted the garage into a wood-floored, mirrored dance studio. Six days a week, the boys would meet for breakfast (often cooked by Jane Carter), work with school tutors until noon, have lunch, and go straight to dance and vocal rehearsal in the garage, where they'd spend the remainder of the day. The group often shared dinner together, too. Lou regularly treated them to meals with flair at T.G.I. Friday's, and it was in that kitschy perch that they brainstormed names for the group. Across the street was a teen hangout called Backstreet Market. Lou suggested "Backstreet," and since they were generally known as "the boys," they settled on Backstreet Boys over a steaming hot plate of fried cheese with zesty marinara dipping sauce.

About six months in, things got rocky for Charles Edwards. He wasn't blending vocally. Plus, the others had an inherent sort of funk or R&B soul about them, but Edwards's movement was a bit stiff and showing no signs of loosening. Pearlman knew it wasn't working with him, but he left the dirty work of firing him to Tanzy Williams and, oddly enough, Julian Benscher. Lou insisted that it be done in a public, group setting. So the crew went out for dinner. Parents were there, too. Jane, recalled Tanzy Williams, was crying. Edwards had a sense that something bad was coming, and after some small talk Pearlman gave Tanzy Williams the nod. She said she was the one who eventually "did the nasty" and fired Edwards. It was the worst part of her early experience with the boys, she said: "It was like drowning a puppy." Benscher told a different story. It was he who was actually having a sidebar conversation with Edwards throughout the awkward dinner. He was blunt with Edwards, insisting straight-up that he wasn't up to snuff. "He was a lovely boy," Benscher said. "But we were trying to put together a singing group, and he just couldn't sing." Julian may not have had an expertise in music or entertainment, but he was at the time a larger shareholder in Trans Continental than Lou himself. "I thought I had the biggest stake in the whole group," he said. By the end of the dinner, he had convinced Edwards that he needed to quit or he'd bring down the group as a whole. Edwards, in tears according to Tanzy Williams's recollection, decided to go.

A few months in, Sam Licata clearly became more interested in his solo career than working as an equal partner in a group. While the other members drilled or hung out together, he headed off with his keyboard to work on his original songs. Various insiders had all sorts of explanations for the Sam's departure, everything from his sexuality to a conflict of interest due to a romantic relationship he'd started up with Sybil Galler. But everyone agreed that he wanted too badly to front the group. Licata added that he wanted to pursue interests on the business side of the group, as well. "It didn't take much convincing for Sam to leave," Benscher said.

Never actually doing any firing himself and always playing the good guy, Pearlman offered Licata a chance as a solo performer under the name Phoenix Stone, but "his fan base never materialized," Lou said. Years after he left the initial group, there was a lawsuit by Licata and a settlement. "I thought it ended amicably," Pearlman said.

Suddenly Backstreet Boys was down two members, but

Tanzy Williams had already hired Scott Hoekstra, a talent agent and manager of several popular acts in the '70s, to line up gigs. He'd made headway with a few shows at high schools, fairs, and shopping malls. The clock was ticking on Backstreet Boys, and every day that passed without the final lineup was a day of missed rehearsals and racked-up bills. "I was running out of boys," Tanzy Williams said. "Every time we had to get a replacement, it got harder and harder to find kids that would fit the bill."

After rounds of unsuccessful auditions, Kevin Richardson came to Lou by way of a Trans Con underling who'd met Richardson around Orlando. He was a model and actor in Walt Disney World's Teenage Mutant Ninja Turtles show. He played Aladdin in the Disney parade. Before moving to Orlando, he had been a football player, a sales rep for a lawn maintenance company, and a wedding singer in the Appalachian foothills of Kentucky. He wasn't the most professionally trained of the Backstreet Boys, but he had model looks, was levelheaded, and would become the mouthpiece for the band. At twenty-one, he was also a sort of built-in chaperone. He started drilling with the others immediately and picked up the moves and parts right away. It was Richardson, in fact, who saved the day when Lou and his crew exhausted their efforts to find a fifth boy for the band. Tanzy Williams brought in a dozen or more candidates, but none of them pushed Lou's buttons, so Richardson convinced him to give his cousin back in Kentucky, Brian Littrell, a crack. Richardson called Littrell, had him yanked out of American history class at Tates Creek High, and had him sing over the phone to Lou. Pearlman put him on a plane—his first-ever flight—and Littrell showed up the next day at fish-themed tourist attraction SeaWorld, for which Lou had flown the Shamu blimp and whose parent company, Anheuser-Busch, had inked some of Lou's earliest deals for the Bud blimp. The group was preparing to play its first real gig at the park. Littrell auditioned right there in the stands, belting out lines from pop songs as a trained orca swam gracefully nearby in the saltwater pool. He was invited to join the group and the lineup was solidified. Shamu jumped through a hoop. The crowd went wild.

The Backstreet Boys debuted for about three thousand people at SeaWorld's high school moneymaker Grad Nite on May 8, 1993, two weeks after Littrell joined up. The stage at the Nautilus Theater that balmy night was still sopping wet from the spray of speedboats and the drippings from stuntman wetsuits—the Boys' opening act was a water-skiing show specializing in human pyramids and long-distance launches, good old Florida entertainment. The teenage singer-dancers braved the conditions nonetheless and kicked and shuffled and waved their arms and jazz hands in unison while their perfectly feathered New Kids on the Block–style mushroom haircuts bobbed in time. The song was the Temptations' "Get Ready." The young girls' screams that would come to underscore so many of their later appearances reached deafening registers for the first time that night. And the SeaWorld gig got them noticed by a deejay at popular local pop radio station XL 106.7. For a spin or two, the boys were the toast of the local dial. Meanwhile, Tanzy Williams, Lou, Scott Hoekstra, and crew went to work searching for a proper label that could propel the group to real, dryer stages. They flew to New York for a showcase for ICM and William Morris Agency, who were considering representing the boys. Hoekstra, who takes credit for the ICM/William Morris tour (as does Tanzy Williams) filmed the whole thing for an "unauthorized" home video he later hawked for $9.95. Aside from the limo, the fancy hotel rooms, and the obviously just-purchased shopping-spree clothes, Hoekstra's hokey collection of VHS moments were indiscernible from any parent's camcorder memories of a grade school field trip. There was lots of waving to the camera, giggling, and goofing around in the airport. As they filed to the terminal, someone accused then fourteen-year-old Nick Carter of picking his nose. He insisted he was only scratching an itch. Pearlman was the ultimate gofer in the tape. He loaded up the bags in the limo. He fetched the boys' boarding passes. In short, he ran the show—quietly, without flash, modestly, even.

Behind the scenes, even he was humbled by the amount of cash he was blowing on his pet project—$3 million, all told. He rented soundstages where the boys would host showcases.

He bought a full stage sound system in case their gigs weren't properly equipped. "We would bring our own sound to engagements," Hoekstra says. "He had vocal coaches, choreographers. He hired them and put them on salary." For the ICM trip, he brought more than two dozen people to New York and put them up in hotel rooms at the Plaza on Central Park. But when it was over, Lou's limos, Rolls-Royces, jets, and lavish hotel rooms weren't enough to sell a bona fide record label on the idea of Backstreet Boys as pop stars. That's when Lou decided to shake up his team. After the New York trip and SeaWorld gig, Tanzy Williams started trying to get the boys back to the blimp warehouse for rehearsal but couldn't summon them on their phones. They weren't returning messages, either. When she called Lou, he told her he'd been in touch with them and that he was giving them a breather—they'd busted their butts up until now, after all. Tanzy Williams agreed and backed off until the group finally reassembled in the warehouse on July 28, 1993. Her husband was already on the soundboard getting ready when the boys straggled in. They were all looking down, around, anywhere but in Tanzy's eyes. Lou asked everyone to come into his office, where he, without someone to push the unpleasant task upon, told Tanzy Williams that the boys needed a bigger, better manager. "I went into tunnel vision," Tanzy Williams said. "I think I fainted." She had been promised a spot in the "family," had turned over almost her entire roster of talent to Lou, and had even agreed to defer her promised weekly salary, taking just $100 a week on top of the living expenses Lou paid her, the boys, and their mothers. Lou promised fame and fortune. He was her best hope for a big break in the music industry. "I really still love the man," she said. "It's practically taken going through therapy to find out why I felt that way. He knows how to use you." Tanzy Williams later filed a lawsuit against Lou alleging, among other things, that he swindled her out of her clients and then started a new corporation in Delaware rather than pay her a share of Backstreet bucks. She settled for an undisclosed sum. Years later, she and a business partner wrote a script for a feature film about the formation of Backstreet Boys and even landed a production deal. She was shopping for funding in 2008. "You know who he reminds me of," she said of Lou, "is the kid who would tear the wings off of flies— not to kill them, just to watch them crawl around and not be able to fly."

Johnny Wright and his wife Donna took over as Backstreet Boys' managers. A former gofer himself and chaperone for New Kids on the Block, Johnny had earned a reputation for making things happen and keeping the wheels grinding on a successful cash cow pop act. If he wasn't a full-fledged wheeler-dealer, he surely had an insider's view of the last boy band explosion, and he had the major league connections neither Lou nor Hoekstra nor Tanzy Williams could provide. Donna constantly worked the phones and hounded labels for attention. She put the boys on the line to sing a cappella to anyone who'd listen just to prove they had the vocal ability New Kids on the Block had lacked. She flew them to New York and L.A. to meet with labels. Mercury Records loved the band and was ready to sign them, Lou said. Its president Ed Eckstine told him, "I feel like a Brinks truck just pulled up to my door!" But before any deal could be inked, it was derailed by longtime Mercury recording artist John Cougar Mellencamp, Lou said. He threatened to walk away from the label if they got in the boy band business. Ain't that America.

Then one of the key BSB allies at Mercury left to go to Zomba/Jive Records and Donna and Johnny saw their opportunity. On her cell phone at a concert, Donna rang Zomba/Jive's Dave McPherson so he could hear the ear-bleeding screams of the young girls going nuts for Backstreet Boys. In 1994, the group signed a deal with the label and flew to Sweden to record with ABBA and Ace of Base producer Denniz PoP. The German audience would gobble up the squeaky-clean boys and they'd go on to score number-one hits in Austria and a platinum record in Germany. Meanwhile, back in America, music fans were flocking to loud guitar noise, tortured, screaming vocalists, and an accompanying fashion trend of scraggly hair, beat-up flannel shirts, and ripped jeans. "Grunge" was de rigueur. The polished, primped, and thoroughly rehearsed Backstreet Boys had miles to go before they scored a stateside hit.

In June of '94, Pearlman stood as best man at Julian Ben-scher's wedding. Backstreet Boys sang. By all accounts, even Lou's, the boys were uncharacteristically off-kilter that day. Benscher said they'd hit the vodka bar too hard, or maybe they were just tired and frazzled from the rigors of searching for a record deal. Either way, they couldn't find their harmonies and they were missing notes all over the place. On the wedding video outtakes, the camera turned toward Benscher's father-in-law, and he could be heard asking, "This is the shit my son-in-law sank his money into?"

## CHAPTER 6

# BUY, BUY, BUY

Since I was a boy, I've had the habit of taking some time right before I go to sleep to think about what I want to do the next day, the next week, the next year, and the next five and ten years. It's Late Nite with Lou and his dream-making machine."

— Lou Pearlman, from *Bands, Brands, and Billions: My Top Ten Rules for Making Any Business Go Platinum*

On June 27, 1994, Lou's Airship Industries Skyship, the one he'd paid Benscher for in Trans Con stock, was ripped to shreds by a windstorm at its Elizabeth City, North Carolina, dock. The ship was moored there after a tour promoting the band Pink Floyd's *Division Bell* album when the gales kicked up. Then on September 11, another one of Lou's blimps flying for Gulf Oil crashed in a Long Island suburban neighborhood on its way to the finals of the U.S. Open tennis tournament in Flushing, Queens, where Lou himself had spotted his first airships (no one was injured in either incident). It was the fifth blimp he'd lost or wrecked in freak incidents; blimp envelopes wear out naturally, but Lou was working on about a 70 percent loss rate from crashes and natural disasters. Alan Gross made noise with letters to the Federal Aviation Authority, and Pearlman and his people caught wind of it. Gross's longtime buddy, the son of his building's maintenance man, Frank Vazquez Jr., called him to warn him not to interfere. He was clearly uncomfortable as a henchman, and he bounced back and forth between being Gross's bro and threatening him. At first he said he was in North Carolina working on Pearlman's blimp for Budweiser, then he said he was in Florida, about to leave for North Carolina. "So what's up, man, how you doin'?" he said, then launched into warnings and sounded like he was reading from a script. His words sounded like Pearlman's earlier heated phone conversations with Gross. "Also called to let you know that you should keep your mouth shut as far as your antics of getting back at Mr. Pearlman . . . especially via the Gulf people. You're only hurting yourself for the future . . . If anything comes of anything you're going to be left out. There's still a possibility of some good things coming together . . . because it's a small world after all . . . When you open your mouth and talk negative, you're hurting me, too." Then Vazquez snapped back into his friendly self and ended the message, "Otherwise how's life, how are the women treating you?"

By 1995, the Gulf Oil and blimp problems were moot. Lou's last blimp lease fizzled out that year, and he never hit the bricks to scour up another. He was busy being a boy band mogul.

Zomba/Jive released "We've Got it Goin' On" in 1995. It reached number 69 on the *Billboard* charts, then it tanked, too. The Boys' record deal hung in the balance. So the Wrights came up with a plan: Export the group to Europe, where they could manipulate a smaller, pop-hungry market and soar back to the U.S. on a current of popularity and experience. "The label didn't want to fund it, so Lou put up his own money," said Wright, who years later went on to manage Britney Spears and Justin Timberlake. Wright had all of the connections and none of the capital to launch a pop group. He'd scrapped his way through tours with New Kids and watched them all get rich but didn't walk away with much in hand to show for his efforts. "Now here was *my* opportunity," he said. And here was Lou. "All I had was time and talent; he put up all the money."

Simply put, Pearlman *bought* his way into the business, starting full-fledged record label, management, promotions, production, and distribution companies in one fell swoop under the Trans Continental moniker (and using Trans Continental Airlines as his corporate umbrella). Including the money Benscher invested in exchange for more Trans Con stock, Pearlman spent $3 million financing the formation of Backstreet Boys, about a million more than he originally planned. Part of his plot was to make the group look and sound successful long before they ever became stars—a fine, if not expensive, art Lou himself had honed as a Rolls-driving, penthouse-dwelling Queens fat cat. A chunk of the Backstreet Boys start-up money paid for vocal coaches, choreographers, musicians, and technicians for computer and musical equipment used to polish the young men's singing. By the time Wright came on the scene, though, they were set up in a house and rehearsal space (Lou's bare-bones blimp warehouse) and had tutors and new clothes—their every need was covered by Pearlman. "I was like, *oh my,*" Wright said. "Some major record companies don't even have that kind of cash flow." On the one hand, Lou was anything but deliberate with his spending decisions; on the other, there was no formula for what he was trying to accomplish. He was a forty-three-year-old man developing raw teen talent into a product that would ultimately live or die by the impetuous whims of an even younger target audience. Lou zeroed in on young girls and their parents, then threw every penny he could at appealing to their pop culture cravings. "Whether he had to rob someone in the middle of the night, the money was there," Wright joked.

It was a spot-on observation.

About the time Backstreet Boys went in search of their European market, Lou's Queens childhood chum Alan Gross had one more interaction with Lou and his companies: He learned his five hundred shares of Airship International stock had been mysteriously transferred out of his name and into Alan Siegel's without his authorization. So he sat down and wrote his first letter to the Securities and Exchange Commission, notifying them in 1995 of Lou's company's failure to give him notification of stockholder meetings, file proper tax documents, and more. "In my opinion, there are serious breaches of both fiscal and operational responsibility and an investigation is needed to determine exactly where millions of dollars of company assets have gone," Gross wrote. He also complained that Siegel had stolen his stock. The SEC acknowledged his complaint with a form letter but nothing came of an investigation, one that likely would have unearthed a massive fraud either with EISA or Trans Con itself. Without apology or explanation, shortly thereafter, Gross received a new stock certificate from Siegel for five hundred shares of Airship International. It was at about this time that Gross took stock of his piles and piles of documents, too—the videos, pictures, and tape recordings from his time with Airship Enterprises, Airship International, and Lou. "I kept it all," Gross said, "because I knew it would come up again one day."

Then that same year an anonymous insider in Lou's shady world of endless investments raised a second red flag. His name was withheld from FDIC documents, but the agent had been contracted to market the EISA plan to unsuspecting investors—nonemployees of Trans Continental Airlines. In a letter to authorities, he questioned the nature of the plan. He couldn't figure out what, exactly, it was. He was told he was hawking CDs and that the company was able to negotiate better-than-prime rates by convincing banks to waive something called a "teller allowance." But there was no such thing as a "teller allowance," at least not in the context Trans Con was using it, and FDIC senior attorney J. Michael Payne confirmed as much in a November 2, 1995, letter to the would-be sales agent. He went on to explore what, exactly, EISA could be, but he was ultimately stumped, too. It seemed like a corporate CD or a brokered deposit, but if either was the case, EISA violated several regulations governing those two products—most importantly, Trans Con wasn't registered as a dealer as the law required. In a final effort to get to the bottom of the investment program, Payne called Pearlman himself to ask about the nature of EISA. Lou told him it was a 401(k) plan, which was available only to employees and shareholders. Payne clearly wasn't satisfied that it made sense. He had, after all, been speaking with the anonymous EISA agent who provided proof that he was tasked with selling the scheme to non–Trans Con employees. Lou had simply lied. But the FDIC, inexplicably gun-shy, hedged in its response to the anonymous EISA sales agent. "Without a complete understanding of exactly what the product is, no definitive determination of deposit insurance coverage can be made," Payne wrote. "In light of the foregoing, I would strongly recommend that you obtain a complete written description of the product prior to making a decision to market it." And with that— a vague insinuation that this agent should not yet sell what was likely an illegal product—the FDIC's first look into EISA effectively ended.

Undaunted by the government's awareness of his shady savings program, Lou went on in '95 to wrangle important high-level investors. Anthony DeCamillis, who with Chatfield Dean had helped Airship International raise $17 million before he was temporarily suspended as a broker, would go on to help Lou secure loans for his flailing public airship company. And that same year, he partnered with Pearlman to start Planet Airways, a charter airline that was separate and apart from Lou's Trans Con. For five years it struggled to secure approval from the FAA but eventually did. Planet would become the only Pearlman-affiliated company to own any commercial jets—three 727s were registered in the company's name, and the company eventually owned three more planes. DeCamillis also invested more than a half million dollars in Trans Con and EISA himself. Lou sent him deposit envelopes emblazoned with the Citibank logo, an aesthetic touch that helped convince investors that their money was going into legitimate, individual CDs. Pearlman told DeCamillis what he told many investors, that EISA was backed by Trans Continental Airlines, which had forty-seven (and later forty-nine) planes—747s, 707s, and L-1011s. In the beginning, it was Lou's access to planes that made him an appealing partner to DeCamillis in Planet Airways. Lou was the second-largest shareholder in the Germany-based airline fleet worth $700 million, he had said, and he produced financial statements to back up claims that Trans Con was raking in about $80 million a year. The statements were audited by Cohen & Siegel of Coral Gables.

But what DeCamillis and none of the investors knew was that in 1995, Lou had dispatched one of his lackeys to a secretarial business called Coral Gables Services, where he set up a dedicated phone line. The freelance secretarial staff was directed to answer the phone, "Good morning/afternoon Cohen and Siegel." He told the service that "most of the calls will be for Stanley Cohen" and said that if anyone called for him or the others, they should be told that "Mr. Cohen/Pearlman/Siegel is out of the office in a meeting" and to take a message. Having been caught off guard by the first queries from authorities at the FDIC, Pearlman wouldn't be so unprepared the next time a government or other official came looking for proof of the legitimacy of Trans Con or its investment schemes. Cohen & Siegel was nothing more than an answering service, a false front for the fake firm, but it would sign off on Lou's fudged financials for years to come. Even its name was an homage to crime: Cohen & Siegel, as in *gangsters* Mickey Cohen and Bugsy Siegel, the founders of Las Vegas.

Lou always kept the names of his biggest investors in the mid- to late 1990s close to the vest. Among them, however, some names were known: Eric Emanuel, a Wall Street investment banker who has since died, appeared on some of Gross's home videos mingling at several of Pearlman's blimp launch events; he was good for several million and brought along Long Island real estate developer Alfonse Fuglioli, who was also good for a few million. Then there was Dr. Joseph Chow.

He had first popped up on the Chatfield Dean call list when the broker was hawking Airship International. Lou himself subsequently reached out to Chow, a Chicago engineering professor whose wife ran a successful health-care business, and came to know him as the sort of investor who preferred loans or promissory notes with better-than-average rates of return to typical stocks. That was exactly the bill of goods Pearlman sold him. Chow did his due diligence and asked Pearlman for company financials. Lou produced regular earnings statements, including one showing $74 million in assets for 1995 and close to $76 million for 1996. Total operating revenues were $76 million in '95, $81 million in '96. On paper, Trans Con was raking in profits and showing no signs of slowing. Lest he had any doubts about the authenticity of the numbers, they were audited by Coral Gables financial firm Cohen & Siegel. Chow was even an early adopter of the EISA plan, which Lou extended to him, he said, as a shareholder in Trans Con. Lou had on hand a letter from Cohen & Siegel confirming the legitimacy of the savings plan, too. It stated:

> With reference to your Employee Investment Savings Account (E.I.S.A.) program, we hereby are responding to your request as to our opinion: We certify that this program meets all . . . Internal Revenue Service requirements and is available to all employees and shareholders of Trans Continental. The reference literature fully depicts the plan as its

*deferment policy as well as insurance coverage by F.D.I.C. and Lloyd's of London as maintained on file in our office...*

Chow was Pearlman's largest and longest-running investor. He and Pearlman even became what Chow's daughter Jennifer considered "friends." Pearlman sat with Chow in the first pew at his other daughter's wedding. Jennifer had fond memories as a young teen of being introduced to members of Backstreet Boys. But even at that age, she didn't trust Lou, and neither did Chow's wife—they occasionally argued over Chow's decision to invest with Lou, but over the course of a decade the two men's business relationship flourished, with Lou constantly pumping Chow full of good news, a positive outlook, and the ever-looming specter of an IPO—it was just around the bend, and it would make all of his investors ungodly rich, Lou promised. In 1997, Pearlman sent a letter out to Chow and other shareholders in the company stating:

*In October, our auditors began the process of determining the current value of the 49 aircraft which are currently owned, and leased, by Trans Continental (TCA). This process is nearing completion and is very favorable in regards to shareholder value . . . All Private Placement shareholders will receive instructions on the procedure for exchanging private stock for shares in the Initial Public Offering (IPO).*

*Your options will be to either cash in your shares at the offering price, or exchange them for IPO shares, which will be unrestricted and free trading.*

He went on to say that the company's underwriter planned to file the necessary paperwork by the end of February and that the IPO should happen within ninety days thereafter, and continued:

*Unfortunately, we are restricted from sharing many of the details with you, but let me say that we are very excited to complete the filing within the next 30 days. The Stock Market is strong, interest rates are healthy, and our Balance Sheet will impress even the most skeptical bears on Wall Street. (Pray for a capital gains tax cut in 1997, we'll need it!)*

He signed it Louis J. Pearlman, president.

By the mid- to late '90s Pearlman had expanded his investor shopping efforts to all kinds of people. At least one investor whose son had an ongoing heart condition transferred his medical savings into EISA (he asked to remain anonymous for his son's sake). Lou personally promised him the account was backed by his company, which he said was worth hundreds of millions, and insured by Lloyd's of London and the FDIC. In Florida, Lou targeted retirees, recruiting along the way local salespeople—known figures in their communities who lived, shopped for groceries, and even attended church with the people to whom they sold EISA (most would later say they had no inkling they were participating in fraud). One of these local salespeople approached Marie Weber, her husband, and her mother-in-law, all of Naples, Florida, about EISA, and in 1997, Weber's mother-in-law, who was in her sixties, invested first. She died shortly afterward and left her son, Weber's husband, an inheritance, which he invested in EISA, too—about $500,000. In a few years, they were getting statements showing a balance of more than $864,000 dollars, Marie, who was fifty-four at the time of our interview, said. It was a hell of a retirement nest egg, and they had already decided where it would go: into their son's college fund and into building their dream home in coastal Georgia. Pearlman kept his Queens relatives and friends pumping money into his ruse, too. On a return trip to Queens, Lou himself pitched Trans Con and EISA to Marc Morelli, his silver-haired, impeccably coiffed, emerald-eyed barber. He became convinced that Pearlman was his shortcut to an early retirement, having already spent years working eight to five on his feet at Lindenview Super Cut on Parsons Boulevard in Flushing. "I was his favorite barber," said Morelli, who was still cutting hair for a wage and tips at age sixty-one. When Pearlman soared to success and moved to Florida, he had even tried to take Marc the barber with him, promising to set him up in his own shop.

Instead, Morelli invested his retirement savings—about $10,000—in shares of Trans Continental Airlines in the late '80s. Later, he and his older brother Alex invested more in EISA, and over the course of almost twenty years, their statements came to show a balance of about $175,000. Throughout the '90s, Pearlman would stop by the shop when he was in town. His own reddish, thinning hair didn't take much work—it had become a mere suggestion of a coiffure—but he did bring the Backstreet Boys by for cuts; Morelli hung signed pictures of all of Lou's bands on the barbershop wall. He did, a couple of times, consider taking his money out of Trans Con's EISA, but Pearlman gave him the inside line. "Marc, don't do it," Lou said. "Don't touch it. Wait a couple of months. When the stock offering comes out, you're going to be a rich man."

Meanwhile, Lou's Boys were overseas building a fan base. In 1996, Backstreet Boys' "I'll Never Break Your Heart" went gold in Austria and platinum in Germany, and they toured playing sold-out shows in massive Asian and Canadian venues. By 1997, the group had sold 8.5 million CDs, and they could barely get around in Europe—they were mobbed wherever they went in scenes seemingly borrowed from a Beatles movie. Young girls wailed. Tears streamed down their faces. Lips quivered. Faces were flushed. And pens and notebooks desperately wagged for autographs. The moment the Boys opened hotel room doors, a wall of girls surged toward it, each hoping for her glimpse. The scene repeated itself everywhere they toured—Germany, Asia, Canada. Everywhere but the United States.

"We have to start from scratch in the U.S.," twenty-six-year-old Kevin Richardson told the *Orlando Sentinel* in September 1997. "A lot of people are skeptical. It's good because it's humbling. In Europe, there would be maybe 500–1,000 people waiting for us at the airport, but when I got off the plane in Orlando, it's like nobody knew who I was." That changed by the end of the year. The boys released "Everybody (Backstreet's Back)" and a self-titled album that compiled their international hits and debuted at number 1 on the U.S. charts. Together, the records sold twenty-eight million copies worldwide, fourteen million in the U.S. While four singles in a row made the top five on the UK charts, "Quit Playing Games (with My Heart)" was a million-selling single in the U.S. In December, the group set off on a sixty-city, twenty-country tour.

Lou celebrated with a massive spending spree. In 1996, his Trans Con record label spent $848,067.31. By 1997, Lou was blowing more than three and a half times that amount, $3,066,751.26. Just as he did as a budding teenage entrepreneur, he started sniffing around other business ideas, too, and in 1996, Trans Con purchased the Chippendales male exotic dancers. In a letter to investors that year, Lou described the successful troupe of buffed peelers—with their synchronized

displays of pelvic thrusting and overstuffed banana ham-
mocks—like they were the greatest thing since *Cats*. Pearlman
also constantly bought clothes, jewelry, and gifts for the boys.
In a show of appreciation that said more about his own geeky
interests than those of his teenage heartthrobs, he promised
them a *blimp* when they reached a certain level of sales.
There's a picture of them standing in front it—it was Benscher's blimp, of course, with a Backstreet Boys logo plastered
on the side. The decal, Julian said, cost Lou about $17,000.
Wright recalled one instance from this era when the Boys
were in danger of missing a show, so Lou chartered a plane to
get them there in time. They actually missed the show by minutes, but the flight cost him about $50,000. "An entourage of
eleven people was flying all over the place," Wright said.
"There were per diems. There were hotel costs. There were
dinners." The biggest single line item in his Trans Con Records financial statements was for "Travel and Entertainment," which in 1996 was $244,075.23. In 1997, it jumped to
$524,995.81. Everyone remembered the dinners the most.
"There were always these entourages of people for dinner,"
Benscher added. "If I had a meeting with Lou or I'd scheduled
a dinner and I wasn't expecting others to be there, I'd actually
get up and leave; I never wanted to be around dinners with
the investors." Scott Hoekstra, who booked Backstreet Boys'
earliest gigs, remembered Lou bringing as many as fifteen or
twenty people to restaurants, and he always picked up the

check: "All the mothers would go, kids, friends of the boys." It was all in service to Pearlman's "we are family" mantra. "He kept driving that home—we're going to take care of our family. That was his main drive, to keep people cohesive, to keep people on an I-got-your-back basis."

As Jeanne Williams puts it, "He wanted everyone to buy into him as Big Papa."

Pearlman treated himself nicely, too. He was sure to be seen in his cornflower-blue Rolls (driven, usually, by strapping young lads with pop star aspirations in peck-hugging tank tops) or getting on board his jet, a Gulfstream II with wing tips modified to make it look like a sleeker, pricier Gulfstream IV or V. His sprawling, iron-gated white house on Ridge Pine Trail in Orlando was outfitted with video games, slot machines, a pool table, a pool, a big-screen TV in a large media room, and plenty of guest bedrooms for sleepovers. If something advanced the celebrity image of his groups or helped him look the part of a mogul or even kept his boys happy, money was no object. Starting in 1992 and running through the '90s, the bulk of Lou's assets—including EISA investors' dollars—went into Backstreet Boys and a vertical pop music factory that supported them. Wright, meanwhile, got a sense that the deep pockets behind Backstreet Boys weren't only in Lou's tent-size trousers (his waistline ballooned in this era, with his weight pushing past three hundred pounds). "Someone would always pop up and say, 'I'm one of Lou's investors; I own a piece of the Backstreet Boys.' We'd laugh and sign autographs, and Lou would say, 'He's invested in the overall company [Trans Con].' We always knew that those were the guys who were funding the recording," Wright said. But all anyone on the outside of his operations seemed to see was that Lou Pearlman knew pop music. Benscher recalled sitting with a senior BMG executive in the late 1990s who said Lou's fortunes in the entertainment industry were beyond astonishing. "It just doesn't work like that. Normally labels have loads of bands that don't go anywhere. It is ridiculous." He meant it in a good way. Another former Zomba/Jive Records consultant with a seasoned, inside view of the Backstreet and *NSYNC deals and who still dealt with the label said it was Jive's billionaire honcho Clive Calder who really saw the opportunity for what was essentially British teen pop in America, but when that happened, Backstreet Boys—then *NSYNC—were perfectly polished and poised to fill that demand. "Somebody put together these kids dancing and singing. Someone had the ability to put together a package. If it wasn't Pearlman, it was obviously whomever he had in his organization orchestrating this stuff. In a sense, it wasn't by accident." He admitted that Lou's endless cash and willingness to spend big where Jive wouldn't probably played into the ultimate success of his bands, but he also insisted that the kind of success Backstreet Boys enjoyed didn't come from Lou's checking account alone: "That has to catch on naturally."

The setting was important, too. Lou's level of "imagineering," as it's known to Mickey's minions, could only happen in the town that Walt Disney built. Orlando boasted a decades-long tradition of molding talented young singers, dancers, and actors into clean-cut teen stars—not to mention the city has year-round balmy weather, no state income tax, and the Homestead Act, which let gazillionaires keep their houses, even if they paid for them with stock fraud money and later declared bankruptcy (as long as they didn't borrow against their homes). It was both a huckster's paradise and a breeding ground for kid stars. Keri Russell, star of TV's *Felicity,* came out of *The Mickey Mouse Club,* as did actor Ryan Gosling and singers Christina Aguilera, Britney Spears, and an extremely talented young vocalist and dancer named Justin Timberlake. He was a *Star Search* loser who'd been doing the skip-and-grin on the *Mickey Mouse Club* television show in the early 1990s when he met up with Joey Fatone and Chris Kirkpatrick; those two had met at Universal Studios—Joey was playing a werewolf in the *Beetlejuice Graveyard Revue* show, and Chris sang in a doo-wop group. When *The Mickey Mouse Club*'s run ended, Chris and Joey called Justin about starting an a cappella ensemble in 1995, and the core of a future pop megaforce was formed.

There are a dozen colloquial versions of how exactly the idea for *NSYNC jelled, but one of the most believable versions involves Lou trying to convince Backstreet Boys to record a song that he himself had penned. The boys straight-up denied him. "I couldn't believe they would take that attitude with him," Julian Benscher remembered. "So I say to Lou, 'Are you thinking what I'm thinking?' and the idea was, okay, we'll show you, we'll start another group." Unlike what he had done with Backstreet Boys, Lou ran with the idea of *NSYNC all on his own; Julian was cut out of the formation and promotion. He didn't have a direct stake in the band this time, either, although he owned a chunk of the companies that backed them—7 percent of Trans Continental Airlines. This time, Lou wanted the golden geese all to himself. He did, however, need the talent-spotting eye of Johnny and Donna Wright, who had come on board as seasoned music industry navigators. Kirkpatrick had just missed the cut for Backstreet Boys, and he came to Lou early in the discussions of forming a second boy band. The formation of *NSYNC was also a cat-and-mouse game played between the Wrights and Lou on one side and Justin Timberlake and his mother Lynn Harless on the other (Fatone and Kirkpatrick joined with little convincing). As Timberlake's parents pondered the opportunity, the Wrights, who recognized the young singer and dancer's star quality instantly, leaned on them hard to join up. In the end, Lou himself joined in the push. Wowed by his rich history and powers of persuasion, Timberlake and his parents signed contracts in 1995. Timberlake, subsequently, suggested recruiting his fellow Mouseketeer JC Chasez. The original choice for the bass slot in the vocal group, Fatone's classmate Jason Galasso, didn't work out. So Justin's former vocal coach, who'd gone on to lead a group called the Mississippi Showstoppers, recommended to Lynn one of that group's standouts, a God-fearing, church-singing Clinton, Mississippi, kid he knew named Lance Bass. It was a combo of Timberlake, Harless, and Lou who all wore down Bass's mom, Diane, until she let him come to Orlando to audition at age sixteen. Pearlman promised to fly her down, put her up, and give her the royal treatment. He knew by then she'd never be able to tell Lance no. True to form, Lou met Lance and his mother at the airport with Lynn Harless in his Rolls and dropped them off at the Enclave, a spacious, well-equipped (if touristy) hideaway in the vacationers' corridor of Orlando, so they could change and unpack. Then Lou fired up the Rolls again and took them to his house, where Bass met the young men who would become his bandmates. Lance, Joey, and Chris got acquainted over a casual game of hockey in Lou's driveway. Kirkpatrick was the most outgoing, and he tried to make Bass feel welcome. Joey was a foul-mouthed New Yorker, a drama-class cutup. He and Bass bonded quickly. Justin, fourteen, laid back and played it aloof. Chasez, whom Bass met inside Lou's house that fall day in '95, also seemed to be in his own world, but he seemed wise at the same time, experienced in life. Though he wasn't the oldest in the group (Kirkpatrick was), he would be the mature one. Later that day in a private room of Lou's house, Bass ran through some vocals for Lou and Robin Wiley, a former vocal coach for *The Mickey Mouse Club*—some scales and a few bars of "Old Man River," a rich bass singer's tune Bass had prepped. Pearlman and Wiley were impressed. Then they brought in the other boys, Wiley showed Bass her arrangement for "The Star-Spangled Banner," and the boys sang in harmony for the first time. When they were done, there was a long, silent pause. Robin smiled and said, "I think we found our bass." Bass was in and the group was solidified on October 1, 1995. Harless was the one who remarked how the boys' vocals seemed perfectly "in sync." The name stuck.

With Backstreet Boys out there as proof that the formula worked, *NSYNC's formation and training were streamlined. They performed together for the first time for about a hundred people at Disney's Pleasure Island on October 22, 1995, just a few weeks after the boys met over a game of driveway hockey. The crowd was just large enough to fill in the front rows for a videotaped promo performance. They were briefly shopped around to labels in the U.S. but were deemed too similar to Backstreet Boys, so the boys followed in the footsteps of their successful predecessors and jetted to Europe, where they recorded and simultaneously promoted their first release. Germany—and Europe and Asia for that matter— couldn't get enough boy band pop, and the group signed to overseas label BMG Ariola Munich. Its first single, "I Want

You Back," was a Top 10 hit in Germany, and subsequent singles, including "Tearin' Up My Heart" were bona fide hits in Europe. The band toured overseas for the better part of two years, during which time RCA's international A&R director Vince Degiorgio saw *NSYNC in Budapest crooning and gyrating for eleven thousand squealing young female fans. He signed them to the U.S. label. The band released "I Want You Back" as a single in the States in 1998. It debuted at number 13 on the *Billboard* Hot 100 chart. *NSYNC's self-titled album dropped in May but debuted at a sluggish number 58. Their break in the States came, fittingly, when Backstreet Boys bailed on a July 1998 televised Disney concert. *NSYNC filled in. "Even after we filmed it, we just thought it was a little concert," Kirkpatrick told *Entertainment Weekly.* But it kicked off a record-breaking streak of sales. By October, the band's first album peaked at number 2 on the charts. MTV featured them on a new show called *Total Request Live* (*TRL* for short) and put their video for "Tearin' Up My Heart" on heavy rotation. They landed an opening slot on Janet Jackson's Velvet Rope tour. And they went on to sell fifty-six million records worldwide.

Bass, a perpetually pie-eyed, sweet-faced aw-shucks kid known as "the manners" in the group, credited its success to its mogul manager, who'd plucked him from the simple life in Clinton and plopped him down in a dream world. He wrote in his 2007 memoir, *Out of Sync:*

*I always liked Lou a lot, right from the first time I met him. He was this large man who seemed so happy all the time. He had a way of making you feel special. He loved to lay out the red carpet every time he saw us, and I thought he must have been the wealthiest man who ever lived to be able to do the kinds of things he did and give us the support he insisted we needed. He had all these limos and Rolls-Royces and was always using them to take us to great dinners in upscale restaurants. I trusted him and felt we were in the right hands. I felt I had a genuine friendship with "Papa Lou," as he insisted we all call him, and that it was going to last forever . . . That blind trust would later come back to haunt us all.*

## CHAPTER 7

# *I WANT IT THAT WAY*

*I*n 1996, while driving down the interstate, a pain stabbed Lou in the gut. It stung so sharply that he had to pull over for fear of passing out. An ambulance picked him up at his car on the side of the road and doctors told him he had a cyst on his liver, which had ruptured. Doctors allowed him to go home, but he was assigned an at-home care nurse until he decided on a permanent solution. Tammie Hilton, a registered nurse, had never heard of Lou Pearlman when she took him on as a patient. Her sister had to tell her he was famous and that he'd started a band Tammie had never heard of and only recognized when she was played a Backstreet track, which she'd heard on the radio. She met Lou in person at his bedside in his Ridge Pine Trail house. The doctors buzzing around him were talking about a transplant. A few bigwig friends were even offering to get him a black market organ, should he need it. Wullenkemper, still close friends with Lou at the time, had quickly caught wind of Lou's illness, showed up and stormed into the house, and tried to take over the scene; he wanted to drag Lou, kicking and screaming if necessary, into an operating room. Instead, he ran smack dab into Tammie, who told him that Lou would *not* be having any surgery, thank you very much, and plainly declared that Pearlman was to have no visitors without her approval. He asked if she knew who he was. She said she didn't care. He was impressed. Lou's mom had died on Mother's Day 1988 following a failed operation, and Lou was terrified of suffering the same fate. He wept freely in Tammie's presence at the prospect of a transplant, and she became his lone ally in a fight against doctors who insisted that they needed to cut him open. In the end, it was Benscher who found a doctor who agreed to do a procedure that could stop the internal bleeding without removing Lou's kidney but might kill him in the process. Without some kind of invasive maneuver, Lou would likely die anyway, so he agreed to it— as long as Tammie was at his side. For weeks following the successful operation, the experienced nurse eased Lou back to health. Along the way Tammie Hilton became his Florida Florence Nightingale.

From that point on, she was a regular fixture by his side. She was often seen with him sporting faded jeans and a T-shirt, and she commonly wore her light brown, wavy hair pulled back in a ponytail with her bangs dangling over her twinkly eyes. She had a cherubic face, though she was far from fat—she was a catch for Lou. When she did smile and laugh it felt hard earned. Mostly she had a tough, intense don't-screw-with-me stare that was equal parts engaging and intimidating, a kind of look that said to those who considered crossing her (and there were plenty of those jealous types throughout her time with Lou), "Damn right you better keep walking." In the beginning, Lou would call her from far-flung stops on his entrepreneurial tour for reassurance about his healing process. Months after his surgery, she told him point-blank that he was just fine on his own, that he didn't need her any longer as his nurse. But Lou kept calling. And for what turned out to be their first date, Lou asked her if she'd take a ride with him. They got in his Rolls, ended up at the Orlando airport, and flew to Ft. Lauderdale on Lou's jet for a friend's wedding. He told Tammie along the way that he had *three hundred* planes (though she never actually *saw* any one but the Gulfstream). He was showing off. She sat next to him at his opulent birthday bashes and star-studded events, many of which she attended reluctantly, knowing she'd barely see Lou as he was pulled every which way but loose by his eager-to-impress cadre of lackeys and wannabe young male pop stars. She did enjoy her share of fancy feasts and jet and limo rides, but she never quit her job or let Lou support her. For the decade the two were together, she usually worked seven days a week and logged twelve or more hours a day caring for a never-ending rotation of patients, her boss said. Her goal was to retire by age fifty, and she rapidly paid down a loan on a $400,000-plus house by working extra hours and pulling in a healthy six-figure salary. She wasn't bowled over Lou's bigger-than-life persona, his cars, his house, or the fact that his boat was parked next to Sir Elton John's at the Atlantis resort in the Bahamas, but it did mean something to her that the life she had essentially saved was that of a man upon whom so many others depended. She was sure she was one of the rarified people who knew "the real Lou," as she often put it, the guy who was just so naïve and sweet to everyone that she had to help him at times show some backbone. She relished that role, in fact. In many ways, she was perfectly cast as the girlfriend character. She'd survived a divorce and raised her son, Michael, by herself and she wasn't quite ready to go headlong into another committed relationship when she met Lou, she said, but that worked just fine for him. Without ever discussing it with her, Lou had started introducing her as his girlfriend, and she let it go because she genuinely cared for him, even if it wasn't in a romantic way. He was on the road a bunch and needed a companion who didn't demand too much in the physical intimacy department. Put in the simplest of terms, she, a nurse both in profession and personality, needed someone to take care of. It helped Lou to have a woman on his arm, especially amid the buzz of rumors about his fondness for attractive young boys.

Though he consistently denied any inappropriateness with his artists, outsiders just assumed something sexual was going on between a man in his late forties who constantly surrounded himself with attractive, nubile, often shirtless and well-toned males. No one above or below the age of consent ever said he had sex—consensual or otherwise—with Lou. Still, someone always knew someone who knew someone who'd heard about Lou doing something inappropriate with one of his boys. The rumors were impossible to ignore and dogged Pearlman from the moment he introduced the world to his flaxen-locked, fresh-faced young artists and then started showing up around Orlando in limos driven by similarly styled young men. The intensity of the whispers about Lou and his boys grew right along with his fame and perceived fortune. If Lou was hiding something, though, he juggled that secret right along with all of his other nefarious acts.

Then in 1997, at the height of Lou's spending spree and budding boy band fame, *something* happened with Nick Carter that changed the way the young artist and his family felt about Lou. Nick suddenly wasn't so interested in hanging out at Lou's house. And his mom Jane went from playing den mother and cooking all the boys breakfast in Lou's rented communal house—and later visiting his own home—to reportedly calling him a "sexual predator" and saying Lou revealed a side that changed her attitude about his relationship with her boys. "Certain things happened, and it almost destroyed our family," Carter told *Vanity Fair* in 2007. "I tried to warn everyone. I tried to warn all the mothers." After the article came out, Lou said, "Jane Carter has been in and out of settlement agreements with my company. I'm sure her boys, like I, have no idea what she is talking about." Neither Jane, Nick, nor Aaron Carter wanted to talk further about Lou Pearlman.

"Lou was a big cuddler more than anything—cuddling with the guys in the limo or at the house watching a movie," said Jonathan Lewandowski, who was barely eighteen when he started working with Backstreet Boys and Lou, and knew several of Pearlman's artists and close associates. "Lou never said, 'Hey, I want to have sex with you,' it was more like 'Here's what you need to do . . . now, let's drink a little wine. I know you're underage, but who cares?' . . . I know it to be true from them directly, the boys, about being with him and such—they may have done some things that they regretted that they knew would advance their career. They would parade around with virtually nothing on. . . . I've seen him throw little parties or get-togethers for these people. I've seen him walking around without his clothes on." The former publicist, an attractive, baby-faced bottle blond who himself is openly gay, said that in 2006 (he was twenty-one), well past the Backstreet era, he met up with Pearlman and a group of others to discuss another project. He got the distinct impression Lou was hitting on him. They were seated next to one another at a party for the premiere of the Uma Thurman film *My Super Ex-Girlfriend*, and Lou put his hand on Lewandowski's leg. "We were on the couch. He started to rub my leg and he'd just smile, then he'd take his hand off and do business, and then put it back on."

Phoenix Stone (born Sam Licata), the original Backstreet Boys member who went on to work with Lou for years before starting his own record label in Los Angeles, said he saw several indications in the mid- to late 1990s that led him to believe Lou was attracted to the young artists and assistants with whom he surrounded himself. "I think it's pretty clear people know he acted inappropriately," Stone said. Simply put, Lou was using his position of power to act out his romantic or sexual desires. If his underlings were young women, Stone said, he'd have been slapped with a sexual harassment suit years ago. "I never saw anything inappropriate with underage boys, but I did see things with guys who were of age— wrestling around, back rubbing . . . There were a few incidents with a couple of the artists, some of the drivers." Stone says he never witnessed Lou engage in any overt sex act with a young man, but added, "There was definitely inappropriate behavior, things that someone in his position of power shouldn't have let happen. I've had this conversation with Lou many times. I'd say that there are plenty of people to have sex with in the world, you don't have to cuddle up with or have sex with or hit on anyone we were working with. He'd always laugh and shrug and say, 'I've got it under control.' "

Despite Lou's denials, rumors swirled about his particular proclivities. "Lou liked to watch," as one insider put it.

Other boys talked about Lou giving them "creepy" massages or rubbing their abs in a purported effort to align their "aura." The aura business rang true with Rich Cronin of LFO, who told *Vanity Fair,* "He was so touchy-feely, always grabbing your shoulders, touching you, rubbing your abs. It was so obvious and disgusting . . . He definitely came at people." And in the same story twenty-year-old Steve Mooney—an aspiring singer with a head full of blond flowing locks and Abercrombie & Fitch model looks who was trying to get into O-Town, the group featured on Lou's MTV show, *Making the Band*—claimed that one night as O-Town was wrapping auditions, Lou called him over at two A.M. under the auspices of either discussing his future in O-Town or "taking out the garbage." Mooney asked what he had to do to get in the band, and Pearlman, clad in a terry cloth robe and white underwear, leaned back in his chair, spread his legs and said, "You're a smart boy. Figure it out." Lou insisted that Mooney was a rejected artist in his company who had a bone to pick. Regarding the robe and underwear incident at two A.M. in 2000, Pearlman said, "This situation never happened. It's a shame he is resorting to slander and can't get on with his life. He never brought any legal action or discussed this with me at any time. No matter what he says, he still can't sing. Mooney was fired." Tammie Hilton said she was there that night and that an argument between Mooney and Pearlman took place. Lou had been displeased with Mooney as an assistant and called him to come take out the garbage in the wee hours of the morning only because he had failed to do so repeatedly as part of his regular daytime duties.

Tim Christofore was thirteen when he joined late-era Pearlman band Take 5. He and his bandmates often slept over at Pearlman's place. "He would let us watch porn and stuff," Christofore said (Pearlman denies ever letting any of his boys watch adult films). "We also saw a room that had video monitors for all the different rooms—one in the room that he had his tanning room." Christofore also said he and another former member of Take 5 had dozed off during one sleepover and awoke to Lou standing at the foot of the bed, wearing only a towel. He dove on the mattress and began to wrestle with them. The towel, Christofore said, came off. Christofore said he thought it was "gross." Pearlman denied the whole incident. "T. J. is making up this story. He sued me in child labor court and lost. If what he says were true, you would think he would have brought it up to help his case. The fact that he never mentioned this in court should tell you where he's coming from. He's just trying to join the lynch party. Besides, I've never owned a towel that could wrap all the way around me anyway."

Julian Benscher, who spent many a long day with Lou and even shared a hotel room with him while they pitched Airship International stock to would-be investors on road trips, said there was absolutely no truth to the allegations of inappropriateness: "It just never happened." If it had, he said, Backstreet Boys and *NSYNC would have used it as a way out of their contracts, which they were desperate to escape as soon as they hit the big time. In fact, Benscher added, he walked in on Lou having sex once in the early '90s—with a woman.

Rape or sexual harassment victims frequently go years before speaking out or just never come forward at all. But in an era when Idaho senator Larry Craig was said to have engaged in anonymous consensual adult bathroom sex, Florida representative Mark Foley was publicly exposed and resigned over allegations of inappropriate behavior with congressional pages, and outing pop culture figures was a daily pastime for entertainment media (a sport that ensnared former *NSYNC member Lance Bass), not even a single alleged victim spoke out or filed suit as a John Doe against Lou for any kind of sexual misconduct.

"There is no merit to any of their discussions regarding inappropriate behavior," Lou said. "It's all BOGUS! We are all good friends and had a normal friendship with no inappropriate activity . . . I don't think there is anything wrong to have [one's] own sexual preference, but no, I've never dated nor have I been interested in men sexually."

Men.

Besides, Lou added, "I've been in a great relationship with my girlfriend Tammie Hilton for nearly a decade."

Talking about his sex life, her place in it, and the rumors surrounding it, Tammie was sure to point out that Lou was a deeply religious man. "He doesn't even believe in premarital sex," she said. And they never had it. Not in ten years. "People draw their conclusions because it's not what the norm is," she said. "But it's amazing."

## CHAPTER 8

# BYE, BYE, BYE

*L*ou didn't wait for the boys to actually earn him a giant wad before he blew it.

In 1998, as *NSYNC and Backstreet dominated U.S. pop sales, he relocated to, and centralized all of his entertainment endeavors in, the Trans Continental Media complex on the outskirts of Orlando, a $6 million recording and multimedia playground he dubbed "O-Town," a nickname for Orlando. His boys practically lived there—whether using the on-site gym equipment, drilling dance moves on stages fully rigged with sound and lights, or recording in lavish studios (where Kenny Rogers and Deep Purple would later lay tracks). The place buzzed with visiting media, and the boys were trained by PR professionals on how to handle them. Part of the successful image Lou was paying for involved schooling his artists on what to say and how to look when cameras and tape recorders were rolling. Lou had a vision of turning his two smashing successes into a pop music factory. He hired vocal coaches, choreographers, musicians, and technicians for the computer and musical equipment. Tutors helped his young artists finish high school. All of the peripheral things no one, including Lou, could have imagined at the outset were taken care of with a stroke of the pen and a bottomless bank account. "The time I was with Lou he backed up everything he said he'd do," Wright said. But along the way, no one slowed down the Trans Con tour long enough to ask exactly where Pearlman was getting his cash. "There used to be a running joke, because Lou used to go to Atlantis [casino] all the time," Wright said. "We'd say, 'Where's Lou? Oh, Lou's going to make payroll this week.'"

In reality, Lou had done his best to run Airship International into the ground—literally, by crashing four blimps, and figuratively, by breaking promises and defaulting on payments due to Julian Benscher, who had once eagerly partnered with Lou in the airship industry and what he believed to be a thriving airline business. After spending a million dollars on the formation of Backstreet Boys and watching Lou lose interest in the lighter-than-air and airline businesses, the ones Benscher considered to be the core of Lou's operations, Julian had begun in 1996 to untangle himself financially from Pearlman. He owned the major assets of Airship International, which had disappeared as a public company. It was renamed and retooled as a different public company before completely fizzling. Lou had been the best man at Benscher's wedding, but then their friendship, much to Julian's surprise, fizzled, too. "I thought he was a really close friend," he said. "He obviously truly didn't value my friendship. After I got married, Lou basically ignored me. I think I was a threat to his story." It didn't help that Wullenkemper, Lou's German mentor and father figure, had actually followed Benscher's blimp empire building closely, even remarking on a visit to Benscher's home—with Pearlman in the room—that he should have gone into business with Julian instead of Lou.

In 1996, the various debts and late payments to Benscher culminated in a sweeping settlement. Benscher agreed to turn over his shares in Trans Con (about 7 percent) for a $2 million lump sum, to be paid in defined installments over the course of several years. Pearlman promptly lagged in those payments, too. Benscher was used to it. He had written into his settlement agreement that until the debt was completely paid, he kept hold of his Trans Con stock and was therefore entitled to any dividends the company issued. But in 1998, he got ahold of internal Trans Con documents that indicated the company was paying a dividend to stockholders that he never received. Questioned as to why Benscher was cut out from the money as the third-largest shareholder, Pearlman said it was

Wullenkemper who had tied up Benscher's money, and he wouldn't release the cash. Lou couldn't have expected Julian to call his bluff. But Benscher was close to Wullenkemper by this point, so he got on a plane to Germany and asked him face-to-face why he wouldn't release the money to Lou so he could settle up on dividends owed for his share in Trans Continental Airlines. "Vat iz zis Trans Continental Airlines?" Benscher said, recalling Wullenkemper's response in a fake German accent. It was supposed to be the company of which Wullenkemper owned 82 percent. The one in which he'd backed Lou, his "son." The one that enticed Julian into deals with Lou and his public company, Airship International. The one that owned Backstreet Boys, *NSYNC, and forty-some-odd jets (depending upon who was asking), and had hundreds of millions in assets there in Germany. Benscher held certificates for a little more than sixty-five thousand shares, and Pearlman and his right-hand man, Bob Fischetti, had certified that only about nine hundred thousand of the potential two million shares in the company had been issued. Lou had given Benscher documents declaring the two of them, plus Wullenkemper, as the three sole owners of Trans Continental Airlines. Lou had even given Julian a letter from Wullenkemper himself on letterhead from the German's Bahamian holdings company thanking Benscher for connecting Trans Con with other airline companies looking to off-load jets. Wullenkemper scoffed at the letter and said it wasn't even his real signature that adorned it. Face-to-face with Benscher in Germany in 1998, the German told him he never had a stake in Trans Continental anything. "He said, 'Julian, *I* own jets, but I don't know anything about Trans Continental Airlines,' " Benscher said. "I just went ice cold." Eighty-two percent of Trans Continental Airlines was a Lou Pearlman fantasy.

Like no one before him, Benscher pulled back the curtain on the corporation that was supposedly backing Backstreet and *NSYNC, exposing the sham that was Trans Continental *everything*. But at the time, even after confronting Theodor Wullenkemper, Benscher didn't shake the pillars of Lou's empire. He had a hard time believing that Wullenkemper was completely uninvolved. He had stacks of documents indicating otherwise. "Just because Wullenkemper claimed not to own Trans Con didn't mean Trans Con was a con," Benscher said. Wullenkemper could have been concealing his involvement to avoid exposure, though Benscher doubted that scenario—"It's just not him," Benscher said, and he remained friendly with Wullenkemper for years. "It's not in his personality." It could have also meant Lou had actually controlled all of the real assets, dozens of planes and hundreds of millions of dollars, and he was using Wullenkemper as a straw man to foil Benscher's attempts to collect debts. Lou had, after all, taken Julian on three different planes that he claimed were his. He even brought him to a hangar in Los Angeles in the late 1990s where he showed him "a real big Trans Continental plane" adorned with the yellow TCA logo. Lou chatted up the guys in the hangar like they were old buddies, asking them how they'd been. "I found out a few years later it was a plane from a different Trans Continental," Benscher said, "an old cargo company that went under." All he knew after leaving Wullenkemper in Germany, however, was that Trans Con was not what it seemed, and the best course of action for Benscher was to get his money out as fast as he could. He continued to apply pressure to Lou and his lackeys to pay him his dividend and keep up with the installments on his stock, which Lou rarely did.

In 1998, Pearlman had bigger problems than Benscher. Backstreet Boys, his golden geese, had grown wiser about their own worth and watched their Big Papa get rich as they labored constantly on tour and in the recording studio. They sued Pearlman, accusing him of pocketing $10 million while they took home a mere $300,000 (split five ways). Pearlman called it a "family disagreement." Though little about the suit was made public, members of Backstreet Boys said in a court complaint that they were treated like "indentured servants," touring and practicing constantly while living on tiny per diems and being told all of the lavish meals, limo rides, hotel rooms, and parties were actually coming out of their own record sales and royalties. On top of that, while touring constantly for the better part of two years, they were never told who was behind *NSYNC, only that the other boy band was their biggest competition and constantly chipping away at their spotlight. When they found out it was Big Papa Lou himself, Kevin Richardson told the *Calgary Herald* in 1999, "That hurt our feelings, because for a while it was like, 'We're a family.' Then all of a sudden, 'It's business, guys, sorry.'"

The shock and reality of the bottom line was Lou's fault, Benscher said. "He just filled the boys' heads with the jets and going to lunch with eighteen people, this BS type of surreal existence that these kids didn't know any better from and thought was real," Benscher said. "We're rich because Lou says we are." But at the same time, they were as hungry for fame as any teenagers would be when teased with the brass ring hanging just out of reach. "When Backstreet Boys signed their early contracts, they'd have signed anything," Benscher said. "I was there."

While the legal drama played out behind closed doors, the Boys won the PR battle in their war against Lou, managing along the way to cast him as a manipulator who tried to make himself, contractually speaking, the sixth Backstreet Boy (and, in fact, he did). The case was settled out of court and the terms have never been disclosed, but Pearlman likely walked away with more than most people thought. After the settlement, the Trans Con dividends and loan payments started flowing a lot more consistently to Benscher. Plus, although it wasn't in his interest as a debtor to Julian, Lou told him the court case worked out in his favor. "He actually had a big smile on his face and said, '*That* turned out well.'"

Backstreet Boys signed with new management, the Firm,

which bought out most of Lou's remaining stake in the band. In 1999, their original self-titled album went diamond, having sold ten million copies. In May, the group released *Millennium* on Jive Records. It debuted at number 1 on the *Billboard* Top 200 chart and stayed there for ten consecutive weeks. Driven by the single "I Want It That Way," the album sold 1,134,000 copies in its first week alone, shattering the record previously held by Garth Brooks (and only broken later by Britney Spears, then *NSYNC). The group went on to sell almost ten million copies of *Millennium* in 1999 and was nominated for five Grammy awards—all without the sixth Backstreet Boy, Lou.

He still had *NSYNC, though, and by 1998, the group had sold three million copies of its first album and a million copies of a Christmas album. Recording and management revenues in 1998 alone, according to Trans Continental Records' internal accounting, were about $4 million. That's to say nothing of the tens of millions of dollars' worth of merchandise they were moving—their faces were on every item of clothing and toy imaginable, and much of those profits went straight into Lou's pockets (and presumably right back out to pay for his robustly expanding collection of businesses and investors).

The band members, meanwhile, were living on a cash per diem of $35 a day.

In November 1998, Jan Bolz, president of BMG Areola Munich and owner of the boys' label, came to visit them in

Las Vegas at the Billboard Awards show, a story Bass tells in his bio. The band members' mothers had been talking when he arrived, and Bass's mother asked "in a good-natured way" when Lance was going to get paid. Double-talk ensued. Bolz explained that all of the limos and dinners and plane tickets and hotel rooms were paid for by the boys' profits—recoupment, that's called—and, despite their paltry per diems and grueling singing and dancing schedules, the boys had been spending most of their earnings living the rock star life with all of the trimmings. But Bolz was too smart to show up empty-handed. He'd planned a surprise, he told the boys and the moms. He'd come to Vegas expressly to present the boys with their first checks. It was a private ceremony, with Lou and Bolz both making doting speeches about the massive movement the boys had created in the pop music world. And that part was true. *NSYNC and Backstreet Boys before them effectively signaled the end of the flannel-clad, angst-addled grunge era. Its pioneer Kurt Cobain died of an apparently self-inflicted gunshot wound in 1994, having seen the artistic statement he set out to make transformed into T-shirt slogans and branded everything—hallmarks of the *NSYNC business plan. Just a few years after Pearl Jam went to testify in front of Congress about Ticketmaster's price gouging, *NSYNC had embarked on its record-setting tour, which, combined with album sales, amounted to revenue of more than $500 million. For all of these reasons and more, when Bolz finally handed out checks to the boys, Bass was expecting two or three hundred thousand dollars. He flipped his over and examined—then reexamined—the number, which seemed to be short a zero. He was holding a note for $25,000. "Without saying a word, I tore up the check, threw the pieces up in the air, and left the room," Bass wrote.

Throughout 1999, *NSYNC tried to renegotiate their contract with Pearlman. Along the way, they discovered more about what they had signed, that they, like Backstreet Boys, had hastily agreed to declare Lou the sixth member of the band. He was collecting 50 percent of all recording royalties, 100 percent of all advances, plus another 25 percent of recording income as a management commission. He pocketed 37.5 percent of the band's profits. As Justin Timberlake would put it to Rolling Stone in 2006 (the only time he's talked frankly about his dealings with Pearlman), "I was being monetarily raped by a Svengali." Eventually the negotiations hit a wall—or, actually, a husky music mogul with a death grip on his boy band bucks. With their lawyers combing over contracts, *NSYNC believed they found a loophole, a tiny out in the contract that required Lou to find a legitimate label to put out the album within a year of its recording, which he technically hadn't done. Based on that, *NSYNC's attorneys claimed their contracts were null and void, and the boys signed a new deal with Calder's Zomba/Jive record label. Pearlman sued the band for $150 million on September 11, 1999, claiming breach of contract. "It is not Trans Continental's intent to cut the throats of those boys," said J. Cheney Mason, the Southern-drawled bulldog attorney Pearlman hired, "but we're going to decapitate the advisers who have been giving them bad advice."

*NSYNC filed a countersuit in November for $25 million, claiming fraud, breach of contract, and breach of fiduciary duty. They wanted out of Pearlman's clutches; the complaint quoted the band as saying Pearlman "picked our pockets" and typically level-headed, worldly-wise Chasez in particular as saying Pearlman is "an unscrupulous, greedy and sophisti-cated businessman who posed as an unselfish, loving father figure and took advantage of our trust." He said the band wanted to continue to record and perform but couldn't do so under Pearlman, and went on, "We are painfully aware our careers may be brief. In truth, our fans made us a success . . . An injunction [blocking their record release] may be the end of *NSYNC. However, we cannot work with people who have lied to us." After months of legal wrangling, the suit came to a head in a public hearing in Orlando. Pearlman's attorneys vigorously argued that Lou was, in effect, *NSYNC, that the other members could be replaced. Then the judge dressed them down. "So you're telling me that Mr. Pearlman is *NSYNC, and these five guys over here my daughter has a poster of on her wall are not *NSYNC?" Lou would never have much luck winning over judges. This one advised Lou and his lawyers to settle fast. The members of *NSYNC exited the courthouse and found hundreds of fans cheering them on. In December 1999, the group settled with Lou. The details have never been disclosed. But they stuck with Johnny Wright, who still awkwardly shared space at O-Town studios with Lou but had initiated a split. Wright had tried to get Lou to renegotiate *NSYNC's contract, a move that would have likely given Lou a smaller piece of the band's revenues over a longer period of time and would have kept him in good graces with the money-minting group. Instead, Lou held his line. "I think that was a concept Lou didn't understand," Wright said. "In the blimp business, if you did a deal, it was done and that was the deal. In the music biz, when the power changes, the deal changes." Shortly afterward, *NSYNC embarked on a world tour and recorded their first album for Zomba/Jive. In a cab in London, Kirkpatrick and Bass finally had a chance to reflect on all they'd been through with Lou. They were free now, Bass said. "Yeah! No strings attached!" The name stuck. *No Strings Attached* was released on March 21, 2000, on Jive; it shattered records once held by the Backstreet Boys, selling 1.2 million copies on the first day of its release and 2.5 million its first week, and was eventually certified diamond, with more than eleven million copies sold.

Outwardly, Lou showed no signs of damage to his entrepreneurial spirit. He backed the pet projects of his hometown homies. With Paul Russo, a former deli worker from Queens who migrated to Orlando to work with Lou, Pearlman opened New York Delicatessen and Pizzeria and a chain of TCBY frozen yogurt shops. He started ShapeCD, a custom compact disc manufacturing company, and installed Alan Siegel at its helm. Then one day in 1999, Pearlman's free-spending reputation found its way to Julian Benscher as he played eighteen holes at Isleworth golf course. One of Benscher's foursome remarked about Pearlman trying to buy a $6 million mansion in the neighborhood. Benscher was flabbergasted. He phoned Lou and asked where the hell he had the money to buy a $6 million house if he couldn't even make the payments on money he already owed. Lou stammered and sputtered and swore the house was his way of getting even more loaned money—he'd already planned to borrow against it—and Benscher came up with a quick solution. He had been looking to offload his mansion and move to the more prestigious Isleworth neighborhood nearby. "I said, 'Buy my house. You'll pay $4.25 million.'" It was a fair enough price, but it worked out better for Benscher than Lou. He closed on the sixteen-thousand-square-foot Italianique mansion in December. Spacious and festooned with cypress trees and Spanish moss, it's situated on the shore of spring-fed Lake Butler. Lou's new place was in the Chaine du Lac section of Windermere, though, a slightly less prestigious, ungated address. Still, it was nothing short of opulent. Plus, Lou was in no position to negotiate. Benscher admitted that he wasn't sure how Lou was even able to pay $4.25 million for his home. "I couldn't understand after the two settlements [Backstreet Boys and *NSYNC] in 1998 where there was any money coming in," he said, but by then, he was an outsider.

It was about that time that Lou came to Johnny Wright and nagged him to get in on Trans Continental's Employee Investment Savings Accounts. Wright resisted initially. He didn't quite understand how the EISA plan worked—and why wouldn't he just put his money in the bank? Lou's interest rates were higher than average but not *that* much higher. Plus, Wright had worked long and hard for his money and managed to put some savings away, even as his partner Lou seemed to spend against some future bank balance that never quite materialized. Wright wanted to put his savings in something tangible—property—even if Lou was promising him 10 percent interest on his principal. Lou persisted, though, and finally Wright relented. "I put a thousand bucks in," he said. "That was my total commitment to it." After *NSYNC's suit, he and Pearlman parted ways. And Wright never saw his thousand bucks again.

In 1999, the business that buoyed Lou's entire empire with its millions of shares and dozens of investors—including Benscher, Joseph Chow, and countless other small-time spenders, retirees, and family and friends in New York and Florida—technically ceased to exist. Pearlman had lied about its assets—there were no planes and no German backer—and in March, the registration for Delaware corporation Trans Continental Airlines expired. Lou never even bothered to renew it. But he kept right on selling its shares and savings plan.

In the same month the corporation officially expired, Lloyd's of London caught wind of Pearlman's claim that it had insured his EISA plan, so to be clear, the company famous for insuring everything from Bruce Springsteen's voice to Betty Grable's legs sent a letter clearly stating that it never insured Trans Con anything. In a March 30 response, Pearlman placated the insurer. "Our company has no policies issued by you with regard to [the EISA program]," he wrote to Lloyd's. A week later, one of Lou's associates sat down behind a computer and conjured from thin air a replacement document that Lou held up as proof that EISA was insured by AIG. The document, called "AIG.doc," sat on Trans Con computer servers available for printing up on demand. Lou and his people even included it in information brochures given to prospective investors, more proof that their money was perfectly safe.

Alan Gross *(left)*, and Lou Pearlman as young teens in Mitchell Gardens in Flushing, Queens. (© ALAN GROSS)

Pearlman's Mitchell Gardens apartment building.
(TYLER GRAY)

Pearlman with his father Hy and mother Reenie at Lou's bar mitzvah in June 1967. (© ALAN GROSS)

The wreck of Pearlma first airship, the Airshi Enterprises blimp for Jordache, on October 1980, in Lakehurst, Ne Jersey. (© ALAN GROSS)

Alan Gross *(right, with an arm around Lou)*, and the Trans Continental Enterprises crew in front of Lou's jet and limousine.
(© ALAN GROSS)

Pearlman with his mother, Reenie *(righ* Theodor Wullenkem *(left)*, and a female companion.
(© ALAN GROSS)

Pearlman and his mother, Reenie in the early 1980s. (© ALAN GROSS)

The remains of Pearlman's second blimp for MetLife, which crashed in Weeksville, North Carolina, in 1992.

Pearlman with *(top, left to right)* *NSYNC's Joey Fatone, Chris Kirkpatrick, JC Chasez, Lance Bass, and Justin Timberlake in 1996 at Pearlman's NYPD Pizza in Miami.
(© MARK WEISS/WIREIMAGE)

Living large on the lam, Pearlman munches on a continental breakfast at the Westin Resort Nusa Dua, Bali, in June 2007, moments before being apprehended by Indonesian authorities.

(above) Leftover FedEx envelopes, teen magazines, headshots, investment plan paperwork, jelly, and other detritus lying around Pearlman's Trans Continental offices in Orlando, Florida, following raids by federal officials and auctions by the bankruptcy trustee.
(© WHEAT WURTZBURGER)

(left) Pearlman's booking photo shortly after his flight to Guam from Bali, Indonesia, in June 2007.

NAME LOUIS JAY
PEARLMAN

A Cadillac Escalade-themed golf cart put up for auction as part of Pearlman's bankruptcy auction on August 25, 2007.

Pearlman's $4.25 million, 16,000-square-foot mansion in the Chaine du Lac section of Windermere, Florida. At press time, bankruptcy officials were unable to sell the property.

In a brochure sent to potential Trans Continental Airlines investors in the mid- to late-'80s, Pearlman included photographs of jets he claimed to own, and aircraft he said were flying for Trans Continental Airlines. In fact, several shots, including this one, were taken of tiny models against the backdrop of airports. Just out of the frame are the fingers of the person holding them up. Lou's childhood friend Alan Gross still has this very model.

This is supposedly what the inside of a Trans Continental Airlines jet looked like—part of Pearlman's marketing materials sent to potential investors in Trans Continental Airlines. But Pearlman never owned a jumbo jet this extravagant.

Lou Pearlman poses with U.S. Congressman Ric Keller *(far left)* (R-FL), Dick Cheney *(far right)*, and an unidentified man. Pearlman donated $16,100 to Republicans between 1997 and 2003.

★ *CHAPTER 9*

# *SYNCING FEELING*

*L*ou never sat down and planned a twenty-year scheme and then just set about bilking. He didn't sweet-talk his investors and then ask for their credit card numbers in the next breath. He listened. He internalized people's dreams. He made them his own. Then he sold them back a share at a time. "He could paint a beautiful picture," Johnny Wright said. "He picks you up in his limo and takes you to his restaurant and takes you to his studio and so-and-so is recording, and on his wall are records from tens of millions of sales. So I can see how people get wrapped up in it and want to invest in it . . . He could sell ice to an Eskimo." At the end of the millennium, however, Pearlman was a boy band mogul without a hit boy band. So he went to work rebuilding his image as the King Midas of the music world. "He had to save face," Wright said. "He had two of the biggest groups in the world that were trying to separate themselves from him. At all costs, I think he was trying to prove to the world that it wasn't about *them*, it was about *him*."

He continued developing his lavish O-Town studios as a Warhol-meets-Disney pop factory, where he spent more than ever grooming a few dozen or more members of new groups to become what he hoped would be his next chart toppers. C Note, a Latin-tinged quintet, had a single, "Wait Till I Get Home," on the *Billboard* charts, but it peaked at number 33. He started Innosense, his first and only girl group, which briefly included a young Britney Spears. The group tanked and Spears migrated over to Johnny Wright's side of the O-Town recording complex as a solo artist. Lou finally scored a minor success with Lyte Funky Ones (LFO, for short), the group formed by Brian "Brizz" Gillis, Rich Cronin, and Brad Fischetti. Trans Con VP Bob Fischetti had first introduced Lou to his brother when Brad was eleven or twelve. Brad had grown up to be a Kevin Richardson–esque, angular-featured, dark-haired, soulfully handsome singer in a pirate-style do-rag. In 1996 and 1997, Lou exported the three boys to Germany and Europe to tour—the tried and true Trans Con formula that propelled BSBs and *NSYNC to superstardom. By 1998, though, LFO still didn't have a hit. Millions were being spent—not quite Backstreet Boys money, but the band was a significant drag on Lou's cash flow. Brizz left to pursue solo interests in 1999. Devin Lima, previously a tool-jerk at a hardware store with a slicked-back, muscle-shirt-ready Italian stallion appeal, landed an audition and stepped into the empty slot. A DJ at the massively popular Z100 pop music station in New York started spinning an older LFO song, "Summer Girls," which got the attention of label types and for a brief stretch inspired Lou to work his magic with LFO. Fischetti remembered it as the time of his life. "Lou is the guy who gave me a chance in the music industry," said the thirty-two-year-old, who went on to run a small record label in Orlando, "and he was a fun guy to hang around." He recalled waiting in the lobby of the Millennium Broadway Hotel in Times Square while Lou negotiated a deal with Clive Davis of Arista Records upstairs. "Lou comes strolling up with a smile on his face," Fischetti said, "and you're just sobbing because you're so excited." Davis, it turned out, heard a hit in "Summer Girls" (reviled since as that sticky-as-bubblegum "Abercrombie & Fitch song" heard by anyone who set foot in a shopping mall at the turn of the millennium). The boys had originally recorded it in 1998 and had, frankly, grown a bit tired of it, but, as Fischetti said, "If Clive Davis tells you to sing 'Happy Birthday,' you sing 'Happy Birthday.'" "Summer Girls" cracked the top 10, selling 2.5 million copies worldwide and 1.5 million in the U.S. Pearlman hadn't found the next Backstreet Boys or

*NSYNC, but LFO had enough juice to keep his hit-making machine humming. In Orlando, Fischetti said, "You couldn't talk to somebody over thirty who wouldn't mention some connection to Trans Con. Everybody wanted to be somebody, and Lou was the way they could do that." That rejuvenated reputation as a dream catcher, Fischetti said, was what pumped up Pearlman the most: "The guy just wants to be liked."

In 1999, Lou took his act to screens big and small, telling friends, "We're going to do in the film industry what we did in the music biz." *Longshot,* his 2000 feature comedy about business corruption and blackmail, was little more than' a PR video for Trans Con people and just about every cousin, friend, or acquaintance that ever wanted to see what it was like to show up on the big screen (however briefly). There were three Garfunkel cousins with appearances and dozens of Trans Con artists, successful and otherwise (everyone from Justin Timberlake and Britney Spears—she plays a flight attendant—to Phoenix Stone and TV band O-Town's Ashley Parker Angel). Kenny Rogers and Dustin Diamond, Screech from TV's *Saved by the Bell,* have cameos. Even Trans Con VP Alan Siegel's wife, Kim, had a part (Teacher #2). Tony DeCamillis cowrote, produced, and starred in the movie. And under Lou's direction, he blew even more Trans Con money on the film than his former firm, Chatfield Dean & Co., once raked in for Airship International—about $20 million. It earned less than $2 million.

The ABC/MTV television series *Making the Band* fared far better. It, too, was mostly a love letter from Lou to himself and his entertainment operation, but the show was a bona fide hit, advancing the *Star Search* and European *Top of the Pops* concepts and priming U.S. audiences for *American Idol*. The show revolved around a nationwide talent search to form a boy band that Lou dubbed O-Town. In 1999, twenty-five young men were picked, then Lou helped whittle them down to eight, who appeared on the show in 2000 to compete for the final five slots. Pearlman popped up from time to time as the Trans Continental Records owner who would sign the winners to a lucrative contract. The national exposure propelled O-Town's first single, "Liquid Dreams," to the number 1 singles sales slot even before it was widely played on the radio—it sold two million copies. The song peaked at number 10 on the *Billboard* Hot 100 chart. The band's spring 2001 follow-up single fared even better, climbing to number 3 on the Hot 100 chart and earning the group second and third seasons on television—though the show was moved from ABC to MTV. Season two followed the development of the band's second album, *O2*, for Clive Davis's new label J Records. But in reality, *O2*, originally scheduled for a summer release, was delayed repeatedly and came out closer to '03. The last season of *Making the Band* chronicled the struggle of the boys to write their own music and prove themselves as legitimate artists. The idea never took, and in 2002 *Making the Band 2* replaced Pearlman with hip-hop vocalist/producer Sean "Diddy" Combs, who swapped out the boy band concept for a hip-hop group; Johnny Wright assisted in the talent search. Combs went on to host the series through 2008. But in 2001, Lou's TV turn and final surge of pop success with O-Town had legitimized him as an enduring pop music mogul. As Johnny Wright put it, "He became as big a star as the artists he was representing."

It was at about this time that young men with pop-star dreams started showing up at O-Town studios' doorstep like abandoned baskets of kittens—three, four, and five to a litter. A few got studio time. Many more got jobs. If things didn't pan out for some young guy striving for a part in the next quintet, there was a good chance he'd land a position as an associate at Trans Con or as Lou's personal driver or assistant or gofer. Pearlman liked the company of vital, popular young men. Trans Con headquarters was this other dimension where it was okay for a guy to walk around in public wearing a wife beater, designer versions of low-hanging, ghetto-style denim affixed with a pointless wallet chain, and hair so gelled and frosted it seemed inspired by a Christmas cookie. Inside the Trans Con bubble dwelled fantastic species of shopping-mall-food-court fro-yo stand bad boys and straight-outta–Long Island, slicked back, pencil-bearded crooners—uniformed soldiers in a pop army. *Fight Club* but prettier, safer. And to anyone who was older than fifteen, male, and experienced in sexual intercourse with a woman, it was just hard to take Lou's clique seriously, even if they were at one time bankable. Nevertheless, his lavish studios, with their on-site gym and pool and more, became a destination for moms with daughters who'd wait in the parking lot for whatever frosty-locked, tanned, toned prince poked his head out. Some even asked for *Lou's* autograph. The musky aroma of his heartthrobs was all over him.

None of the legal bills, lack of cash flow, or exorbitant overhead at the time kept Pearlman from living the life of a mogul. He'd bought Benscher's mansion for $4.25 million in 1999 and he purchased a beachfront condo in Clearwater, two penthouses in Las Vegas, an apartment in Manhattan, a condo in Atlantic City, a new limo, a skybox at Raymond James Stadium in Tampa, and more toys than anyone could keep track of. For a remarkable video segment on a rarely watched show called *Livin' Large* produced in the early 2000s, Pearlman gave a boastful tour of his home and showed off some of the possessions paid for by his "multimillion-dollar" business empire. There was a Salvador Dali print hanging in his home, a refurbished Louis XIV bed. He pointed to a picture of one of the planes in what he described as his "Planet Airways fleet." Though as a seasoned salesman, he was particularly careful how he described the plane, saying it was "one of a half a dozen 727s that we operate." Planet did eventually own and operate as many as six 727s by 2000 and had even achieved

FAA certification. Pearlman backed the company financially, but he was not involved in any of the operations. Tony DeCamillis ran it. Later in the TV-show tour of Pearlman's wealth, a private jet came to a stop behind him in a scene shot on an Orlando tarmac; he told the camera it was his and said very carefully, "This is my new jet." There was a quick cut and edit then Lou continues, "A new Gulfstream IV ST probably runs somewhere around thirty-eight million dollars." Of course, his was neither new nor a Gulfstream IV. It was a thirty-year-old Gulfstream II—a fancy toy but hardly worth $38 million. Deeper into his mansion, he cracked open a safe and pulled out a watch collection, whose crown jewel was a $250,000 diamond-studded Rolex with matching ring and cufflinks, worth a total of about $425,000, he said. The cameras then followed him to his own jewelry store in the Florida Mall, Rocks (he owned a stake in it, not the whole thing). There, viewers were shown a $1.3 million pink diamond ring and a $2,000 pen "good for signing big contracts." And finally, back at the house, Lou showed off his fleet of cars: a Mercedes coupe, his cornflower-blue Rolls, his Cadillac Escalade with a video game system and speaker boxes that resembled a crater-dimpled lunar landscape. Viewers saw his $135,000 limo pulling through the front gates of his Chaine du Lac home, and out back on the docks, he showed off $50,000 worth of personal watercraft. "If these Jet Skis could talk," he said, "they would tell you about all of our artists who have been riding them." They might have also revealed that Lou himself couldn't swim, and that when several of the Backstreet Boys jokingly threatened to throw him in his own pool during his fortieth birthday, he wet his pants with fear.

"It's great to be livin' large," Pearlman said.

So confident was Pearlman of his reach in the entertainment world that he bought the Options Talent Group in 2002. It touted itself as the largest model-scouting network in the country, and Lou bragged about it being an ingenious business model, but it was doomed from the get-go. Thousands of people in cities all over the United States had fallen for what was essentially a bait-and-switch scam. Hawkers lured them in with flattering blind approaches on the street, asking questions such as "Have you ever considered modeling?" Those who bit were told to show up for casting calls that were, in essence, massive sales pitches. In the presentations, wannabes were teased with glimpses of glamorous lives in front of cameras, then asked to drop about $1,000 to $2,000 apiece on photo and promotional packages. Options promised to get the packages seen by top talent agents and perpetuated a fantasy of high-dollar work and placement in top fashion magazines. Teams were dispatched on "photo tours," but even with professional-level makeup, lighting, and photography, many of the clients were far from what the average person would consider model material, like the young hopeful on a New York leg of a photo tour who had a lazy eye. On another stop one woman who turned up was an amputee. The model scout salespeople told her she could get specialty work, despite the fact that she was missing an arm. She'd forked over her hard-earned savings for the shoot, and the crew did their thing on her. But she never turned up in *Vogue*.

The state attorney general's office had been investigating Options for a month when Pearlman bought it in September. They and the Orlando Better Business Bureau were flooded by complaints and were actively warning the owners of Options to clean up its act and warning consumers against what appeared to be a scam. Lou's real reasons for getting into the fashion business, especially through a company that was the subject of a criminal investigation, were never quite clear, even to his closest friends and associates. Some said Pearlman, with his rosy-cheeked optimism, overlooked the dirty and devious principals in the company because he believed the concept would net him some quick cash, or that he'd turn around Options' problems with his direct line to the minds and desires of teenage girls. He had satisfied their craving for cute, nonthreatening boys, and now he was going to help them fulfill their own dreams of becoming the models those boys were interested in. He made a superficial effort to revamp the image of the company, taking it through a series of name changes, from Options Talent to eModel, Wilhelmina Scouting Network, Web Style Network, and eventually Trans Continental Talent. But the best theory, held by several former

Trans Con insiders, is that Lou thought Options Talent, a pub-licly traded company when he got ahold of it, would be easy to bore out and pump full of his other Trans Con entertain-ment companies. In other words, it could become his Wall Street vessel, and Lou could live up to those boastful and rosy statements to Trans Con investors about going public. The Lou Pearlman dream-making machine was in overdrive. So he threw his fat assets behind the model scouting business, believing that with a little cleaning up, some organization, and that golden Pearlman touch, it would secure him a spot not only as a mogul who knew from singing, dancing, and cute boys but as a modeling pioneer who knew a fresh female face when he spotted it, too.

What he got instead was an *Ocean's Eleven*–style assembly of hucksters as his new business partners. Options' principals were scam artists, ex-cons and felons. Alec Defrawi (a.k.a. Ayman Ahmed El-Difrawi, a.k.a. Michael Difrawi), the man responsible for starting the scouting business, was convicted in 1995 of wire and bank fraud and served time. More fright-ening, he'd been arrested and charged with child abuse after a girlfriend accused him of scalding her four-year-old's geni-tals in a bathtub. (Difrawi negotiated a plea agreement that involved him staying away from the girlfriend and enrolling in a parenting course.) An Egyptian immigrant, he explained his aliases as ways he sought to get around bias. It was un-clear whether he meant the bias of those who would think twice about working with an Egyptian or of those who would shy away from doing business with someone who had a felony conviction and had been charged with child abuse. Also deeply embedded in the Pearlman-run scouting agency was a dis-barred attorney named Gregory Jans. Jans had previously confessed to looting the trust of two brothers who'd hired him to manage a half million dollars. Instead, he wrote checks from the account to himself, his law firm, and his offshore ac-counts—Jans had a background in international finance that left him with a unique expertise in hiding money in places with tight-lipped, eager banks. Pearlman hired him as a finan-cial adviser, and according to several reports, the disbarred attorney was called upon for legal advice. Another principal in Options and Trans Continental Talent, Ralph Edward Bell, had run a talent scouting agency in Baltimore, Maryland, and Washington, DC, and its methods were practically identical to those of Options and Trans Con Talent, even though Bell had been barred by the Federal Trade Commission from operating another business in the same field. Bell's specialty was riding a company into bankruptcy while figuring out a way to be first in line to get paid back personally when assets were un-earthed.

Cort (sometimes referred to as Cortes) Randell, another key player in Trans Con Talent and its various incarnations, had a different, nefarious specialty that had earned him national attention. He'd started the National Student Marketing Network in 1965 while still in college. It used an army of young salespeople to push a line of essentials—school supplies, coffee mugs, etc.—to students. Buoyed by lucrative contracts with several major suppliers, the company went public, and the stock price soared in 1969 to $144 a share. But the whole thing was deflated by Andrew Tobias, a young protégé of Randall who exposed the scam in his book *The Funny Money Game*. Randell's army of salespeople, it turned out, did little more than hand out brochures. The big contracts that buoyed NSMN's projected sales never came through. Those sales figures were massively inflated and, in some cases, forged. Even as he was accused of scamming stockholders out of $100 million, Randell landed at another company in DC, a consumer mortgage business called the National Commercial Credit Corporation. But by 1976, he and a partner in that corporation were indicted for bleeding the company dry, declaring bankruptcy, then secretly bleeding it some more. Randell was convicted on five counts of securities fraud, seven counts of mail fraud, and five other various fraud charges and sentenced to seven years in prison and five years' probation.

The list of hucksters and their shady dealings at Trans Con filled five-hundred-plus pages of the 2006 book *Under Investigation*, by author and web watchdog Les Henderson. He suggested that the Florida attorney general Charlie Crist, who would later become a high-profile governor of Florida, pushed to have the investigation into Options and Trans Con Talent dropped because of political contributions made by Pearlman (about $10,000 all told). In reality, the investigation into Options Talent was tainted by the use of possibly illegally gotten e-mails from Trans Continental's computers. Henderson references "leaked" documents frequently in his book, and they paint the picture of a deeply fraudulent operation. The state attorney's investigator was fed some of these same e-mails, but they never added up to a case against Options or Pearlman—the investigator, Jacqueline Dowd, was reassigned. If the government ever tried to bring a case to court that was potentially built on intercepted private e-mails, the privacy violations and ensuing scandal would have far outshined the conspiracy theories that swirled when the government dropped its case against Options and Pearlman in July 2004. But even the exoneration and a slew of name changes wasn't enough to save the flawed model-search business. So Lou formed a new company, Fashion Rock, using essentially the same staff and resources as Options and a slightly different business model—he held massive meetings where prospective talent and agents would mingle at convention booths. Fashion Rock gave the old Options a loan just before Pearlman declared it bankrupt, then Options paid back Lou's new company out of its assets, a maneuver that must have made Cort Randell proud. Fashion Rock, meanwhile, briefly succeeded, and Lou even paraded potential investors in Trans Con or EISA through the conventions, showing off his creation.

Johnny Wright, who had split from Lou at this point, recalled trying to fly out of Orlando one morning when the airport was clogged with "thousands of people in the airport leaving with all of these Fashion Rock bags . . . The people at the airport that day were happy! For, it was like, Lou strikes again!"

In actuality, nearly two years of investigations into the company that represented his best hope for an IPO put a major dent in his reputation. "He did say to me that he wishes he would have never gotten into that whole talent business," Pearlman's girlfriend and confidant, Tammie Hilton, said, a rare admission of defeat for Pearlman. More problematic, the investigation also fell smack-dab in the middle of his efforts to buy a massive office complex in the heart of downtown Orlando and almost undid the deal. In 2002, Lou agreed to buy a former crown jewel of hokey tourism called Church Street Station, a four-acre, two-hundred-thousand-square-foot complex decorated with hand-carved wood accoutrements, chandeliers, fountains, a glass elevator, and authentic bi- and tri-wing planes hanging from the ceilings of its main building. Originally an old train depot, Church Street Station was turned into a mustache-and-pantaloon-themed ragtime attraction in the late '70s, drawing 1.7 million yearly visitors at its peak in 1985. Then Disney and Universal opened their own theme park expansions, which included fake downtowns, celebrity-chef-branded restaurants, and squeaky-clean clubs that pulled tourists away from downtown proper and out to the attractions. The once vibrant hub had turned mostly into a ghost town, an eyesore and public humiliation to city leaders who couldn't keep up with the Mouse.

Lou wanted to turn Church Street Station into the headquarters of Trans Continental everything. And to leaders in Orlando, he seemed a likely savior. None of the bad press from the sour Options dealings seemed to stick with them. They agreed to give him $1.5 million in loans to be repaid over fourteen years and five hundred parking spaces if he redeveloped Church Street. Pearlman promised to stage a minimum of 150 nighttime outdoor events in 2004, 200 in 2005, and at least 250 every year thereafter. He also promised to bring 500 jobs (later cut to 300) to the city's center. The papers, in particular the alternative *Orlando Weekly,* that had railed against the city for letting the most prominent, historic piece of real estate in the town go to hell railed even harder against trusting Pearlman to revitalize it. But leaders were desperate, and the deal was done. City councilwoman Daisy Lynum even handed Lou the key to the city in a public ceremony. "It was an expression of gratitude," she told *Orlando Sentinel* political columnist Scott Maxwell. "I gave him a key because everyone else was giving him hell."

Even in 2002, the national media was still on board for Lou's thrill ride. Reporters toured his lavish digs, put his personal worth as high as $950 million, and credited him with putting Orlando on the entertainment map. Even newsmagazines *20/20* and *60 Minutes,* known more for hard-hitting reports and exposés than puffery, kissed the ring. A doting 2002 profile of Pearlman (one of the last of its kind) on *60 Minutes II* called him a "super mogul with his finger on the pulse of young America." Prodded about the lingering claims by *NSYNC and Backstreet Boys that he bilked his artists for too big of a chunk of change, he quipped to the *Orlando Sentinel*, "If you're going to make $50 million, and I'm going to get $100 million, who's going to complain?" In 2003, Pearlman conducted an interview with Jim Abbott, music writer for the *Orlando Sentinel*, while cruising at forty thousand feet on his private plane. He was flying to Atlanta for appearances with his last semisuccessful stateside act, Natural. While there, Lou was also planning to drop by CNN to plug his book, *Bands, Brands, and Billions*, written with another *Orlando Sentinel* reporter, Wes Smith. Pearlman did a signing for the book a few days before the trip, and the line to meet him stretched around the Virgin Megastore building in Orlando. But instead of housewives and bookworms clamoring for their copy of the bio, most of the people in line were teens who'd brought demos, headshots, and their parents. Lou took the photos and tapes and had all wannabes sign release forms for the materials, which they did without a second glance. One mother of a fourteen-year-old daughter said of Orlando and Lou, "We moved down here specifically to get into this market . . . If you want to get your foot in the door, he's the guy to see."

The press had also begun to highlight more of the lawsuits filed against Pearlman—the famous Backstreet Boys and *NSYNC suits but also smaller suits brought by people like Donna Wright, former wife of Johnny, who sought a six-figure sum for the credit Lou took for what she says was her work making his boys (and him) famous. And there was Clay Goodell, a former member of the Pearlman flop Take 5, who had filed a Department of Labor complaint against Lou claiming violations of child labor laws (the complaint was dismissed). He commented to Abbott about Natural being the latest group to get taken advantage of by Lou: "It makes me laugh to see what happens and see it happen all over again. They're forming a band and they don't really question it at all. I feel sorry for them. Then again, I don't."

Former Natural member Ben Bledsoe said he knew the history of Backstreet Boys and *NSYNC going in, the whole sixth-member thing, which Lou contractually made himself with Natural from the get-go. (He wasn't as greedy on song rights and other back-end points, Bledsoe said.) But rather than angle for something more equitable in the contract, he just went into the agreement knowing what he'd probably get out of it. At age twenty-six, five years after the height of his boy band success, Bledsoe said he was still benefiting from his Natural experience. He was touring as a solo artist and living in Los Angeles, doing occasional voice-over work and scoring music for TV and movies while working to land roles as an actor. Although Natural never made Bledsoe (or Pearlman) rich, it did pioneer a corporate deal with the Claire's accessory store, which sold the band's single "Put Your Arms Around Me" at a special reduced rate with every purchase worth $12 or more. The Claire's partnership also helped back a tour with the Monkees and propelled them on their own solo tour. It first occurred to Bledsoe that his band was breaking big when they sold out the Orlando House of Blues, then again when a group of random girls erupted in a fit of screaming at the sight of them in a town where the band had no direct ties. "Little moments like that . . . It just seemed like, 'Oh my god, something's happening.' The concept that we didn't have to earn every fan directly." Lou started them out in a converted Greyhound bus, but they did eventually get the Pearlman treatment: planes, hotel rooms, limos. "There's no doubt there was a lot of money spent on promoting us," Bledsoe said. The group peaked in 2004, then split up. "I walked away with very little to show for it, monetarily. I feel like I knew getting into it that it was going to be more about the experience than the money. I lived the dream."

"I'm having a lot of fun" was Pearlman's mantra during his last high-flying, largely positive interview. When he landed in Atlanta, he put up the members of Natural in the Four Seasons, dropping $300 a pop for their rooms and $14 apiece for deli sandwiches (Natural knew it was all recoupable, Bledsoe said). He bragged about *Making the Band 2*, which had actually been taken over by Sean Combs. He slipped in a plug for a home-studio, do-it-yourself pop star kit he was starting to market called Making the Hit, which let buyers use their computers to create demos (that sort of thing would later come standard on most Macs). For $59.95, the kit also included a CD-ROM tour of Trans Con Studios and a catalog of industry contacts. He was just beginning his migration to the Church Street complex, and he talked about his plans for an outdoor street concert series there (part of his deal to buy the distressed city blocks), which he intended to call "Motown to O-Town," in keeping with his tradition of shallowly treading in the footsteps of Motown's Berry Gordy.

"You're not going to be in an elevator a year from now and hear any rap songs," Pearlman said in the interview. "You're not going to hear Eminem in a restaurant when you're having a nice five-course meal. But you will hear the Backstreet Boys and *NSYNC. Our music lasts. It has melodies, and it's clean, wholesome fun. And you know what? The majority of America really wants that." For a finisher, he barked some directions about shortening Natural's guitar intro during a rehearsal for their TV performance—the band actually played instruments—then Lou himself picked up a guitar and strummed through "Scarborough Fair," his cousin Art's tune, in what's described as a "soft, quavering tenor."

In reality, when he agreed to a deal to buy the Church Street property and all of its darkened amenities for $34 million, he hadn't had a hit in years. His image of success was an elaborate false front. As Pearlman cultivated his public image as a slightly doughier, creepier, white teenager's Berry Gordy, he had quietly reported in 2001 to the IRS that he was personally worth *negative* $3 million. Then he just quit filing tax returns. His bands weren't making enough money to cover the bills. His film was a flop. He had long since abandoned his interest in airships. And Trans Continental Airlines, unbeknownst to his giant pool of shareholders, didn't exist. Money was going out to buoy all sorts of businesses—Trans Con Foods, which ran NYPD pizza and Pearlman's TCBY yogurt franchises, for example—but the only real discernible income came to Lou's offices in Citibank-logo-adorned envelopes: checks from EISA investors. On October 26, 2001, the FDIC had, for the second time, caught wind of Lou's scheme. This time, a concerned investor alerted the corporation to the fact that Lou was claiming his EISA was FDIC insured. "I am writing you concerning FDIC insurance of Employee Investment Savings Accounts at Trans Continental Airlines," an FDIC official wrote. "My concerns center around the use of the word 'FDIC' and the confusing manner in which insurance on the Employee Investment Savings Account is discussed." Particularly confusing was the part saying the FDIC insured the accounts when it never did. Pearlman replied in writing: "Our company is Trans Continental Airlines Inc. We do not offer to anyone other than employees or our private shareholders our Employee Investment Savings Account plan. Our employees have their own individual accounts set up with approved banking institutions. Our matching plan is based on years of service. We have not solicited anyone nor have accepted anyone to this plan that does not qualify and certainly not the general public . . ." It was the same lie he'd told the same organization in 1995. And it staved them off again.

The state of Florida's Office of Financial Regulation was more tenacious. Responding to a 2003 consumer complaint, the agency quietly launched an independent look into the sale of shares in Pearlman's Trans Con companies and the claims that EISA was FDIC insured. They spoke with Charlotte Oliver, an EISA sales agent who told the OFR that Pearlman promised investors that their funds were held in U.S. bank accounts, that they were FDIC insured up to $100,000, that Lloyd's of London and then AIG insured the accounts, and that Cohen & Siegel had audited the program and determined it to be aboveboard in every way. The OFR found one person it identified only as "Investor M" who got a letter on August 1, 1995, from EISA sales agent Stephen Meunch, offering a chance to participate in the program, which was said to be FDIC and Lloyd's of London insured, and a two-page attachment to the pitch was what appeared to be the Lloyd's policy. In January 2004, responding to an earlier letter from the OFR asking about the two investment schemes, Pearlman attorney Peter Antonacci responded, "Neither of these products has been offered for sale to the public by the company since at least 2002." Unconvinced, the OFR continued to monitor EISA.

What they didn't yet know was that Pearlman and his agents had collected $13.8 million in EISA money in 2003 alone—from all kinds of investors, including members of the public. In fact, EISA sales agents would be paid out $7.5 million in commissions for hawking the program. Most of the money would go to Kristen Finger, who managed EISA operations, and Michael Crudele, who marketed the program. Pearlman even deposited more than $30,000 in a prepaid college tuition program for Crudele's daughter. Lou had raked in so much cash from EISA that by 2004 he had even paid back some of his EISA investors—in the end, he returned a total of $43 million in interest and principals. That's how the Ponzi scheme worked. New investors' money paid off the older debts, and although Lou could never indefinitely maintain the debt he racked up in the early 2000s, some early investors got out unscathed. There was always a Trans Con Airlines shareholder or even EISA participants to whom Lou could point as happy customers. For a long time, Dr. Joseph Chow was the biggest one of them. An accounting statement from Trans Continental Travel Service issued to Chow in December 2003 covering stock he owned and investments in the company he'd made since 1997 reflected an available balance of $5,196,984.35. Another heap of Trans Con Travel stock purchased by Chow in 2001 was worth an additional $1,168,630.37.

At the time, he was Pearlman's single largest source of cash. Chow even loaned out $100,000 to the Trans Con–underwritten East West Entertainment, too, the primary purpose of which was setting up a tour in China for Whitney Houston. Chow was also an early adopter of EISA. On a biannual EISA statement issued to Chow in December 2003, one of his accounts showed a balance of $846,255.28 (grown from $826,954.08 invested in July of that same year). "He just believed in Lou," said Chow's daughter Jennifer. "He had complete faith in this man. It was really kind of amazing to see." All told, her father sank about $14 million into Lou's companies.

Then in 2004, saddled with the Church Street debt, having failed to produce any band that earned him any profits even approaching those of Backstreet Boys and *NSYNC and relying primarily on new EISA money to get him by, Pearlman was dealt a slap of reality. Dr. Joseph Chow succumbed to pancreatic cancer. Lou's angel investor died and Chow's family was saddled with his estate taxes. So they came calling to Lou to get their father's money back.

## CHAPTER 10

# HIT, HIT, PUMP

*I*n 2004, the same year Chow died, Lou's employees threw him a fiftieth birth-day party so big it filled a massive banquet room at Walt Disney World's Dolphin resort. It was fully catered, with a carving station and open bar. K. C. and the Sunshine Band performed, along with a slew of Trans Continental artists, most of whom would never make it much farther than that night's gig. A toned, tanned, frosty-blond, expertly trained dancer named Sean van der Wilt put on the most elaborate show of the night (his relationship with Lou would end without anything close to a hit). "Some of the stuff Lou's created . . . ," a nearly out of breath Van der Wilt said onstage, "the term 'boy band,' he originated it. Aviation, he didn't create it, but I bet this man has a percentage with the Wright Brothers. A lot of these moves up here, Lou created them. He taught me 'hit, hit, pump,' " he said as he performed a clench-fisted, three-step hip thrust maneuver. Then he called Lou to stand up and join him in it. In what may have been the first and only public display of Pearlman's pelvic prowess, he obliged.

Brooke Hogan, Hulk's daughter, who signed with Pearlman as an artist, sang a few songs and played piano. Then she slinked down into the crowd and serenaded Pearlman like Marilyn Monroe serenaded JFK, singing an inappropriately sultry rendition of "Happy Birthday" to Lou. It was made even more awkward by the fact that her father and Lou's girlfriend, Tammie, watched from just a few feet away.

Howie D, who also remained cordial with Pearlman even after Backstreet sued him, got up and told the story of how he almost missed his chance to join Backstreet Boys because he used the stage name Tony Donetti and Lou and crew couldn't find him for a callback—until he stumbled into the same audition again. Aaron Carter, Backstreet Boy Nick's younger brother, who was one of Lou's last real hopefuls, sang along to a prerecorded track about "partying" on "Saturday night," slipping Lou's name into the lyrics occasionally.

Photo montages flashed on giant screens showing Lou and his planes and blimps, Lou in Queens with Alan Gross and his mom and all of the neighborhood guys whom he brought with him to Florida. There was a picture of Lou posing with Dick Cheney, though no one has ever been able to say if it was real. There were videotaped messages from Kool of Kool & the Gang, cousin Art Garfunkel, Kevin DuBrow of the metal band Quiet Riot, and more. The staff of his office delivered messages into the lens: "They wanted me to give a picture of you and me together, but we're not going to make it that easy for them to make wanted posters," said one be-Dockered manager. A member of the accounting department deadpanned: "Always remember, Lou, your money is secure here, because this is where the buck stops."

From the stage, C Note, Pearlman's streetwise, Latin-tinged act, rapped a personal message to him: "From the blimps to the airships to the G4 / C Note concerts, sold out tours / Late nights at the yogurt store / You never hesitated to open doors / Make it happen keep it rollin' that's what you say / So we try to pursue that every day / Haha we love your sense of humor, thank you / Lou P, from me and the crew." They end with a call-and-response: "When we say 'happy' ya'll say 'birthday' . . . When we say 'big,' ya'll say 'papa' . . ."

Lou himself took the stage toward the end of the show. He was sober as always but sweating and visibly drunk with pride. If there was stress or chaos in his mind, it didn't show. "I don't know what to say, it's just unbelievable," he gushed. "I have to tell you that I didn't have anything to do with this night's event. All I did was show up . . ." In reality, he paid the bill. "It's just mind blowing. There's close to a thousand people here tonight. It's unbelievable . . . I only thought weddings and Fashion Rock events were this big." Not one of the artists in attendance would go on to have a major hit, but Lou continued, "To see our artists . . . I gotta say, just about everybody is here tonight or is represented. It's been a lot of fun over the years . . . from aviation to entertainment to pizza to jewelry, I want to thank everyone in our company for making this special . . . As we're moving into our Church Street Station offices, people were saying let's see if we can top everything, and we did . . . It truly shows if you can dream it you can do it!"

K. C. took the stage in a sparkly Ed Hardy–style T-shirt bedazzled with the message: "That's The Way (I Like It)," and he belted out, "Happy birthday, happy birthday to ya . . . to ya!" It went on for what seemed like forever.

Two years after he'd bought his downtown complex, Pearlman's heap of debt and lack of real income had started manifesting themselves in ways the pop Svengali could no longer control. By the time he celebrated his fiftieth birthday in 2004, his grip on his financial juggling act had started to slip. Though the executive Trans Con offices had been completed at Church Street and Lou had moved in, overall renovations were frozen. Lou and his business partner Robert Kling had failed to pay contractors, and ten companies had filed construction liens against Church Street Station, claiming they were owed $2.1 million. Planet Airways, once one of Lou's most legitimate hopes for enduring success, had for years been propelled by a

$4.5 million Civil Aeronautics Fleet contract, under which Planet flew members of the U.S. military to and from bases. But keeping up with maintenance and newer, more efficient planes flown by Planet's competitors was more than Lou could afford. After 2004, the airline fell into a nosedive and never pulled out. In 2005, Lou tried to introduce a new financial group into the Planet partnership, Nevada corporation PHC Holdings. There was debate about whether PHC was created as a shell into which Lou could dump Planet Airways (and thus try to escape its debts) or whether PHC would legitimately infuse money into Planet to update its aging fleet. Regardless, the deal never went through. Tony DeCamillis, who was running the airline, learned that one of PHC's principals, Kevin James Quinn, was actually a disbarred attorney who was banned for life by the Securities and Exchange Commission from serving as an officer or director of a public company. Quinn was also banned for life from participating at all in any offerings of stocks under five dollars per share, so he couldn't legally raise money for the airline with a penny stock offering. The SEC started calling Quinn at an office he'd set up at Planet with questions in 2005. DeCamillis, who had suffered his own trouble with securities officials at Chatfield Dean, caught wind of the calls and reached out to the SEC himself, learned the truth about Quinn's background, and told him to immediately stop any actions he might take with regard to acquiring Planet. The PHC deal fell apart. Lou, in turn, quit funding the airline and DeCamillis was forced to resign. Planet subsequently failed to keep up with FAA standards. It lost its Civil Aeronautics Fleet contract and was grounded by the FAA in May 2005. One last vestige of Planet, a decaying 727, sat on a back corner of Orlando International Airport for years, a public monument to Pearlman's dwindling fortunes.

Unbeknownst to the public at large and even some of Lou's associates, his inability to keep Planet, Church Street, and various other projects afloat was a side effect of a legal battle he was locked in with the family of his biggest backer. At Dr. Joseph Chow's funeral in mid-2004, his family had approached Lou about the money he still owed them and their father's trust. They were staring down estate taxes, and the loans Chow had given Lou were already past due. Pearlman was never easy to get ahold of, so family members decided the funeral was the best time to catch him and deal with that piece of leftover business between the decade-long friends. True to form, Pearlman made a commitment on the spot to pay back what he owed—or at least a significant chunk of the $14 million (including interest) that Chow had invested. Then, with his former friend, business associate, and biggest source of cash lowered into his grave, Pearlman started trying to figure out a way to claw out of his own deep hole of debt. Chow's brother was the first to question Lou about the IPO he frequently dangled to keep investors like his brother hanging on, but suddenly Lou had no such high hopes. The stock offering, he said, was a dwindling prospect in the current market. Moreover, if the family did decide to take their money out of Trans Con and EISA, Lou said, he could only give them about ten cents on every dollar. When the family got the news, things between them and Lou turned ugly.

The Chow estate, known as the Thorndale Investment Company and headed up by Chow's daughter Jennifer, hired attorney Edwin Brooks to start the process of going after Pearlman for what he owed, but Lou beat them to the punch. In late 2004, he sued *them*. Baffled at first, they learned that Pearlman, who had been sued in virtually every business he started, could detect even the faintest aroma of brewing legal action, and in Florida, his notoriety as a defendant had begun to compete with his notoriety as a music mogul. So he filed the suit against the Chows in Chicago. The family counter-sued. And then what was once a merely ugly legal battle turned downright nasty.

Brooks, a plainspoken, no-nonsense litigator who side-lined as an adjunct professor at Northwestern School of Law and specialized in loan default and restructuring litigation, filed his complaint in 2004 and set about proving, first, that Chow had written stacks of checks to Lou. Chow's own bank and financial records made that a cinch. Slightly more diffi-cult was proving that Chow had given the money to Pearlman as loans, not in exchange for stock in Trans Continental anything. Pearlman did give Chow stock as a good-faith gesture but never in exchange for his money. That would be a sticky point, but without question—beginning with Julian Benscher and running through the late-'80s, early-'90s era of big-bucks investor scouting—Pearlman had handed out Trans Con stock like gold stars. It was his funny money, and, following the success of Backstreet Boys and *NSYNC, a share in what was a nonexistent company with no real assets was assumed to be worth far more than the $10 it originally cost. The IPO was coming, after all.

With a stack of promissory notes and IOUs between Pearlman and Chow, Brooks built the case on behalf of the trust that Chow never intended his money to suffer any great risk. Based on the deep assets Pearlman claimed to have, he always assured his investor he'd at least return his principal, but Chow stuck with Lou for the better-than-average interest on the loans and the golden IPO at the end of the rainbow. Another tough part of Brooks's job involved what's known as "piercing the corporate veil," a legal term for looking beneath an umbrella company like Trans Continental Airlines to see what other subsidiaries it's funding, then going after those companies' assets, too. Documents trickled in, but Brooks faced resistance at every step— missed and postponed delivery dates and lame excuses when it came to the whereabouts of financial statements. "They actually said 'a hurricane came and blew away my documents,'" at one point, Brooks said—

the Carl Hiaasen version of "My dog ate my homework." Then, early in the back-and-forth, Pearlman came into Brooks's office and tried to settle; that ended with Brooks basically throwing Pearlman out for offering emotional ploys and an insultingly low sum. "He would always say that he thought my client was a wonderful man. He would always try to pull that bullshit on me. I didn't buy it."

As strong as his position seemed to be, Brooks ran up against delay after delay from Pearlman's camp in turning over financial documents—and a judge who refused to hold Lou's feet to the fire didn't help. Then late one night, he was sitting in his office perusing documents. One in particular was bugging him. Known as a forbearance letter, it was the cornerstone of Lou's argument against paying back the Chows. It said, essentially, that Chow's repayment was conditioned upon the "convenient repayment schedule" set by Trans Con's board of directors, a payback "that does not place economic constraint on any of the respective companies." In other words, Lou didn't have to pay him back a dime if doing so threatened the financial well-being of his company. It was signed by Joseph C. F. Chow and dated June 22, 2002. "I couldn't figure out why in god's name somebody would sign something like that," Brooks said. He knew Chow believed wholeheartedly in Lou and that his bottomless faith was the subject of arguments between him and his wife, who suggested unsuccessfully for years that he pull back in his involvement with Trans Con. "I struggled with the idea that maybe he did sign it," Brooks said. Then, as the evening waned, Chow's distinctive, angular signature on the bottom of the forbearance kept catching the lawyer's eye. As practiced as it clearly was, it looked a bit too much like his signature on another document, a promissory note, ironically. Brooks riffled through his stacks and found his copy of that promissory note, and it bore what appeared to be the *exact* same signature. He held the two documents together up to a lamp with the forbearance letter on top and lined up the signatures. They were almost indistinguishable. "With that, I said, 'Holy crap, this is a forgery.' " He could almost picture Lou hunched over the document on his desk, $2,000 pen in hand, biting his hanging tongue and bottom lip, sweating a little, tracing Chow's John Hancock.

A sharp lawyer, he went out and hired two handwriting analysts, one a forensics expert who analyzed the ink and the speed with which the pen strokes were made and determined that the signature on the forbearance document was microscopically identical to the promissory note signed in ink by Chow. This was, beyond a shadow of a doubt, a case of forgery. But although he had the original copy of the forbearance letter, he only had a copy of the promissory note. He knew without originals of both documents Lou could make the argument in court that *he* was the one who got the legitimate signature on the forbearance letter and *Brooks* had the forged signature on the copy of the promissory note. Frustrated, Brooks knew he was a step away from a smoking gun—a step too far to force a settlement in his clients' favor and keep the case out of the hands of an unpredictable jury. So Brooks stuck the letter and the proof of the forgery in his back pocket and sat on it. Through most of 2005, he and attorneys for Pearlman played cat and mouse. Brooks sent out dozens of requests for documents and traded e-mails and messages too numerous to count in which document delivery and pickup times were shuffled or rescheduled, appointments were missed, phone calls went straight to voice mail and were never returned, and new promises to comply were made only under the threat of further court action. Even when a reluctant judge finally did agree to force Pearlman's hand, he stalled some more. In the end, it would take almost two years and eventual threats of contempt of court for Brooks to wrangle the discovery materials Pearlman was required to turn over.

By mid-2005, the Chows' lawyer realized that if he ever was going to get anything out of Pearlman and his companies, he'd have better luck going after Lou's personal assets. Doing so meant getting Lou to turn over personal financial statements. Surprisingly, he did—documents audited by the same Cohen & Siegel accounting firm that had put its stamp on Chow's account statements and virtually every financial record given to investors since the late 1980s. The documents might have looked legit to Brooks, but he had already unearthed one forgery and was deeply skeptical of Pearlman, so he decided to serve Cohen & Siegel with a subpoena. Online, he found offices for the firm in South Florida and Germany, so he hired a process server to call upon their Coral Gables office. Shortly afterward, he got a call from the server. "There's no Cohen & Siegel here," he told Brooks. It was just an office complex with some secretarial service. "I figured out that he had a false accounting firm, and my thinking at that point was, *This guy is doing some pretty bad stuff.*"

He wouldn't get at just how bad Lou's stuff was, though, until Pearlman invited him to the opulent Church Street Station headquarters of Trans Continental. From November 30 to December 1, 2005, Brooks was allowed to look through Trans Con's financials as part of the discovery process. It was a warm, sunny winter day when Brooks landed in Orlando. Lou was not waiting in his cornflower-blue Rolls-Royce Phantom at Orlando International, though. He did not chauffeur Brooks to the Enclave to drop off his luggage, nor did they swing by his mansion for Jet Ski rides. Brooks was shown straight to a back room of the massive complex by a security guard built like a railroad spike. He lingered as Pearlman's in-house legal minion, Mike Ferderigos, brought box after box of documents. Ferderigos, it's worth noting, was a caretaker of Lou's boats in New York who'd moved to Orlando at Lou's behest and decided to go to law school with the express purpose of working for Trans Con. He was far outmatched by

Brooks. During his first day spent in the dank room, the Chows' attorney pored over documents for companies that seemed to run on no income other than giant cash infusions from LJP (for "Louis Jay Pearlman") Enterprises. The money actually came from investors, of which Chow was the largest. "It was pretty clear to me at that point that this guy is running a Ponzi scheme," Brooks said. He didn't know how big it was or how many people it involved, but he knew his client had been duped on a massive level. "I saw enough to know I could pierce the corporate veil."

Lou personally visited Brooks throughout his stay, looking visibly shaken, sweaty, concerned, and at times just plain nervous. On the second day, Brooks found the original letter that he needed to prove Pearlman's signature was a fraud. "I knew I had a forgery," Brooks said. "Here I am sitting down at this basement with an original note thinking, *Oh, crap, what do I do?* It was the key to the case, and I couldn't walk out with it or I'd be accused of all kinds of stuff." So he stuck it in a folder, made note of what he was doing, handed it to Ferderigos, and told him he would need the original letter at a later date. A judge subsequently backed his demand to have the letter sent to him so he could have his experts examine it. "Then once I had it, I refused to return it," Brooks said. As for other documents that proved the Ponzi, he began flagging them to be copied but had a sneaking suspicion they'd end up "in the river," he said—or blown away by another precision hurricane. Pearlman himself came down to visit Brooks one more time that winter day at Trans Con before the lawyer left to go back to Chicago. This time, he offered him a settlement of a couple million, to be paid over time. Brooks, now with evidence of a Ponzi scheme and a forged letter, countered with a $9 million offer. No deal was made.

For the first time, Brooks knew he had the ammo to force a settlement that would please the Chows. He also had an opportunity to turn Pearlman over to the authorities. Like a good attorney, he chose the interest of his clients. "If I turn all this stuff over, the house of cards comes down . . . that doesn't help my client," he said. "So we kept pursuing it, hoping that Lou would know we had the goods on him."

What he couldn't have known from such a brief look through Lou's labyrinthine subterfuge was that Pearlman had already tapped into a far greater replacement source of cash than Chow: banks. He'd borrowed $2.8 million in July 2000 from Integra Bank NA (of Kentucky, Illinois, Ohio, and Indiana) to cover Planet Airways's sucking debt. And no one inside or outside his organization had blinked when Lou convinced Florida bank Mercantile to loan him $6 million in 2001. Even those inside the company who handled the details of the loan assumed it was a temporary measure—Lou borrowed money all the time to cover businesses they were sure became profitable. Ditto the 2002 loan of $5 million from MB Financial; Lou put that money into Planet Airways, which was still struggling to gain altitude. Then in '03, Washington Mutual gave the airline and music mogul a $5 million line of credit, Mercantile gave him another $6 million loan, and in the same month Bank of America gave him a $10 million loan. All of them were secured by the bogus Cohen & Siegel financials, worthless Trans Con stock, personal assets he put up over and over as collateral to multiple lenders, and the same phony reputation as a tycoon that he'd sold for years to unsuspecting investors. On October 20, 2003, Pearlman sent FNB Bank in Pennsylvania a 2002 federal income tax return that put his income in the millions and a Form 4868 for the year ending December 31, 2002, claiming falsely that he had paid over $4.8 million in estimated taxes. In reality, he'd not filed his taxes since 2001, when he reported his net worth to be negative $3 million. The bogus tax return was doctored to look like it had been prepared by the ever diligent and constantly on-call Cohen & Siegel. On April 30, 2004, he sent more false income tax filings for Trans Con Airlines to Bank of America. They, too, were fake and prepped by Cohen & Siegel—in other words, Lou. Bank of America forked over $34 million, supposedly for Fashion Rock, Church Street, and various television and concert plans. He used the same bogus financial info in January 2005 to get $2 million more from Mercantile Bank. Then on March 18, 2005, he pulled a move that was even more brazen than forging Joseph Chow's signature on the forbearance letter—at times the sheer temerity of Lou's swindling was what kept him from getting caught. In the process of landing a $3 million revolving credit note and a $16 million term note loan, he sent a false income tax return for Trans Con Airlines to Integra Bank for the 2004 fiscal year. Cohen & Siegel had audited it, and it was signed by Harry Milner, Lou's old former friend from Chicago who had paved the way for the Budweiser blimp deal, the man whose hard work he had rewarded with the title of Trans Con's corporate finance officer. Milner, however, had been dead since 2003.

"Lou was going to use my father as the big fall guy," Milner's son Harry Milner III said. He had e-mailed Lou via the Trans Con corporate website three months after his father's death to tell him the news. He heard back from a Trans Con associate, who told him his e-mail would be forwarded to Lou. Either Lou never got the message or figured a dead man would tell no tales. "It wasn't important to him that he was dead," Milner's son said, "because the idiot never got my e-mail."

On March 21, 2006, Lou sent his EISA investors good news: Their interest rates would be going up!

On August 21, 2006, one of Pearlman's associates sent more bogus financials to NorthSide Bank in Georgia seeking $2.5 million for Trans Con studios. Along with it was a letter from Cohen & Siegel verifying the existence of a $50 million contingency reserve fund at German Investment und Finanzberatung GmbH, also known as German Savings Bank, for the benefit of Trans Continental Airlines. In October, another Pearlman associate sent a fake letter from German Savings Bank to NorthSide as proof that the $50 million fund existed and that it was about to release $5 million to Pearlman. The fund's name was TW Trust. TW as in Theodor Wullenkemper.

All told, Lou rounded up about $160 million from more than a dozen bank loans. None of the financial institutions called the others; if they had, they'd have learned that Lou promised his same handful of assets over and over to secure cash: his home in Chaine du Lac, Windermere (rendering it vulnerable to seizure under Florida's Homestead Act); "jet shares" in his Gulfstream; thousands of shares of bogus Trans Con stock; his studios; his Rolls-Royce; even *Top of the Pops*, the British TV show that inspired *American Idol*—Lou aspired to become Simon Cowell, too, but he never actually sealed the deal to import the program to America and didn't have rights to the title.

U.S. Bancorp, which had inherited Lou's first multimillion loan from Integra, was the first to sue Lou and Trans Con, for more than $2 million in unpaid loans in 2004. It demanded Lou turn over one of Planet's 727s, which he'd used to secure the loan, and a chunk of Trans Continental Airlines. Lou didn't. Other banks started calling in defaulted loans in the fall of 2006, the same time the Florida Office of Financial Regulation intensified its investigation into Lou's EISA and hit him with another round of questions. Lou told investigators in December 2006 that German Savings Bank was holding $39.5 million in EISA money that covered investors' principals. He blamed his delinquencies on the same German Savings Bank, explaining at one point that money for payments that was supposed to be wired to him was held up by Homeland Security (ironically, Lou was a big Republican campaign donor). The funds were not ever held up by Tom Ridge and crew. There were no funds. In fact, there was never a record of any of Lou's or his investors' money ever going to German Savings, or, for that matter, that there even existed a banking institution by that name—certainly not at the address Pearlman gave for the bank, the same address he provided as the German headquarters of Cohen & Siegel.

On December 20, 2006, the same time Pearlman's attorneys agreed with OFR to stop selling EISA, another EISA sale went through—to a Clearwater, Florida, investor for $1 million.

For the better part of 2006, Pearlman and his attorneys dodged a deposition, even though it was they who had originally sued Chow. Dozens of times, all chronicled in furious back-and-forth e-mails, Pearlman and his people changed appointment times, stalled for all sorts of reasons or for no reason at all, then finally showed up in November, offering to pay back pennies on the dollar. "I told him straight to his face, at least one of three things is going to happen," Brooks says. "You're going to go to prison. You're going to go bankrupt and your companies are going to go bankrupt. Or you're going to pay me the money." Pearlman settled with Brooks and Chow's estate for about $9 million and arranged a payment schedule.

Then that same year, Lou dropped a huge bundle of money on his own fine dining restaurant. Inspired by and perhaps hungering for the Peter Luger cuts of beef he'd feasted on when he first hit the big time in Queens, he opened Pearl Steakhouse at Church Street. Aged beef with all the trimmings was always just a stone's throw away from his office, and Pearl had all the signatures of a Pearlman enterprise, including falsely inflated prices. "Pearl might be an OK, average kind of place if it weren't so ridiculously overpriced," wrote *Orlando Sentinel* food critic Scott Joseph, refusing, despite Pearlman's reputation as the man saving Church Street, to fall in line. "What set a bad tone for the evening was when the waiter approached the table holding what he said was the featured wine of the night. Because I've learned from lessons past, I asked how much the wine cost. The muttered answer was $100. No wonder it's featured. Instead, I chose a $50 bottle of Sterling cabernet sauvignon . . . I was startled to find the price had grown to $85 on my check. It was reduced when I pointed out the error."

## CHAPTER 11

# FAREWELL TOUR

The resplendent Trans Continental offices in Orlando were more like a clubhouse than an executive headquarters for a multimillion-dollar entertainment empire. Lou referred to everyone there as his family and pretended to hold their best interests close to his heart. They called him Big Papa. And to his partners and execs—former deli counter workers, drivers, disbarred or otherwise clientless attorneys, ex-cons, traders who'd been banned from the financial world—Lou was their way back in. The longer they stuck with him, the more they turned a blind eye to what was really happening. Everyone assumed it would last forever. But when Lou wasn't in the office (frequently), many of his minions would show up late, take long lunches, and leave early. When he was there, they jockeyed for face time with him. Secretly, Lou pitted his employees against each other with office gossip but shuffled off the resolution of personnel problems to his underlings. He played the good guy, constantly dangling the prospect of financially backing his executives' side projects if they pitched him a promising business plan or pumping them up with inflated titles they'd never land with their level of education, experience, and skills in the outside world. He gave them wide-ranging responsibilities, too. The buddy system at Trans Con awarded Lou's former Queens pal Paul Russo his own New York Pizzeria and Deli (NYPD). It's how Bob Fischetti came to help manage the intricacies of EISA, run Trans Con's country music label, host a singer/songwriter night at a local nightclub, and even take over a large club space of his own with plans to turn it into a restaurant, comedy, and entertainment venue. Loyalty, more than any particular business skill, catapulted Alan Siegel to the top of Lou's companies and landed him a position running a custom CD manufacturing company. And the same undying commitment to Pearlman is what gave Frank Vazquez Jr., the son of the maintenance man at Mitchell Gardens, the chance to oversee all of Trans Con's operations; it also gave him his first glimpse of Lou's complete fraud, which he had helped pull off for years. Lou always called on Frankie, in particular, to handle his dirty work—keeping the loyal lackeys in line or fending off creditors. He learned from Lou how to stave them off with promises of repayment or forthcoming fortunes. Then on October 27, 2006, Pearlman opened a new checking account at Bank of America for Trans Continental Enterprises, LLC. Between then and December 31, 2006, he deposited $3,833,000 in EISA money into the account—he knew the authorities were closing in on the bogus savings account program. One week later, on Louis J. Pearlman letterhead, in his own handwriting, Lou wrote, "Please transfer from our Trans Continental Enterprises Account . . . $500,000 to Global Investments and Services Ltd. . . . The Netherlands." As a high-ranking Trans Con exec in an office rife with gossip, Vazquez had a front-row seat for the whole nefarious final act. In the first week of November, he asked Lou for a meeting and told him he needed to talk about some of the things he'd seen at Trans Con. Then on November 11, the bank sent Lou's money overseas. That same afternoon, Vazquez, who'd kept up appearances as a smooth-talking wheeler-dealer in Trans Con's upper echelons but had privately become stressed out about the company's future, climbed into his beloved 1987 Porsche, cranked it, and asphyxiated himself to death in the garage of an Orlando home, the one paid for with an inflated salary from his job as a fake executive for a nonexistent company.

Neighbors reported hearing Vazquez's car run for several hours; one of them knocked on his garage door and found it hot to the touch. Orange County sheriff's deputies found bills, computer passwords, a will, and other personal effects neatly laid out. His friends said that was just Frankie's obsessive nature, but Orange County sheriff's investigators described it like a neatly organized farewell. Vazquez was sitting in the still-idling Porsche (the gas tank was three quarters full), dead from carbon monoxide poisoning, a green T-shirt wrapped around his head to help him tolerate the smell of the exhaust fumes. The medical examiner ruled the death a suicide, finding nothing suspicious in an autopsy or toxicology reports— only caffeine was found in his system. But much later, Lou would call his childhood chum Alan Gross and tell him about the meeting Frankie had asked for a week before he died, the one in which he wanted to share some very strange goings-on he'd discovered at Trans Con. Another friend of Trans Con had died, too, Lou pointed out, from an apparent heart attack. Plus deep-pocketed Trans Con and Backstreet backer Eric Emanuel had died in a car crash. As usual, Lou was all hints and insinuations and never forthcoming with anything concrete. "If you hear anything about me dying of suicide or a heart attack you better go to the FBI," he told Alan Gross in a phone conversation. "He found out a lot of shit, Frankie." It was fodder for the conspiracy theories of friends and relatives of Vazquez who couldn't fathom the idea that anxiety, depression, and, for Vazquez, getting so deeply screwed both professionally and financially by his lifelong friend led him to a dark end at his own hands. Plus, although there wasn't one shred of evidence of foul play, Lou perpetuated those rumors, hinting that one of his creditors might have come after him via Vazquez. Missing from the equation was the emotion usually involved in the loss of a childhood friend. Even to those who knew him best, Pearlman didn't seem outwardly distraught. He told his girlfriend, Tammie, about Frankie's death, but he didn't come looking for a shoulder to cry on. He was all business, Hilton said. Lou *briefed* her. "He was very matter-of-fact about it. He said, 'Hey, babe, you're going to hear some stuff coming out about Frankie's death . . . ' " For him, it was a PR crisis, she said. But in reality, it was that and more. Vazquez's death ramped up press coverage of Lou's troubles—the banks' lawsuits, the OFR's investigation, his late payments and broken promises at Church Street. It was all coming apart.

By late 2006, the Trans Con headquarters, whose doors were once stormed by starry-eyed wannabe pop stars, was now deluged with angry, often elderly investors. Lou's executive assistant Mandy Newland fielded most of their calls, as well as calls from banks looking for payment on loans. Bob Fischetti, Mike Crudele, and Kristen Finger dealt with EISA payments and investors. By November 1, however, Finger had departed, and she cashed a $5,000 check from Lou. In the memo portion of the check, Lou wrote: "Best wishes!" The same security guards who once pushed back eager teens were suddenly keeping old folks from marching up to the executive offices to demand checks, and a few were paid after angry visits. Newland says she pleaded with Lou to just talk to some of the debtors, and when he did, it was usually to make empty promises. Some who visited did get paid, Newland said. "They just wanted their money. Or else they wanted an answer as to when they could get their money. They just wanted answers—we all sort of wanted answers. We realized that the ship was sinking a little bit. But Lou would assure us all that he was going to take care of it. That either he was going to get a loan or downsize the company. Nobody knew the extent of the money involved."

The first weeks of the new year, 2007, brought more civil suits, adding to the heaps of complaints from banks, investors from New York, disgruntled wannabe models, and more. Some of them named Lou's executives, EISA salespeople, and more and called the EISA program a fraud. Lou had stopped paying the banks altogether, and they were coming after him with a particular vengeance, foreclosing on his properties along the way. He made superficial attempts at cutting back staff at Trans Con but then just sort of left everyone hanging around to read the writing on the wall. In one last-ditch effort Lou allowed accountant Paul Glover to comb through his books. Unlike Edwin Brooks, the last outsider to take a gander at the inner workings of Trans Con, Glover had been given full and cooperative access to anything he wanted. He was sent into Trans Con by Frank Amodeo, a mysterious former attorney who had been disbarred in Georgia after his alleged role in a scheme to bilk seniors out of money. Amodeo had done what so many exposed hucksters do in a pinch: He migrated to Florida. And he began working as an agent to liquidate real estate for those who'd declared bankruptcy, but in 1995, he was arrested and charged with forgery and grand theft. The charges were dropped. In 1996, however, the IRS smacked him for $83,000 in back taxes, and in 1998, he served two years in a federal pen. His next firm, Mirabilis Ventures, a venture capital firm, was later investigated for swiping more than a half million dollars from a bankruptcy company. He had staged one hell of a comeback in the wake of all of this, forging connections through the good-old-boy-meets-Washington network jokingly referred to in Florida as the Cracker Mafia. He sat two spaces away from George W. Bush at a NATO summit. He employed ex-cops and at least one ex–Secret Service member who had run security for Bush's visit to Iraq. Amodeo described his role as a "distressed business manager" with AQMI Strategy, whose website proclaims, "More than a consulting business, more than strategists, we solve problems when no solution seems evident." Amodeo saw Lou's situation as one in which he could play the role of a white knight. He needed Lou in many regards. In other words, Pearlman had attracted him for the same reasons he attracted so many others. Nevertheless, Amodeo called Glover into his office prior to his Trans Con visit and told him he had a team in place—everyone from money men to political operatives to

PR pros—ready to try to save Lou's bacon. He wanted Glover to go in and figure out what assets Lou could pledge as a way to make restitution on the money he'd made disappear, something he could offer state regulators, the banks, and hundreds of investors, all of whom were coming down on Lou hard in late 2006. Amodeo assured Glover his interests were in recovering money for investors. "We had a plan in place," Glover said, one that would have let Lou make restitution, avoid jail, and keep his house and some modicum of his high-flying lifestyle. "It would have been quite a thing if Lou would have signed the agreement we prepared." But he hadn't yet when Glover went rifling through his financials. "Lou was clearly looking to run," said Glover.

On January 5, 2007, Glover holed up in Pearlman's corner office at his Church Street complex. Lou wasn't there. Initially Glover was sharing space with OFR investigators, who were also rifling through stacks of documents. At about 3:30 P.M., they mysteriously and abruptly got up and left without saying a word, as if they were done. In a sense, they were, having learned that Lou went right on selling EISA after his attorneys had agreed with them to stop. A bit later, Glover picked up his mobile phone and dialed Cohen & Siegel, the auditing firm that had signed off on nearly every key financial document in Trans Continental's history since the late 1980s. Cohen & Siegel's standard accounting language was outdated by years—just a few old words that everyone in the industry had agreed to ditch were bugging Glover, and he wanted to ask the firm's principals directly for an explanation. He hit "send" on the phone, put it to his ear, heard the Cohen & Siegel line ring, and watched the line on Lou's desk simultaneously light up, not once, but twice. In that instant, having started a search for assets but stumbling upon hundreds of EISA statements and certified letters from investors demanding their money back, he knew he was neck-deep in a Ponzi scheme, the biggest one he'd ever seen.

Unlike those before him who'd unearthed possible evidence of massive fraud—Benscher and Brooks among them—Glover wasn't beholden to Lou or tied up in any of his investments. So he started asking for more paperwork. The execs in Pearlman's office—Bob Fischetti, executive assistant Janet Hart, and others—gladly handed over boxes of documents Glover asked for. Vazquez's recent suicide was a wake-up call to them all, Fischetti in particular. A convincingly naïve right-hand man to Lou, he had signed the last December 2006 million-dollar EISA sale. Now he was panicked that he might get snagged and thrown in jail with everyone in the place. "I think it was Bob Fischetti who was most street-smart and recognized: We've got to do something. We can't just run from this stuff. They were looking for answers," Glover said. "Here was his surrogate executive team that is now waking up to the fact that there could be some personal liability. They got a little freaked."

At about nine P.M. on January 5, Glover made a fateful shift in purpose. Hired to stave off Trans Con's implosion and feeling the pull of Lou's lackeys on his coattails, begging him to help them bail out of the company that had lined their pockets with cash for decades, he decided to blow the whistle instead. Glover gathered up as many boxes as he could carry, stuffed them with evidence of Pearlman's shady dealings, and put on his best poker face for the office crew. "I didn't want to tell them it's a fraud and scam and anyone associated with it is going to jail," he said. "I was trying to pretend I wasn't cognizant of what I was staring at, operating as though I was going to help them out." He told Fischetti and Hart that he needed a week to come up with a plan of action. And with his heart pounding, he made a break for the door. "I was wondering, *Are these people going to jump me on the way out of the office?*" Beefy guards stood between him and the door. They held it open for him. "I ended up taking along a box of documents that could indict virtually everyone there."

That weekend he tried to get ahold of Amodeo but couldn't. On Monday he got another person in Amodeo's office on the phone and told her what he'd discovered, and she told him she'd pass it on to the state attorney's office. But that wasn't good enough for Glover. He called the state's fraud hotline himself and got a call back from authorities who dutifully took his evidence and finally took action—twelve years after suspicious investors and associates first filed complaints about Lou, Trans Con, and EISA, time in which Lou had bilked banks and investors out of a combined $500 million.

But Pearlman wasn't done. He did one last deal, on the veranda of his Orlando mansion. Protected by a cordon of guards armed with Uzi submachine guns, he agreed to sell off what was perhaps the only legitimate asset he had left, the city-block-size, honky-tonk Trans Con headquarters—along with its restaurants, massive bars and ballrooms, and even the celebrity-themed Club Paris nightclub space decorated in soft pink and adorned with pictures and monuments to new fame icon Paris Hilton—to Orlando developer Cameron Kuhn for $34 million. Pearlman even asked Kuhn if he'd send four million directly to his German account—he owed some people some cash there, he said. (Kuhn did not.) On February 1, the Office of Financial Regulation filed a civil suit against Pearlman detailing what it said was fifteen years' worth of fraud in hawking the Employee Investment Savings Accounts. The suit detailed the bogus claims Lou made about the plan being FDIC, AIG, and Lloyd's of London insured. It echoed what Glover had seen and what Lou's associates and investors had begun to figure out, that his entire empire was built on lies.

Watching it all come down on their heads, Lou's executives couldn't help but grab leftovers. They'd unwittingly provided Glover and, subsequently, state and federal investigators with all they needed to nail their boss and reveal the full Ponzi scheme, but in many ways they remained typically oblivious—or perhaps they just panicked. The documents were shredded and boxes were carted off. The last chunk of Trans Con cash was divvied up, too, about $5 million, that Lou moved into his personal account in his final days in the states. An EISA marketing manager, for one, moved $1.5 million into his personal bank account. And in what amounted to a smash-and-grab, scrambling, greedy Trans Con employees carted off plasma TVs, crystal vases, surround-sound setups, a conference room table and chairs, and more, worth about $20,000. When receiver Jerry McHale stepped in, he traced several of the hard goods to boat-custodian-turned–Trans Con–lawyer Mike Ferderigos. McHale was assigned as a sort of financial cop initially tasked with taking control of and liquidating Pearlman's assets. His first order of business was freezing Trans Con in its tracks. "When I went into the accounting offices, the areas south of Lou's offices, there were personal effects left lying around . . . it was clear that they left in a hurry," McHale said. Garbage had started to pile up because Trans Con quit paying its collection bill. "The restaurant below the offices complained that they hadn't had any room for trash because of all the shredded documents . . . There was scrambling at the last moments, but by that time we were down to the carcass."

Following the Office of Financial Regulation's February 1 suit, a judge had ordered a raid on Pearlman's offices and home. On February 15, the FBI and other federal officials stormed in. They backed a Budget rental truck up to the Trans Con headquarters and began loading it with boxes of leftover documents. At Lou's Windermere home, more documents were loaded into vans. On February 20, 2007, the Alamo of Pearlman's Ponzi, the opulent Trans Con headquarters, known to banks as FF Station, entered into voluntary bankruptcy. On March 1, Pearlman personally was put into involuntary bankruptcy.

The only thing missing in the equation was Lou. He was gone. The last Trans Con employee to see him was his executive assistant Mandy Newland. She met him in Dublin, Ireland—Lou had flown from Orlando International—where he was checking out a potential new boy band called Streetwize. He told Newland he was going to go on to Germany and that he'd be gone for a while, adding, "Don't worry, I'm going to take care of everything. I'll be calling you every day." Newland added, "That's when I got very concerned." He left on a flight with Patrick King, one of the boys from Natural who had been living at his house. "That was it," Newland said. "I never saw him again. I was in touch with him, but I was very angry with him. I wanted to know, do I have a job?"

From his undisclosed location in Europe, Lou was free of the day-to-day hassle of investor and bank calls, state investigators, bad publicity, and hounding reporters. But he seemed to miss the spotlight that bathed him back in the States. He mailed a letter from Germany to the *Orlando Sentinel*, promising that everything would be all right, that his investors would be made whole. Lou was on the lam, but that's not how he spun it. He was touting himself as a still-bankable pop music mogul. He bragged about his recent successes with US5, with whom he'd picked up a Goldene Kamera Pop International Band award in Germany. During the awards ceremony, the camera cut from the band to an exiled but tuxedoed Pearlman, who, caught unawares, looked haggard, a frown and a dazed look plastered across his swollen, sullen mug. The US5 boys looked like a supergroup cloned from the members of Backstreet Boys and *NSYNC, a caricature, with spikier, blonder hair; sharper, more confident dance moves; and better-fitting suits. Their long acceptance speech was mostly in German, except the part where they name-dropped Lou and said in English, "We love you, baby." "I'm an optimist," Lou wrote to the *Sentinel*. "Rebuilding and making things better is what I do." The letter came February 2, the same day McHale first walked into Pearlman's office to find it picked apart and in shambles.

Pearlman's home and offices remained mostly dark until June 12, when fans, friends, and enemies of him and his bands descended on his Trans Continental headquarters and began furiously bidding in a bankruptcy auction on everything from parts to his Gulfstream jet and his gold nameplate on his desk to the desk itself, boy band gold plaques and records that went for up to $4,500, and even motorized draperies from Big

Papa's office. Grown men hoisted *NSYNC gold records above their heads like trophies. Others quietly slipped off with bargain office supplies. Clay Townsend, the lawyer for former Pearlman talent scout Jeanne "Tanzy" Williams and the man who sued Pearlman repeatedly on behalf of former Backstreet Boy Phoenix Stone and late-era Pearlman artist Aaron Carter, just barely lost out on the bidding for Lou's desk but settled for buying his ski boat for $11,000. "I need one this summer for my three sons," he told the *Orlando Sentinel*. All told, the auction raised about $200,000, a drop in the bucket of money Lou had stolen and used to pay his employees, his businesses, and himself.

A fire sale of Pearlman's household goods followed, and that's where the real picture of Pearlman's overgrown teenager tastes emerged. There was plenty of furniture and fine china, but most of the notable knickknacks could have come from a fifteen-year-old boy's dream house: spacey artwork (including the painting called *Lavender Nebula* that Gross owned, too); life-sized R2D2, Anakin Skywalker, and frozen Han Solo figures; vintage microphones; toy jets; a fake million-dollar bill; a tangle of backstage passes; Disney kitsch; and more. There were also handguns, an assault rifle, and an Uzi machine gun. For the most discriminating, high-end shopper, there was a golf cart version of a Cadillac Escalade. Meanwhile, Soneet Kapila, the extremely aggressive bankruptcy trustee appointed by the state to squeeze every penny possible out of Lou's assets, went after everything from Pearlman's stake in the Orlando Predators arena football team to the Italian-style mansion situated at one of Orlando's most coveted lakefront addresses. (He gave up trying to sell the house— as well as other upside-down Pearlman properties—in March 2008 after an auction failed to produce a bid higher than $3.75 million; for his primary home alone, Lou owed $5.8 million to the Bank of America, including back taxes.) His Rolls had long since been repossessed, and the Orange County sheriff's department had seized his Gulfstream II private jet and turned it over to one of the banks Lou owed.

When all was said and done, the former nerve center of the boy band boom and headquarters for one of the largest financial frauds in history appeared frozen in a particularly turbulent moment in time when people were being laid off, the bills for operating costs were stacking up, and everyone was scrambling to shred or steal anything of value. Lou's signature Pearl steakhouse, the on-site fine-dining restaurant where it's said Pearlman routinely ordered three-pound lobsters as appetizers, was dark and barren. In the cavernous mall outside of the Trans Con executive offices, real restored vintage bi- and tri-wing World War I planes emblazoned with the Trans Con logo hung from the building's ceiling, props originally hoisted as part of the complex's kitschy tourist trap past. Inside, the place was like a freakish amalgam of a busted boiler room operation and the bedroom of a teenage girl, littered with shredded documents, canceled checks, old office supplies, *Bop* magazines, half-empty jelly containers, and a pair of 4XL sweat shorts on the floor. A bunch of Queen Elizabeth II cruise ship literature was stacked in the corner (Lou had a trip planned, it turns out). The walls were festooned with posters of his last active boy band, US5, which was still selling records in Germany; former New Kids on the Block frontboy Jordan Knight; and other recording artists, along with a slightly askew Chippendales calendar. Among the leftovers in Lou's nerve center was a youth soccer practice schedule with games highlighted in hot pink.

Lou, meanwhile, was still hustling. He had fake seals made and fake documents drawn up to try to make German Savings Bank—the repository of his imaginary assets—look real. He e-mailed a few of his former associates back home instructing them on what they could do stateside to make German Savings look legit, too. He paired up with Mitchell Louis van Balen, the twenty-two-year-old man supposedly behind the bogus German Savings Bank, and started working on a new scheme, an online poker training school called Poker Kindergarten. Van Balen had possibly even mortgaged his house to front the startup money. Far from sharing the intricacies of Texas Hold 'Em with online card sharks, Lou launched a furious salvo of attempts to get his hands on what little assets might remain of Trans Con, committing bankruptcy fraud along the way. On March 6, 2007, a desperate Pearlman filed a claim against his own company in the name of German Savings Bank and van Balen in the amount of $5,200,853, based on a $5 million promissory note van Balen had supposedly given Lou. There was no loan. There was no German Savings. Just Lou trying to get his hands on the cash. He also sold a stake that one of his companies, Louis J. Pearlman Enterprises LLC, had in Trans Con Mobile LLC, a seemingly legitimate cell phone company, for $1 million. In May, he had the buyer wire $250,000 to Germany, just as he'd tried to have his Church Street Station buyer, Cameron Kuhn, do with $4 million. Receiver McHale had been tipped about the money transfer, though. He moved quickly, adding Louis J. Pearlman Enterprises to the list of his companies in bankruptcy, freezing the wire transfer the next day in April and seizing the $250,000. In a stroke of unparalleled audacity, Pearlman filed *another* fraudulent bankruptcy claim, stating that German Savings owned 100 percent of Louis J. Pearlman Enterprises and shouldn't be included in the bankruptcy. As proof, he filed fake notarized, backdated documents with the bankruptcy court—all from overseas. And still, authorities couldn't put a finger on the whereabouts of the three-hundred-pound man with a penchant for cornflower-blue *everything*.

Pearlman traveled from Germany to Madrid, Spain, then to Panama, where he looked into citizenship. From there, he swung through Singapore and tried to do a quick million-dollar deal in Hong Kong. He spent the majority of his days on the lam in Bali, Indonesia. Thorsten Iborg, a German tourist, was walking on the beach in front of the Westin Resort Nusa Dua in Bali, when he spotted the gargantuan Pearlman sunning. He recognized him as the American behind the boy bands that had been such a rage in Germany. Later he saw Pearlman attending a cocktail party and watching YouTube music videos in the hotel's Internet café. "He looked a little bit sad and bored. I think he wanted to be caught," Iborg said. He sent an e-mail about his discovery to *St. Petersburg Times* reporter Helen Huntley with the subject line "We've seen Mr. Pearlman." "At the moment we are in the hollaydays [sic] in SE-Asia," wrote Iborg, a thirty-two-year-old computer programmer. "In our hotel there is a guy, who's locking [sic] like Mr. Pearlman . . . Perhaps this information is useful to investigators." Iborg, who, admittedly, was hoping for cash in exchange for his Lou spotting, eventually snapped a picture of Lou pawing at a pancake and waffle breakfast. Then, with his permission, Huntley passed the tip on to the FBI. Iborg e-mailed with FBI special agent Scott Skinner, who, when he learned that Iborg might have a line on Pearlman, tried to feign disinterest, presumably to guard against tipping off someone who could have been a Pearlman associate in disguise. "Mr. Thorsten Iborg, thank you for your reply," Skinner wrote in mid-June. "As of the current date, we do not have an existing arrest warrant for Mr. Pearlman . . . I am sorry to say that we have no extradition treaty with Indonesia, so he is free to travel within Indonesia. In any event, please let me know if you see him again as we would like to at least talk to him to get his side of the story." In reality, the FBI moved quickly, going to work with the Indonesian National Police–Bali, who agreed to expel Pearlman as an "undesirable visitor." They caught up with Pearlman hours after Iborg snapped the photo, and Pearlman agreed to fly to Guam, where he was indicted on bank and wire fraud charges on June 14. He was dressed in a cornflower-blue T-shirt and carrying a credit card and several thousand dollars' worth of local currency. He had been registered at the Westin under the name "A. Incognito Johnson."

## CHAPTER 12

# FACING THE MUSIC

> My idea of hell would be to know that I'd have to face elderly aunts or uncles who've had to go on welfare because they believed in me and I let them down. I couldn't live with that. I'd move to a remote desert island rather than face that.
>
> —Lou Pearlman, *Bands, Brands, and Billions: My Top Ten Rules for Making Any Business Go Platinum*

Six months before he was nabbed, Lou Pearlman sprawled out with his frequent boy guests in a six-bedroom, eleven-and-a-half-bathroom mansion on a spring-fed lake. His neighbor, basketball megastar Shaquille O'Neal, let some of his boys use his home recording studio. Another, Tiger Woods, could have knocked on Lou's back door with a well-placed drive. By mid-July, Lou had settled into a sixteen-by-eight-foot cell in Orlando's Orange County Jail. Given his propensity for extended European and Asian tours, a judge deemed him a "serious flight risk" and denied him the opportunity for bail. His jailers separated him from the general population because of his fame and fears that someone would try to take him hostage or extort him, but Lou had convinced a judge he was so strapped for cash that he needed a public defender. Fletcher Peacock, a tall, buzz-cut drill-sergeant-looking lawyer straight out of central casting, tackled the case with vigor, meeting regularly with Pearlman. Toward the end, Peacock resigned from the public defender's office to go into private practice, but he saw Lou's case through. In the Orange County Jail, inmate no. 07031368 got only got a couple hours a day to mingle with his fellow inmates, exercise, or use the phone—if jail held any punishment for Pearlman, that was it. He got three visits a week, conducted via videoconference. Most weeks, Tammie took up all three and often brought along her eighteen-year-old son Michael—he was friends with Lou, too.

A month in, the reality of his surroundings had not yet permeated his fantastic bubble of denial. Clad in a jumpsuit that was almost the color of his old Rolls, he hobbled into the frame of the videoconference center, squinted at the screen, and issued a blanket refusal to talk about anything having to do with the charges against him. "I'd love to come out about a lot of things," he said. "I think there are things missing from the story. Nobody's heard my side, which is unfortunate, but my lawyer has advised against talking about anything having to do with the case." In fact, *his* side was what he sold to hundreds of investors, banks, friends, and family for years. Given the opportunity, though, he happily hopped on one last chance to sell his myth.

He was feeling great, he said, even shedding pounds by doing one to two hundred sit-ups a day, though no jail officials could recall ever *seeing* him in the act. "I've definitely been dieting," Lou said. "I'm on a low-fat diet, low sugar. It's only been a few weeks. In another couple of weeks I might be able to weigh myself, figure out where I am. But I feel a lot healthier. My pants feel looser." Months later, his commissary purchase records would reveal that Lou, a diabetic, was supplementing his three daily "hots" with creamy peanut butter; peanut butter and vanilla wafers; iced honey buns and cinnamon rolls; "Butterscotch Buttons"; banana marshmallow pie; root beer; Tang; something called Whole Shebang; "bold & zesty" Chex Mix; "ripple potato chips"; cheddar popcorn; "Sharp Cheddar Cheese Squeeze"; onion dip; Cheese Nips; pickles; beef salami; "fresh catch tuna"; swiss rolls; Oreos; M&Ms; Atomic Fireballs; "dunking sticks"; Hershey Take 5 (the name of one of his last bands), Butterfinger, Three Musketeers, and Almond Joy candy bars; bear claws and blueberry, strawberry, and "chocolate thunder" donuts; and more. He also bought Tums.

"I'm planning on this chapter ending relatively soon," Lou said on July 16, 2007. He talked about his blimp company, "the first to rival Goodyear," and reminisced about old successes and accolades. "I got the World Award from Mikhail Gorbachev," he said, noting proudly that other recipients included Steven Spielberg, Morgan Freeman, and Michael

Jackson. "I got that two years ago at the Hofberg Palace in Vienna."

He clearly fancied himself a king in exile, and he flashed the quality that lured so many investors and friends, the warm but awkward half smile, his pitifully pudgy cheeks, and his rock-solid conviction that no amount of wrongdoing—not even making $500 million disappear—could overshadow his contribution to music and the millions of teenyboppers who swooned to the tunes of the bands he introduced. "I've had a good past," he said. "We did the first-ever reality show and had a big impact with that, *Making the Band*. We've had a lot of great things. I've helped a lot of people. We've brought the world a lot of young talent. I've just had a great, great time. I've just enjoyed all of the people throughout my career. We were the pioneers of a new regime."

Lists—of accomplishments and things to accomplish— were always Lou's bailiwick. He always had a little calendar in his wallet pocket and relied on it for everything. Once behind bars, he must have felt naked without it, and he wasn't one to let a little thing like a looming life sentence cramp his style. After a few months of visiting several times a week, keeping funds up in his commissary accounts, passing along news from the outside, and making phone calls on Lou's behalf, his girlfriend, Tammie, noticed he usually hobbled into the frame of the video screen carrying stacks of paper. One day, she realized he'd hand-drawn calendars and had continued scrawling down to-do lists. "He has papers and papers where that's all he's doing is drawing calendars and making lists of things to do," Tammie said. The first thing he'd do when she'd visit was grill her on the things he had asked her to do since her last visit. He asked for times, dates, plans, calls she made on his behalf, updates on commissary money. "All the while he is going down these things to do, and I can see him putting a star by them or whatever he does." He also started telling friends that he'd call, or the few that visited, about an idea for a new television show he'd been inspired to create from his jail experience. Called *Second Chances*, it would feature the losers from *American Idol, America's Next Top Model,* and other such competitive shows. It would be hosted by celebrities who had their own legal run-ins or career crashes, "Paris Hilton or Mel Gibson or Kelsey Grammer . . . everybody who's been to jail," he said. Lou, with his own golden touch, would engineer their comeback. Also, he said, he still kept tabs on his successful pop acts, even with just an hour a day or less for phone calls. "A typical day includes just handling all facets of the business. You know, it's always going from one act to another, handling all aspects of that, focusing on one act then another then another . . . I have less of that to focus on now," Pearlman joked. "Today I'm focusing on something a little different. I'm making notes for my lawyer, getting the facts together for him." Then he paused and kind of looked around for a second and added, "It's not the Four Seasons here."

As Lou began his incarceration, FBI and U.S. attorney's investigators were hard at work untangling his businesses. By the accounting of Paul Glover—who had the most intimate, recent knowledge of Lou's companies but, unlike government investigators, wasn't banned from commenting—Lou was juggling eighty-four businesses, a number that sounded about right to court-appointed receiver Jerry McHale. The Florida Department of State's Division of Corporations had on file about eighty corporate names with Pearlman as an officer or registered agent. Trans Continental Entertainment, Travel, Productions, and Merchandising and Leasing; restaurants; a gym; his Rocks jewelry store and its spin-offs, Rocks Timepieces and Rocks Management; Fashion Rock and its spin-off Talent Rock; companies for each of his bands (US5, Backstreet Boys, O-Town, LFO); and individual corporations named after Lou—Louis J. Pearlman Enterprises, LJP Productions, LP Productions, Pearl Pictures; and various registrations that were never more than ideas. A lot of the companies were "part and parcel" to his bands, Lou said. "You have to have a lot of different businesses to put together a tour so the artists themselves aren't liable for anything." Not even their jewelry.

Even after a month-long ordeal in which he was found to be scrambling for cash, trying to perpetuate his fraud, and setting up a new one, Lou still spun the idea that he was never on the lam but was actually just on an extended overseas business trip working with US5 and scouting for new acts. "When I'm traveling with my artists, it's always a pleasure," he said. "I've been working with US5 most recently. I'm guiding their careers. It's tough. There's a lot involved. You have to give the right guidance, get the right vocal coaches. Plus, it's a cycle. Boy bands always change their course . . . US5 is doing well. I'm proud of all of my artists. And there will be more artists we'll develop in the future as well. I think the time is right for it again. I mean, the Spice Girls just got back together. The Backstreet Boys are about to get going again. They had a band member quit, but they're about to get started again . . . We are still entitled to a share of the revenues."

No, he wasn't. But the idea seemed to excite him, and he followed it deep into the recesses of his fantasy world. "I mean, look at Justin's career—it's taking off," he said, glossing over the fact that he hadn't had a thing to do with Timberlake since he and his band split from Trans Con and Lou in 1999. "I think Britney will get back on the bandwagon, too . . . My thing—and I've said it before—is that I'll know the exact moment when boy bands are over, and that'll be when God stops making little girls."

As he sat charged with crimes that carried a combined maximum sentence of 130 years, as banks and bilked investors came forward to claim losses in the millions, as the FBI pieced together his Ponzi scheme, Lou said, "I'm proud of everything I've done to date . . . This is just one of those hurdles in life that you have to get past. There are a lot of nice young fans out there who will always love what I've done.

"I've brought a lot of joy to the world."

For the next seven months, Lou whiled away his time by working up notes for investigators and his attorneys. He phoned old friends, taking stock of who might still be on his side. He talked to them about generalities but rarely specifics. He met with and talked to Dave Hedrick, a mysterious forty-six-year-old audio-video specialist from Apopka, Florida, who never met Lou before he started buying up his possessions at the various auctions. He spent $6,000 on clothes alone and then just gave them back to Lou after meeting him via video-conference. He promised to return other pictures and effects, and he even tried briefly to piece together a bid for Lou's mansion when it went on the block. In the end, he was a shining example of the sway Lou had over certain personalities. In a series of calls made shortly after he was jailed in the summer of 2007, Pearlman also talked to Alan Gross about having a barbecue after his bond came through. He said he felt "used" by Theodor Wullenkemper. "He always told me he'd be there for me, but where is he now?" he asked. "I really trusted him a lot." At one point, Gross asked Pearlman what he'd say to these people who are saying he stole millions of their EISA money. Lou said, "I'd tell them the truth. I'd tell them the truth that I feel very bad. I wish I would have met the majority of them, I never did. Some of them I spoke with on the phone after they invested. Of course with those people and everybody involved, I would do my damnedest to make sure they're made whole. I'm not stopping 'til that's done. And I'm going to cooperate one hundred percent as I did . . . Some people who are involved will be coming to light."

He continued, "The plan to plot to hurt people with their life savings and all that, come on. No way. Not in a million years. I'd never hurt my family, my friends, okay? Nobody. I would never do that. And I feel sorry for them and I'm going to make them restitute [*sic*]. It's a crazy, crazy world we live in . . . I own up to the stuff that I was president of the company, that everything that happened was under my watch. And I have to own up to that, unfortunately. I have to own up to the fact that everything got out of hand. But I never sat down to plot to hurt anybody."

He ended by telling Gross, "You're one of the few people who know the facts." Over and over again, Gross said the same thing about his former childhood friend: "Lou's whole life is all about deception."

For the next couple of months, Lou tried to feed investigators tidbits about where his missing money might be. Bits and pieces of his last-ditch wrangling leaked out, and he seemed desperate to make one more power move, the kind that would set him free—or at least allow him to keep wheeling and dealing. On the outside, his former investors and colleagues speculated about hidden money. Lou always needed to be needed, and the rumors about a hidden savings that only he could help find perpetuated his myth. "I believe he's stashed somewhere between one hundred fifty and two hundred million dollars," said J. Cheney Mason, Pearlman's lawyer in numerous lawsuits, including those filed by Backstreet Boys and *NSYNC. Lou disappeared owing him $15.5 million in legal fees. "If he had any concept of reality at all, he'd be directing the bankruptcy court that money so he could make restitution," Mason said, adding, however, that he wouldn't know where to begin to look himself. "If I knew, I'd be over there with my shovel getting it myself!" But Lou had already been presented that opportunity by Paul Glover and his boss Frank Amodeo. He chose instead to flee. "It's obviously hidden somewhere," said Soneet Kapila, the court-appointed trustee who, at the federal level, took over the liquidating of assets from receiver Jerry McHale. "It's too early to say where."

The more time passed, however, the more obvious it became that there was no pot of gold buried in the backyard of Lou's mansion.

A confidant like no other, Tammie knew Lou as a man who relied upon many of his longtime employees so much that even when a couple of them stole money from him—and he busted them—he kept them on board. Lou had ceded much of his operation to his triumvirate of insiders, she said—Alan Siegel, Greg McDonald, and Bob Fischetti. But when he got locked up, she was the one to whom he confessed the *real* story, she said, that it was his executives who perpetrated the schemes. She even helped him work on a deal from jail worth "a couple million dollars" with a mysterious German who wouldn't ever tell her his name (it was Mitchell Louis van Balen) for the online gambling school Poker Kindergarten. (For a while, a website came up at pokerkindergarten.net, and there was a basic framework of a business online, but by March 2008, the site had been replaced by an error page.) Van Balen called Tammie to get messages to Lou, and as the weeks passed he became more and more desperate, especially when the German told her he was being questioned by authorities in relation to Lou's case.

Then in early October 2007, Lou shared with Hilton the darkest secret he could possibly share, the thing that would exonerate him and reunite them, she said—reunite them at her house, of course, since his home was on the block. "It's like double-oh seven, I know," she said. "It sounds like something out of James Bond." When it came out, it wouldn't just change perceptions about Lou, it would completely recast the allegations against him: "The charges against Lou are going to be dropped." They had the wrong guy, she said, without a stitch of sarcasm: "When they reveal who the real people behind this are, it's going to set this town on fire." These weren't just industry insiders. These were prominent people that most pop music fans and certainly any Orlandoan would know. Orlando mayor Buddy Dyer was wrapped up in it, she said. The only holdup was that the prosecutors were trying to find some way to make some small charge stick so that they could save face and Lou couldn't turn around and sue them for false imprisonment, she said.

Referring to Lou's get-out-of-jail card, Tammie said, "Only four people know about this . . . Three of them are dead"—Frankie Vazquez, who'd climbed inside his Porsche, lowered his garage door, and asphyxiated himself; Joseph Chow, who'd died of cancer; and Eric Emanuel, the fat-cat investor who'd died in a car crash. Conveniently, she was the fourth. Back when Orlando developer Bob Snow built Church Street Station—the former ragtime-themed tourist attraction that became the headquarters of Trans Con everything, the massive monument to Lou's ultimate con in the heart of Orlando—Snow installed a system that tracked every keystroke of every computer in all of Church Street Station all the time. That machine was located in Tampa, Tammie said. Snow built it—in the 1970s—so that only he could access it, with his thumbprint. What a man in the garter-belt-and-pantaloon business needed with cloak-and-dagger spy gear was unclear, but when he sold Lou Church Street Station, Tammie said, he changed the codes so that Lou's thumbprint activated the system. In that system was every piece of evidence the FBI would need to track down the *real* culprits in the massive fraud.

Her unsubstantiated fantasies—Lou's theories—evolved

over the weeks: Everyone was on the take, from the governor of Florida and the mayor of Orlando to the bankruptcy trustee. The missing millions were supposedly stolen and divvied up by former crooked Pearlman associates, a charge that had a kernel of truth to it, but Tammie, clearly channeling Lou, fingered former Trans Con bigwig Greg McDonald and former ex-con Options Talent partner Alec Defrawi. She spun the tale that, along with Bob Fischetti, they were the triumvirate that really controlled the operation. They were involved with the scheme to hide the money in Dubai. Some people involved had ties to al Qaeda, and the Patriot Act came into play—Lou, remember, had bogusly claimed the Department of Homeland Security held up a money transfer from German Savings when he was scrambling to stall banks and investigators. Tammie could never give specific details. It was clear that Lou was using her to disseminate wild conspiracy theories and dilute the fact that he'd spent most or all of the money that he solicited from investors. Along the way, he'd convinced her that investigators *needed* him as an ally to satisfy the demands of 1,800 clamoring investors. If they were lucky, Lou would even hold off suing them once he was cleared of all the charges. He was the only one who could track the trail of tens of millions, the only one with the thumbprint that would unlock the secret system in Tampa—in her words, "Lou has a *clone computer.*"

By the end of October 2007, she was giddy with anticipation. "Last week was a huge week," she said. "Nobody can know this . . . It's so cool." The authorities had sneaked Lou out of the jail and whisked him over to the courthouse. They drove him into an underground garage and closed the garage door before they let him get out; they didn't want the media catching wind of any of this. Lou was taken to a private conference room where representatives from the FDIC, the IRS, and the state and federal prosecutors' offices were present. They wanted to talk to him about what he knew. Tammie said she, unfortunately, wasn't allowed to attend, "but they did bring him McDonald's food for lunch. He was so excited. He calls me up, he's like, 'Babe, I got a Big Mac and Chicken Mc-Nuggets and French fries and a Diet Coke. I laughed, and they laughed at me and didn't care, and I told them this was better than any steak I could ever have!' "

"I laughed all day long," Tammie said. "I'm sure that Mc-Donald's was gone in a few seconds.

"More or less, they apologized to him for the whole situation. They were like, 'Look, we had to start someplace, and you had guilt written all over you, but we've had the opportunity to see what you've said and we can tell you're telling the truth.' " The plan was to get a sidebar meeting with the judge and do some things off the record that would eventually lead to a new bail hearing: "That way the judge is on the same page as everyone else." Lou would get to come home after a couple more meetings, and there would be new rounds of arrests.

"They told Lou, 'Look, we're the government, we do everything slow, especially when we thought you were guilty,'" Tammie said. They were also concerned that a hit would be taken out on him. Other than the inevitable delays involved in everyone trying to avoid looking bad for arresting the wrong guy, Tammie said, "It's going really, really well."

Of course, no secret meeting had ever happened. Lou was never secretly whisked away from the jail and into the courthouse. There was certainly no apology or admission that they had the wrong guy. There were no more rounds of arrests in his case. And there definitely was no McDonald's.

In late November Tammie was deposed by federal prosecutors. It was quick and painless, she said, and seemed like a formality. She didn't reveal anything top secret, and they didn't ask about the clone computer. Then in December, something about her changed. Tammie showed signs of losing faith. "I'm very angry with him this week. I have been for two weeks," she said on January 4. "He just pulled a Lou." At Christmastime, he had told other inmates that Tammie would buy their wives Christmas presents. Then he gave them her cell phone number. When one inmate called, he commiserated with Tammie about the unreliable mail system in the jail and told her he'd heard that she'd been trying unsuccessfully to get Lou a picture of his motorcycle, the one that looked so much like this inmate's own bike that Lou had asked him earnestly if he had stolen it from him. "And I'm going, *That fat fucker had never been on a motorcycle in his life!"* Tammie said, laughing. "I know why he does it. He does it because he doesn't want to be the one to say no. He wants me to say no, but in the meantime they've got my phone number. They think I'm going to be sending them money and gifts, which makes it look like I may have all of [Lou's] money . . . He's just put me in a couple of positions like that." Meanwhile, Lou continued to tell her he was working with the FBI to lead them to the assets and real culprits in the fraud. She said she understood that he was going stir-crazy, but if he had all this information they valued, then surely he could arrange bail and they could come interview him on the outside. "It doesn't make any sense," she said.

As local news headlines about the progress of his case trickled out and nothing seemed to move ahead, Tammie said she was starting to doubt Lou's story. She took a deep breath. "I . . . don't know. Today I do, because he said something to me that was a complete lie . . . I will have that conversation with him face-to-face when I see him on Sunday. I don't like to do things like that over the phone, because I don't want him to sit there and get depressed and miserable and think, *Oh my God, I've lost her* . . . Today I doubt some of the things he's said. Tomorrow I'll be back on track."

But she didn't ever get fully back on track. By early 2008, she was still sympathetic to Lou, but she knew he was lying. "I don't think *he* knows what the truth is anymore . . . He's in

denial so much, it just escapes him. He has a story for everything." Later she added, "I feel bad for him, because I know
that all he wanted was for these people to be his family, and
he thought he had to be a crook to get that."

In February, talk started to circulate that there would be
a plea deal. Tammie, of course, got the news from Lou, and
he'd asked her to pass on a statement. He wanted it framed
this way:

> *As chairman of Trans Continental Airlines Inc. and Trans
> Continental Airlines Travel Services Inc., the only two
> Pearlman companies involved, Pearlman takes on full re-
> sponsibility for questionable corporate activities that had
> occurred. His entertainment entities and other companies
> are uninvolved in this plea agreement. Pearlman will help
> to fully restore victims up to $200 million. Others will be
> charged as part of a conspiracy scheme. Other than Trans
> Continental Airlines and Trans Continental Airlines Travel
> Services, this plea does not name any other Pearlman enti-
> ties such as Trans Continental Records, videos, manage-
> ment, publishing, entertainment, Making the Band and
> television shows, Talent Rock, Backstreet Boys, \*NSYNC,
> or any other artists. Although Pearlman didn't steal or hide
> $200 million, he will take full responsibility and ensure full
> restitution. Although a maximum penalty could be up to
> 25 years in prison, which would include four total counts*

> *of: money laundering, stock and investment funds fraud,*
> *bank fraud, and bankruptcy fraud, based on Pearlman's as-*
> *sistance and cooperation, a judge will decide his fate. Pearl-*
> *man is looking forward to resolving this matter as soon as*
> *possible.*

It was exactly the sort of thing Lou always wanted Tammie disseminating. Throughout the years, she was the first to know when something bad was about to come out—about Options, or Church Street, or whatever. Of course, she always got the *real* story from Lou himself. Subsequent media reports were exaggerated and wrong. This time, she laughed at the prospect that anyone would publish his statement as it was written in advance of a completed plea agreement— if there even was one.

On March 3, Lou's plea deal did go public. The documents that went along with it outlined twenty years' worth of theft to which Lou admitted, signing his initials on the bottom of each of the forty-seven pages in the document. It defined Trans Con Airlines and Travel Service as two bogus companies at the core of his entire empire. It revealed the EISA program to be fraudulent and it placed the blame for hundreds of millions of dollars bilked from banks and individual investors squarely on Lou and outlined how the money had gone to finance the full spread of his companies. It defined his entire operation as a Ponzi scheme and even spelled out how fraudulently gathered money had been funneled to more than a dozen different companies Pearlman had created. It did not offer a clue about where a penny of the missing millions had gone, but in exchange for a maximum twenty-five-year sentence, Lou agreed to plead guilty to money laundering and bank, bankruptcy, and investment fraud charges. He also committed to help the government find any assets that might be left, up to $200 million—he had to cooperate truthfully (a tall order) but he didn't actually have to come up with a cent. The "questionable corporate activities," as Pearlman called them in his statement, were defined in his plea agreement as straight-up theft.

On March 6, he appeared before a judge to declare his plea in person. Rather than use the words "I'm guilty," Pearlman said, "I'm accepting full responsibility." In a con that started more than twenty years ago, Tammie was one of the most unique victims. Lou never went after her for money, but the fact that he drew her into his world at all spoke to his mind-set: Whether it was boys or investors or a woman he could call his girlfriend, Lou would lure trusting targets to fill the holes in his businesses, his life, or his personality. She was the last person standing by his side, and she'd be the last one to walk away. Virtually everything Lou had been telling Tammie for the past year was directly contradicted by the plea agreement. "I've busted him in lie after lie," an exasperated Tammie said after the document hit the media. She believed Lou would never lead authorities to any more money. "He's gonna keep lying, I know he is," she said. "I'm going to go see him one time face-to-face—not just through the video—and have that conversation with him . . ." Then she rehearsed it: "Look, I'm sorry that you're here, and I'm sorry that you thought for years and years and years that I'm not smart enough to know that you lied. When you get transferred, I'm not putting any more money in your commissary account. I'm not coming to visit three times a week. I lost about twenty-five thousand dollars of my salary doing things for him," she said. "I'm not doing that anymore."

Lou begged her for one last face-to-face meeting. He swore he had something he needed to tell her. Tammie wasn't sure what to expect and speculated that it was more likely more lies than a map to a hidden $100 million. She was sure that she wanted nothing more than the truth. "If the FBI asked me, I would tell them point-blank . . . I don't know anything. And I can't believe that he really has any money or anything to turn over, but I also have a hard time believing that he's run this scheme for so long and he is such a smart businessman that he hasn't stashed some money." She said she was surprised the FBI hadn't asked her to wear a wire for that final conversation with Lou: "If they wanted me to do it, I'd do it."

Early in 2008, she met with a longtime Pearlman employee who worked closely with Lou and who Tammie considered trustworthy. The former associate had reached out to her, and the two met and commiserated about a turn of events for Lou that they both considered pathetic. It was then that the friend confessed something to Tammie. The friend had been in a hotel room with Lou and one of his young male associates. The band member was lying on the edge of the bed, and he sensed that Lou clearly wanted privacy. This friend never saw Lou actually do anything inappropriate with any of his boys. But it wasn't the first time Tammie heard insinuations that Lou secretly lusted for young men—they were the machinations of jealous Trans Con employees, she always figured—but this time the report was coming from someone Tammie trusted. In early 2008, she banned her eighteen-year-old son, Michael, from coming with her to visit Lou in jail. Her son had no aspirations in the music industry, but he was friendly with Lou through Tammie, who started realizing how frequently Lou asked about her son when they'd talk on the phone, and it gave her an ill feeling. "You can't go back to see Lou," she told her son. "I can't lose sleep at night thinking that Lou might be dreaming about you. Because I'd kill him."

A judge was assigned to Lou's sentencing, and a date was set for May 21, 2008. Defense attorney Peacock asked for more time to prepare what's called a presentencing memorandum, a document that essentially begged for mercy, and prosecutors agreed that they, too, would benefit from more time. But Judge G. Kendall Sharp refused the requests for delays, saying succinctly that nothing in the requests merited a delay in some bit of justice for fraud victims. They had already waited almost a year since his arrest for some kind of closure. They'd flooded Judge Sharp's office with letters begging him to give Pearlman the maximum sentence under the plea agreement or, if possible, even longer.

Alan Gross was among them. "I saw the early patterns of Mr. Pearlman's fraudulent business practices. I feel as though I was victimized by Lou Pearlman even though I did not participate in the EISA investment plan or any of the recent transgressions. Besides losing investment money, my career goals were thwarted by my association with Mr. Pearlman," Gross wrote. "I would like to give testimony to encourage Judge Sharp to mete out the harshest sentence that is possible because there are so many victims of Pearlman's Ponzi scheme who feel that they have no voice or representation and no chance of compensation."

Boyd H. Wheeler, an eighty-one-year-old disabled World War II veteran, wrote Sharp and detailed the predicament he found himself in after investing more than $102,000 with Pearlman, the entire contents of his savings account.

> My social security is now my only income. Due to my financial status I was unable to continue my health insurance through AARP. Approximately one year ago I was hospitalized for surgery at South Bay Hospital in Sun City Center, Florida. Therefore, I owe South Bay Hospital

*approximately $2,000 for which I am paying $50 a month to reduce the debt. I am seriously in need of dental work costing me approximately $8,000. The VA Hospital will not cover this cost. The trip to the VA Hospital is about 90 miles, round trip. I must rely on friends to drive me there. I do have a car but do not feel comfortable driving in traffic. My home needs repair . . . the list goes on . . . Mr. Pearlman has ruined my life. No amount of money would restore my dignity or peace . . . I believe $150,000 is what Mr. Pearlman owes me.*

Another victim, Lois Nevler, wrote to Sharp, "Lou stole from me my financial future by performing a scam which is unfathomable for me to imagine. I cannot reiterate enough how violated I feel . . . Please do not be lenient on him. He does not deserve it. He deserves to pay deeply for his numerous crimes."

She poured her heart out in the letter, describing to the judge why she felt especially hurt—she was his cousin.

*I was robbed and deceived by my own family member. What Lou has done to me is the ultimate betrayal.*

*Due to the fact that Lou was an only child, we were extremely close, like brother and sister. I was continuously told how much he loved me, like a sister. Obviously, that was one of the many tactics Lou used so that I would be-*

*lieve in him. In my wildest dreams I would never expect a family member to be so evil. I don't know how any human being can do such horrific things as to scam so many innocent and trusting people (mostly family and friends) out of their life savings. And to make things worse, not only did Lou lie verbally for so many years, but to give statements in writing that all the money was FDIC insured, showing documents regarding how great the company was doing, etc. Obviously we all know now that all the documents were fraudulent. This has been devastating to me. Lou Pearlman was robbing me of my savings, while smiling and saying everything was great, with full intent of what he was doing. Any human being that can intentionally do what he has done is a horrible, evil man, without a conscience and definitely without a soul.*

*Lou took away my spirit to trust. How can I ever trust again if my own family member intentionally deceived me so deeply . . .*

Five days before his scheduled sentencing, Lou made one last-ditch effort to perpetuate his con. It was as audacious as anything he'd pulled off thus far. He asked the court to grant him a delay in sentencing so he could continue to develop boy bands from jail. It was his best, quickest hope for coming up with the $200 million he'd pledged to return to investors, he said. "Transcontinental [*sic*] Records and Mr. Pearlman have demonstrated a legitimate track record of developing and managing hugely successful international pop music stars. These include The Backstreet Boys, In Sync [sic], and O-Town," Pearlman's attorney wrote in a motion to delay his sentencing, and continued:

> At the time of his arrest, Mr. Pearlman was in the process of developing another pop music band in Europe. That band, "US 5" [sic] has had several commercial "hits" in the European market and continues to be very popular and perform there on a regular basis. However, due to Mr. Pearlman's detention, he was unable to take "US 5" to the next step, i.e., promoting them in Asia and the United States. It is this "next step" that would potentially reap large profits for Transcontinental Records, and in turn, the victims.

He wanted a telephone and Internet connection two days a week, to start by June 1. By June 15, the court would have an idea if his efforts were successful. Essentially, he wanted everyone to invest in him all over again. Presumably, since he was claiming to be so broke he needed a public defender, these new efforts from jail would involve luring even more investors. He was asking the government to become a partner in a Ponzi scheme. Prosecutors strongly objected. "It is the position of the United States that the Defendant—who has pled guilty to conducting hundreds of millions of dollars of fraud by use of his businesses—should never be allowed to conduct business while in custody . . . The Defendant is in jail. He should be treated in the same manner as any other prisoner."

Judge Sharp quickly denied the request.

The sentencing was scheduled for nine A.M. on May 21, 2008, and elderly folks, some with canes and younger aides, began filing into the federal courthouse in downtown Orlando as soon as the doors opened. A few showed up as early as seven A.M. to guarantee they'd get a seat. On a slightly cooler-and-windier-than-average day, news cameras lingered by the entrance and correspondents caught as many of them as they could for sound bites. Some chose not to speak and said they were embarrassed to be named. They felt stupid for falling for Pearlman's Ponzi, despite the fact that they were, figuratively, in the company of about 1,800 others—financial institutions such as Bank of America among them. Inside, the wooden pewlike benches in the gallery filled up immediately. All told, there were about 125 inside the plainly adorned wood-and-white courtroom; more people filled the hallway just outside. Assistant U.S. Attorney Roger Handberg, a slim, angular, young-looking by-the-booker, turned to the right half of the gallery and instructed anyone wishing to speak to give his name—a mere five would be selected by Handberg and be allowed to speak. Then bailiffs instructed those who had scored seats in the first row to move and make way for the media. Already in a foul mood on a tense day, protests erupted, many from the young caretakers of the elderly victims. Bailiffs firmly but politely held their ground on the seating arrangement. Tammie Hilton was flanked by Dave Hedrick and Mandy Newland, Lou's former executive assistant. In a room full of scam victims, representatives from bilked banks, Joseph Chow's daughter Jennifer, and others, Tammie, Dave, and Mandy represented the three lone supporters of Lou, though even they had begun to doubt his intentions. Pearlman filed in wearing leg irons, handcuffs, and a navy jumpsuit with the words "5X Orange County Corrections" screened onto the back in white block letters. "He's lost a lot of weight," someone in the gallery quipped sarcastically. Tammie sniffed at that comment, and later she and Mandy cracked snide quips and scoffed at the groans and remarks of others who openly derided Pearlman. Lou looked back and smiled at Tammie before taking his seat at a wood table with his back to the audience.

As the sentencing got under way, Judge Sharp, a silver-and-gray-haired man with a gravelly voice, leaned back in his chair and started off the morning by calling Pearlman to the podium and questioning yet another one of his claims: Lou stated in the presentencing memo that he had a Ph.D. from Century University, which he'd earned online in 1983. "Our office did some checking," Sharp said, and they could not confirm Pearlman's degree. In fact, he said, "They weren't even issuing online diplomas in 1983."

"It wasn't online," Pearlman responded. "It was a correspondence course."

"It says 'online' in the report," Sharp answered.

The fact that the judge had, on Lou's day of reckoning, found another bogus claim caused a few scoffs and snorts in the audience. Attorney Peacock then began to outline his defense. When he claimed that Pearlman willingly gave himself up in Indonesia and went to Guam without attempting to flee, a female member of the audience, wailed, "No, *no!*" sounding as if she'd been wounded. "Quiet!" Judge Sharp barked, banging his gavel. Peacock's argument hinged on a few key claims: Pearlman wasn't on the lam while in Europe, he was doing business, and he freely agreed to go to Guam to face FBI questioning when authorities kicked him out of Indonesia, which saved the U.S. government time and money; he'd cooperated with the bankruptcy trustee to recover assets; throughout the course of his EISA program and Trans Con scam, he'd actually paid out $103 million, which wasn't being taken into account by those who said he stole $500 million or more; he was almost fifty-four, not a young man; and finally, twenty-five years was a long time to give someone for this sort of crime, based on comparable cases, Peacock said. He also argued that once Pearlman had established Trans Continental Airlines and Airship International, he was unable to leave it and its numerous investors behind. In a backward bit of logic, he blamed Pearlman's subsequent scams on his desire to do right by his earliest investors. "In Mr. Pearlman's mind," Peacock said, "he honestly thought he would pay everybody off."

Sharp asked Pearlman if he had anything to add. Lou read a statement:

> *I'm truly sorry, Your Honor, to all the people who have been hurt and victimized by my actions. Over the past nine months since my arrest I've come to realize the harm that has been done. I now want to do whatever I can to help resolve that harm. I'm working with the prosecutor and the bankruptcy trustee to recover whatever money I can for the victims, and hopefully in this way I can help repay the loss. Again, I'm truly sorry and I apologize for what has happened.*

With Judge Sharp's permission, Handberg called Waneta Reynolds, seventy-five, of St. Pete Beach, Florida, to the podium. Clad in a purple pantsuit and sandals and wearing her hair up in a banana clip, she walked slowly, measuring every step, right past Pearlman. She and her husband invested $3 million in EISA in June 2005 through a local financial firm. In January 2006, they invested $400,000 more. Her husband, Roger, eighty-seven, contacted the state about Pearlman's businesses, she said, and found them to be legit. He got a "glowing" Dun & Bradstreet report, too. "He was an astute businessman," she said. When he started trying to take out the money and found out it was all gone, "Tears ran down his face," Reynolds said. "He said, 'I've lost all of my self-confidence.' He died seven months later." Perfectly composed until that point, she broke into tears. "He thought that he couldn't provide for me . . . My husband's dead and I'm alone . . . I'm sorry for my tears."

Ted Granowski, a dignified elderly man in a navy blazer, told the judge how he questioned Pearlman's plan before investing and said Lou had him up to his office and showed him an insurance policy with a raised seal on it. Before he could finish, he, too, broke down into tears. The final sentence he could muster was: "He hurt my family."

Marie Weber, fifty-four, had one of the saddest stories. She and her husband, both of Naples, Florida, had invested $606,000. Her last EISA statement showed a balance of $864,000. The couple had earmarked the money to pay off their son's college education and what was owed on their retirement home in Georgia. It was gone. "This man," she had said shortly after Lou was first jailed, "I just would like to look him in the eye and ask him how in the world could he enjoy his life." Her voice quivered, but she held back tears. "I would just love to take him and put my hands around his neck and choke him until his eyeballs pop out." By the time she faced Pearlman in court, she wasn't able to hold her tears anymore. She wept openly and poured out her exasperation to the judge. Pearlman sat behind her, motionless. Her son, she said, has suffered emotional problems while worrying whether his parents would be able to hold it together. She herself had gone on antidepressants. Once on the path to retirement, she was now working two jobs—at a post office and a pet store—just to make ends meet. "But I will work until my dying day," she said through her tears. "The emotional part is going to go on for the rest of my life . . . You can give me all of the money in the world, but I'll never get this time back. He's absolutely sick," she said of Pearlman, and begged of Judge Sharp, "Please. Give us some justice here. We're living on the edge."

The audience erupted in claps and cheers. Judge Sharp let it go. Tammie and Mandy huffed.

Lou, his back to the audience, didn't seem to react at all.

Finally, James Taylor, a sturdy man who appeared to be in his fifties, wore a deep scowl as he walked by Pearlman and fixed him with an angry stare. Bailiffs leaned forward slightly in their seats. Taylor had built his own house and spent "thirty-eight years in the union," he told the judge. He identified himself as a "relatively small investor." "He deserves every minute he can get," Taylor told the judge, and intimated that he hoped Pearlman's fellow inmates doled out physical justice on him behind bars. "I'd like to see him come out of there wearing pink pants," he said. Bailiffs perked up again when Taylor left the podium, raised his hand to Lou, and wagged a pointed finger at him. It was clear he desired to do much worse.

When it was Handberg's turn, he took shots at the defense

arguments, reminding the judge that the very nature of a Ponzi scheme is that its architect pays back early investors to make the scam seem legitimate. He cited cases of his own in which defendants tried for similar scams were given even more than the twenty-five-year max Pearlman faced. He seemed confident that the judge was on his side. Sharp held a book several inches thick that he said was full of hundreds of letters from victims. He'd read them all, he said, adding:

> It's confusing to me why nobody noticed that there weren't any Transcontinental Airline planes flying around. All you need to do is go to JFK, O'Hare or something, where are the Trans Continental planes? Nobody saw any flying around. The banks, you used the same collateral on many, many different banks. Why didn't anybody check and see why it's the same collateral in different banks? It's a little confusing to me.

Several representatives from banks who had run Lou's financials, called in Dun & Bradstreet reports, audited financial statements, and even seen pictures of planes Lou supposedly owned grew wide-eyed in response to being reprimanded and looked at one another in disbelief.

Without much more fanfare, Sharp went through the counts one by one, eventually handing out the maximum sentence under the plea agreement. Lou got twenty-five years in prison. Under federal truth-in-sentencing laws, he'd have to serve at least 85 percent of the time, twenty-one and a quarter years. For a man of Lou's health it was possibly a life sentence. But Sharp wasn't done. He added:

> *The guidelines and the Federal Rules of Criminal Procedure have what's called a Rule 35 in which when you cooperate you can get reduction in sentence. And I'm going to give you an incentive because the mathematics work out fine. You've pled guilty to defrauding your investors [out of] 300 million dollars in this case. There may be more out there, but that's what you pled to, $300 million. And you've got 300 months in the Bureau of Prisons. So I'm going to give you an incentive. I'm going to give you the keys to your jail cell. I'm going to give you a one-month reduction of sentence for every million dollars that you get back into the pockets of these investors.*

All throughout the process, victims had pushed for the maximum sentence—life behind bars—for Lou if they could get it. Their biggest fear was that Pearlman would one day go free and dig up a barrel of money, then just go right back to the fat-cat lifestyle he was living for twenty years. Judge Sharp made turning over that money irresistible for Lou. But his demeanor and tone—which made his addendum feel like a just-in-case clause—indicated he wanted to give Lou's victims as much solace as he could, but he didn't hold out much hope for Lou getting out of prison anytime soon. He knew what most of the victims knew in the pits of their stomachs: There was no more money. Lou spent it all.

Tammie Hilton wasn't surprised by the ruling. She had spoken to Lou the night before via phone, she said, and he had expected the maximum sentence, too—or he told her that, anyway. She had fallen off the weekly visits and had drifted apart from him, and she took the opportunity to scold him. "You don't sit there and say that 'I want to run boy bands from jail' when you stole three hundred million dollars," she told him, adding, "I've told you, people were your friends to your face but behind your back they hated you. . . . The money got to you and made you greedy." All he could say in response was, "I know." She had always said she would follow him through a trial and sentencing, but if he was found guilty and went to jail for a long time the two of them were over. "This is where it has to stop," she said.

By then, their sham love affair was in tatters, anyway. Tammie was engaged to another man named Keith. She had dated him from 1996 to 1998, but he moved to Houston, Texas, for work. She had tried to convince him to stay. He told her he didn't want to leave her but couldn't pass up the job. She wasn't about to start a long-distance relationship, so they split up. After Tammie nursed Lou out of his deathbed, she had played along when he called her his girlfriend in public. He just seemed so pathetic, she said. She tried several times, starting as early as 2000, to tell him they were just friends, but he didn't want to hear it. "I always tried to be his friend," she said. Playing girlfriend was an easy gig, not that she was ever paid for it, not directly, anyway. It did involve hanging out, and that part was occasionally entertaining, though the glitzy parties felt like torture to her. She genuinely liked Lou. The only girlfriend-like thing she ever asked of him was to treat her nice on a date on her birthday, July 5—just the two of them. She may have even been trying to see if they could work as a couple. But the evening they had planned quickly turned into a group setting and people were chewing Lou's ear off about business during Tammie's supposed celebration. She was furious. "I told him, 'You were supposed to meet me alone one day out of the year.'"

He responded, "I told you my life is like a fireman's."

"I don't give a God-damn," Tammie said. "If anyone's life is like a fireman's it's mine, because I actually save lives, re-member? I saved yours!"

By the time Lou was locked up, Tammie had just turned thirty-seven. Lou would call fairly regularly and update her on what he was up to—"just doin' my thing," he'd say. "No you're not, you're in jail!" Tammie quipped. Lou was still call-ing her his girlfriend in the weeks heading into the trial. It was only his crazy life—and then legal problems—that had kept him from making an honest woman of her. "I never got married because of my crazy travel schedule," Lou said in July 2007. Tammie was still his closest confidant, but in reality, the two were little more than phone buddies by then.

Tammie got a call from Keith out of the blue in 2002. She recognized his radio-DJ-sounding voice immediately. He missed her. She missed him. They talked for ten hours. They started taking trips to see each other. She explained to him the situation with Lou and Keith was, inexplicably, a good sport. When they got engaged, she had to cut the cord with Lou; she and Keith planned to wed in late 2008. But on May 21, the day of Lou's sentencing, she hadn't told him the girlfriend act was over. She'd tell him about Keith during an upcoming visit or call, she said—or face-to-face if she got the chance. Any normal person would be devastated, but she didn't know for sure whether Lou was capable of processing emotional trauma at this point or his failure on so many levels. She suspected he would weave this one more bit of bad news into his deep fabric of denial. Hours after he was sentenced to spend what would likely be the rest of his life behind bars, Tammie said, "He doesn't realize that he doesn't have one person who he could call a friend . . . He is going to die alone, and he has no idea."

Lou's ability to pull off any significant swindles ended May 21, 2008. But his impact endured. In 2007, Backstreet Boys, minus Kevin Richardson, released *Unbreakable,* their first re-cording since 2005's flop *Never Gone.* The album's first single, a ballad called "Inconsolable," peaked at number 21 on the Adult Contemporary charts but only climbed to number 86 on the tell-tale *Billboard* Hot 100. The group did what they always have done: They went on tour in Europe. More U.S. dates were planned. New Kids on the Block, Lou's alleged inspiration for his entrée into the boy band world, reformed and toured with the next generation of teen titans, including boy band torchbearers the Jonas Brothers. Together they sold out some arenas. In 2008, almost all of the major labels started pushing new boy bands: Warner Bros. got behind a group called V Factory, and Capitol released a record by Backstreet-like quintet Varsity Fanclub—assembled by former Backstreet Boy Phoenix Stone and original Backstreet talent scout Sybil Hall. Johnny Wright was putting together a new version of Latin boy band Menudo, for which Backstreet founding member Howie Dorough had tried out unsuccessfully. *Rolling Stone* ran a story with the headline "In Dark Times, Labels Look to Boy Bands."

At last count, court records put Pearlman's victims at 1,400—though most involved put that number closer to 1,800. It varies when taking into account not only the names on checks written to Pearlman and his companies but the people from whom the money was stolen—husbands, wives, children, grandchildren. Prosecutors put the amount Lou disappeared at $424 million, though investors say that number is more like $500 million. He was only on the hook for $300 million to banks and individuals according to his plea agreement. As he and his victims parted ways on May 21, 2008, several of the bilked investors shrugged and said it was the best the judge could do; it didn't feel much like a victory. Several of them would go to work the next day when they should have been living out their retirement in leisure. Others said they just felt stupid. Jennifer Chow, who along with a group of investors had formed a committee and written a concise, factually impeccable letter to Judge Sharp before the sentencing, didn't want to talk about the ruling. She was reserved and hardly in a celebratory mode immediately afterward. Alan Gross, who planned right up until the last minute to come to the sentencing, decided not to fly down—his health was too fragile, he said. He had also been virtually smacked around by commenters on a *St. Petersburg Times* blog, Helen Huntley's blog, for what some perceived to be his grandstanding in the media. The trustee had given up on selling several of Lou's properties, including his home. He continued to hunt for assets, but he no longer believed there was a hidden pot of money out there. At last count, he'd recovered about $4 million. About $400,000 was spent in the recovery process, though. And trustee Kapila and his attorneys had not submitted a bill for their work.

The crowd milled around outside of the courtroom for about a half hour before dispersing. Outside, a man handed out CDs of his son's local band to victims and members of the press, telling anyone who would listen that Pearlman was going to help him produce and promote the band from jail. Local news outlets would take the bait and lead that evening's stories—and subsequent reports—with the news that Lou was planning to promote a new group from lockup. Several showed video of the confrontation outside of the courtroom between an investor and the man handing out discs. The victim, a woman who had darted out of the courtroom just after the sentencing, ran right into the man hawking his music and marketing scheme. "We don't want your stupid CDs," she snapped at him. "We want our money!"

On July 15th, 2008, Tammie Hilton got one final letter from Pearlman, sent just before he was transferred from Orange County, Florida, to an Atlanta, Georgia, federal prison. In it, he repeated his usual litany of updates and to-dos. Then he added this: "I'm so pissed that I've been forced into this position of becoming a martyr."

## ★ N O T E S

Most of the sourcing for this book is explained in the course of the narrative, but there were some instances when doing so would have interrupted the story itself. For that reason, the following notes are offered as backup. Also, covering a story in which everyone involved has an angle proved treacherous, so no amount of transparency is too much. What follows is my attempt to fill in some blanks with regard to the sources who proved most valuable. In general, some of Lou's story was told through the daily reporting of papers such as the *Orlando Sentinel* and the *St. Petersburg Times*. And, as I'd hoped from the inception of this book, much of the drama has played out in court, and thus in the public records. I've never appreciated Florida's Government in the Sunshine laws more.

### CHAPTERS 1–3

Accountant Paul Glover, the one who first reported the depth and breadth of Lou's fraud to the authorities, was one of the first people I talked to about this story. He was referred to me by a mutual friend, Cameron Kuhn, who bought Lou's Church Street Station complex just before Pearlman fled the country. I interviewed Glover for hours for my *Radar* magazine story on Pearlman, and then months later, I reinterviewed him and got into even more detail. His story was corroborated by my friend Cameron; neither he nor Paul had anything to gain from telling it. And when I did revisit old material with Paul, his anecdotes didn't change much at all over the course of the months. As was the case with much of this book, media accounts of the developments in the case—the FBI raids, the lawsuits, etc.—were used. I also visited Pearlman's offices and sifted through many of the items that are detailed in these chapters and in later chapters in the book. Other details were gathered from Glover, Kuhn, and press accounts by those who had also visited his offices during Lou's heyday. I also called upon memories of Church Street Station from my own youth. It was a mainstay of my teenage life, and I covered that entertainment corridor for the *Orlando Sentinel* as it started to come back to life in the early 2000s.

Many of the details of Lou's early life started with *Bands, Brands, and Billions: My Top Ten Rules for Making Any Business Go Platinum* (2002, McGraw Hill), Lou's self-help book/biography written with *Orlando Sentinel* reporter Wes Smith. It proved an invaluable source for this entire book—not necessarily as a fact-check but more as a map to a treasure of lies. (Smith declined to comment on his work with Lou on the book.) I reinterviewed many of the people mentioned in his book and those who knew Lou as a child: former kid newsies Danny and David Lebenstein, former Pearlman school chum and later associate Ray Seiden, and acquaintance Michelle Novak, who gave me a tour of Lou's old neighborhood.

Alan Gross is a pack rat, plain and simple. He admitted as much. He's collected mementos from every stage of his life.

And the first third or so of his life ran concurrent with Lou's, so many of the documents, letters, videos, audiotapes, and pictures that he's kept involve Lou and his businesses. He shared many of these documents, archives, and stories too numerous to count over the course of a half dozen visits to his home and hours of conversations. Gross also recorded several key phone conversations he had with Lou. He has aspirations of writing his own book or helping produce a documentary on Pearlman. Because he was interested in the story being told thoroughly, Gross often connected me with other sources— gratis. I did, however, agree to pay him a nominal fee for rights to his photography and images.

Details of Frank Vazquez's death were culled together from press accounts but mostly from the Orange County Sheriff's investigation summaries and the coroner's autopsy report, which I got through public records requests.

Don Guth spoke via phone in detail about the shoddy design of Lou's first blimp. Avi Nakash, one of three brothers who founded Jordache, scoffed when I mentioned to him Lou's claim in his book that everything worked out for Jordache, PR-wise. He promised to call me back for a longer discussion but didn't, and he didn't reply to repeated requests for interviews.

I interviewed Paul Lofaro at length about his time with Airship Enterprises. He had not read Pearlman's book but was surprised at the way Lou described Lofaro's efforts as his own. He refuted several of Pearlman's claims and verified a few others.

The members of Flyer were extremely gracious in sharing their memories of their band days with Lou as manager. I visited singer Willie Colon's home, and all of the band members were there. We listened to music and audio and video recordings of Lou in Colon's basement recording studio. His wife made brownies and delicious pigs in a blanket.

Harold Milner III eagerly spoke in an interview about how Lou used his father—and then his father's name—well after his death. He was extremely displeased, to say the least.

Press accounts and public records filled in many details about Lou's blimp and business attempts. The detailed plea agreement, which Lou signed in 2008, helped color some of the facts of Lou's early life as well.

## CHAPTER 4

Julian Benscher was extremely helpful and a primary source for much of this period in Lou's life. Admittedly, Benscher had an interest in portraying himself as one of many who were fooled by Lou, but he cooperated with the FBI as they investigated Lou and was never accused of any wrongdoing. He did buy out several of Lou's life insurance policies after Pearlman went to jail, and, simply put, he stood to profit if Lou died.

He was suspicious of me in the beginning and insisted that we meet in person, which actually put me at ease. I visited his home twice for extensive interviews, and he provided key documents that verified his stories. He spoke on and off the record and was very clear about which was which. Occasionally, things he said off the record were later deemed to be usable. Benscher had a knack for storytelling, and although he may have spiced up small details here and there, almost everything he said was vetted with documents, media accounts, and corroborating interviews. The story of his own inheritance and beginnings in business were corroborated by David Kleeman, who knew Benscher's father, Campari Group Chairman and CEO Gabi, and worked for Benscher's mother as an attorney in the battle over the inheritance.

Theordor Wullenkemper took months to reply and only did so via letter, almost the whole of which is reproduced in this chapter.

## CHAPTER 5

Maurice Starr was brief during a phone call and seemed not to want to be associated with Lou at all. Jordan Knight, via a representative, declined requests for interviews. Once a Trans Continental recording artist, he didn't want anything to do with Lou anymore. The New Kids were selling out arenas with the help of younger, newer boy bands as this book went to print.

Burton J. Dodge, who painted all of Lou's blimps, eagerly spoke about the negligence behind the 1992 crash of Lou's MetLife blimp in Weeksville, NC. National Transportation Safety Board records also proved helpful.

The story of the foundation of and auditions for Backstreet Boys was reassembled through press accounts; Pearlman's book; interviews with Scott Hoekstra, Jeanne Tanzy Williams, and Phoenix Stone (Sam Licata); a speech made by Howie Dorough at one of Lou's birthday parties (on video); and other sources.

Several background sources provided information about this era that was corroborated by documents.

## CHAPTER 6

I interviewed Johnny Wright once via phone. He indicated clearly which parts he wanted off the record, and I stuck to those instructions.

Public records from the FDIC, the result of Freedom of Information Act requests, helped establish some of the first attempts to alert government authorities to Lou's schemes.

Jennifer Chow, daughter of Lou's largest single investor, Dr. Joseph Chow, was helpful in corroborating and characterizing Lou's relationship with her father. The Chows' attorney, Edwin Brooks, was extremely helpful. He shared hundreds of pages of documents, including Trans Con financials (though some he could not share), and spoke extensively in interviews.

Several background sources were used in this chapter, usually to lead to other on-the-record sources or documents.

Lance Bass's bestselling book *Out of Sync* was a primary source for stories about the formation of *NSYNC.

## CHAPTER 7

Tammie Hilton was an extremely forthcoming source for many of the details of Lou's life, beginning as early as 1997. When I first contacted her, we agreed to speak off the record, but she agreed that I could use information and comments she made if I didn't publish anything before Lou's case had played out. I reminded her of this agreement throughout the months' worth of conversations we had, and she was always aware that I would use the information she gave me and quote from her when appropriate. She also acted as a go-between with Pearlman in prison, although I only directly used that mode of information gathering once—when getting Lou's reactions to the claims of inappropriate sexual behavior published in the 2007 *Vanity Fair* article. That story, "Mad About the Boys" was also a good jumping-off point for those sexual allegations. I spoke to many off-the-record or background sources with regard to Lou's alleged sexual misconduct, and almost everyone who knew him commented on rumors about inappropriate behavior between him and his artists or other associates. I tried to use those comments sparingly, if at all. Jane Carter, mother of Trans Con artists Nick and Aaron, declined through her lawyer to comment further, saying she was working on repairing her relationship with her boys, one that seemed to have been damaged in part by her speaking in the past.

### CHAPTER 8

FAA documents, court records, and other public records were used extensively to put together this chapter. I also relied on recollections of tours I took of Trans Continental's studios during the company's heyday. Bass's book, Benscher, and press accounts were also helpful.

### CHAPTER 9

Brad Fischetti was an informative, if not overly upbeat, source who was helpful in describing how Lou dealt with his bands in this era. He declined to speak again as Lou approached a plea deal and it looked more and more like he was going to be found guilty and sentenced to jail time.

A video called "Lou Pearlman Livin' Large"—part of a TV show, apparently, called *Livin' Large*—was key in establishing some of Lou's most costly possessions. He went on camera and bragged about them. The exact date of the taping was never clear, but based on the artists he was working with at the time, his house, and the possessions he claimed, I surmised that the piece was shot in the early 2000s. I was first apprised of the video by Helen Huntley, a reporter and blogger for the *St. Petersburg Times*. Helen was a dogged reporter on this case who steered me toward several sources she was kind enough to share.

Information about Planet Airways was culled from public records as well as on- and off-the-record sources.

Les Henderson's *Under Investigation* was also a helpful resource for this chapter, as were the recollections of several former Trans Continental Talent (or Options Talent or Wilhelmina Models) employees, including my longtime friend and associate Wheat Wurtzburger.

Ben Bledsoe was very forthcoming but mostly positive about his experience with Lou. He seemed to know what he was getting into and played his stake accordingly.

Many public records also went into this chapter.

### CHAPTER 10

A DVD of Lou's fiftieth birthday was extremely insightful for this chapter. The recollections of Tammie Hilton, who sat next to Lou for much of the celebration, proved vital.

On- and off-the-record sources helped fill in blanks about Planet Airways, as did court and financial documents and interviews given by Chow family attorney Edwin Brooks. Lou's plea agreement as well as other government documents provided additional information.

More details from a visit to Lou's offices were used in this chapter.

Interviews with Thorsten Iborg, the German tourist who spotted Pearlman in Bali, Indonesia, were informative, and Helen Huntley shared information about e-mails between Iborg, her, and FBI special agent Scott Skinner.

## CHAPTER 11

This chapter was driven by my visit to Lou in jail and public records from the Orange County, Florida, jail. Allen Moore, the jail's public information officer, was a consummate professional whenever I requested these documents, which I was entitled to see.

Information about Pearlman's planned reality show came from press accounts, recorded phone calls between Pearlman and a source, and Tammie Hilton.

## CHAPTER 12

Most of this chapter came from previously cited sources, Tammie Hilton, and my own coverage of Pearlman's sentencing. Follow-up interviews were conducted with various victims, including several outside of the courtroom who preferred not to have their names used.

# ★ ACKNOWLEDGMENTS

This book wouldn't have happened had Maer Roshan, editor in chief of *Radar* magazine, not agreed that Lou Pearlman was worthy of a feature. Later, he held my job as I took a month off from *Radar* to work on this book. I also benefited greatly from the focus given to me during the editing process by then executive editor Aaron Gell. He helped shape my vision on an early, much shorter draft of this story, but his advice and editing comments reverberated in my head as I worked on this book.

Going back even further, Mary Frances Emmons, my editor at the *Orlando Sentinel,* helped put me in the position—as the paper's nightlife writer—to see much of Lou's machinations close-up.

Kathy Huck, my first editor at Collins, was ultimately patient and understanding as this story came together in real time. Serena Jones, who took over this book, was nothing like a replacement editor and everything I needed, an enthusiastic and wise guide through the process.

Byrd Leavell, my agent, was my champion every step of

the way with this book. He treated me like a bestselling author from day one.

Christopher Olsen, a friend and other-worldly writer, was an amazing sounding board throughout this process.

# ★ INDEX

In thirteen years as a journalist, Tyler Gray has covered everything from a teenager's death penalty trial for murder to the drug-and-sex-fueled shenanigans of fuzzy theme park characters. His stories have appeared in the *New York Times*, *Esquire*, *Radar* magazine, *Men's Journal*, the New York *Daily News*, the *Orlando Sentinel*, the *St. Petersburg Times*, and others. He has appeared as a pop culture and news commentator on ABC, CNN, MSNBC, FOX, Comedy Central's *The Daily Show with Jon Stewart*, and others. Gray is a senior editor at *Blender* magazine in New York City.